DIONYSUS
GROUP

Who Killed Teresa?
Unknown Facts and New Developments Beyond Making a Murderer

ISBN13: 978-1977511553

ISBN 10: 197751554

First Print Edition: September 2017

Manufactured in the U.S.A

Dionysus Press

DIONYSUS
GROUP

CONTENTS

OUR NOTE

In this *Dionysus Group* book release, we assume the reader to have watched the *Making a Murderer* docu-series, or have knowledge of the story. Other books on the subject repeat one another in recounting basic details and we do not want to bog the educated reader down in redundancy, re-hashing what they already know.

Here, in *Who Killed Teresa,* we present the unknown facts, the new evidence, and fresh conclusions gleaned from the new information and global focus on the trial and appeals going forward, for Steven Avery, Brendan Dassey, Ryan Hillegas, Manitowoc Law Enforcement, and the American Judicial system.

Strong opinion combined with limited information creates false perception. False perception is a non-reality. The post *Making a Murderer* saga is rife with the good intentioned creating false perceptions of a highly complex criminal case, where all sides used deception and cunning. *The Dionysus Group* Think-Tank attempts to gain a higher understanding of truth and reality through a concerted and focused think-tank process, which draws not only from the group's expertise, but the combined researching and debating power of a professional focus group.

The Dionysus Group consists of nine individuals that initially met monthly to discuss a single, predetermined, major issue, event, or mystery in human affairs, primarily to discover what really happened, or *the truth*. We present and debate ideas by means of a robust, think-tank style working-group.

The Dionysus Group are not 'truthers', nor are we conspiracy oriented. *The Dionysus Group* deals with real-world issues, and understands that media gained knowledge is only a start point; *The Dionysus Group* is a research group that reaches conclusions.

The members of the think-tank wish to remain anonymous due to physical threats, and to protect themselves in their various careers.

When we first agreed that the 'D Group' *had* to know the reality underlying *Making a Murderer* and the Avery/Halbach mystery, we shifted gear and started meeting weekly. What happened was quite astonishing.

The day *Making a Murderer* was raised within the group, it was instantly clear that opinions were strong. The tone changed to aggression. Voices shouted one other down.

We had to regain composure.

Why were we so emotionally stirred?

Our resident psychologist gave enlightening insight. With composure regained, a show-of-hands revealed that eight members believed strongly in Steven Avery's innocence; only I thought he, along with his nephew, was potentially guilty of Teresa Halbach's murder.

Did any of us have a right to such strong opinions, with our *only* knowledge coming from the gripping docu-series, *Making a Murderer?*

Thoughtfully, we all agreed, *no*.

We did *not* have all the facts and information required to form the strong opinions that we felt, however, we all decided that *Making a Murderer* raised questions that once asked, could not go unanswered.

We could not un-ring this bell.

There was a powerful drive to know what happened.

The Dionysus Group had to know - *Who Killed Teresa?*

At the conclusion of eight months and fifteen days of research, meetings, argument, and debate, we reached unanimous agreement.

We know who killed Teresa Halbach.

But as one who has studied the *Making a Murderer* saga knows, there lurk yet new questions and deepening mysteries; sinister skeletons are still cloaked in Wisconsin's darkest closets.

The book you are about to read will answer the questions left hanging for over a decade:

Did Brendan do it? Is his confession true?
Is Steven Avery a psychopath?
Did Law Enforcement frame Steven Avery?
Will they be freed?
Who Killed Teresa? And;
What will happen next?

The Dionysus Group, October, 2017

I

WAS HE FRAMED?

Steven Avery was certainly framed by Manitowoc Law Enforcement in 1985, when charged with Penny Beerntsen's assault and rape.

We know this from depositions taken twenty years later in 2005, after Avery's exoneration through DNA testing and analysis of pubic hair found on the victim.

As it turns out, and as we know, multiple sources at the time, in 1985 pointed to another, more likely rapist, the infamous Gregory Allen.

In an epic move of fraudulence, the Manitowoc County Sheriff's Department created a false alibi for the rapist Gregory Allen when he had none. Despite multiple and ongoing suggestions that Allen, and not Avery was Penny's assailant, Law Enforcement ignored Allen, allowing him to commit further sexual crimes when he should have been in prison.

Significantly, the rapist Gregory Allen still continued to harass Penny Beerntsen *after* Avery's arrest; stalking her home, and making threatening phone calls - and in doing so, bolstering Avery's defense, which should have been solid with fourteen strong, reliable alibis.

However, our purpose here is not to delve into the gory details of Avery's 1985 'fit-up' by the Wisconsin DA's office, namely Denis Vogel, but we must re-confirm that Avery *was indeed framed* in a ruthless and complex scheme initiated and maintained for 18 years by Manitowoc officials.

Why they did this to Steven Avery will become clear later, but the point now is to show that Manitowoc Law Enforcement was capable and willing to use foul-play to get what they wanted. If this method was their culture, the culture never changed along with the faces.

Note here that this is an observation based in fact, and this statement while true, does not mean the *Dionysus Thought Group* has a pre-conceived notion of Avery's innocence in the Halbach case; but the fact that Wisconsin State doesn't let the process of law get in the way of their hard stance on justice is a clear problem for the man they charged in the matter, any jury, and us as investigators going forward.

We will search for reality by exploring all evidence - physical, circumstantial, admissible, inadmissible, discovery material, speculative, and historical.

The conclusion by all, a conclusion that led to *The Criminal Justice Reform Bill, 2005*, was that Wisconsin Law Enforcement, in particular, the Manitowoc County Sheriff's Department and the DA Denis Vogel, framed Avery knowing that he was innocent of Penny Beerntsen's rape, and dumped him in prison. Also, as further information came to them, the Manitowoc County Sheriff's Department and the DA's office *knowingly* prolonged Avery's wrongful incarceration.

In 2003, a single pubic hair from the 1985 trial evidence was DNA tested by Sherry Culhane of the Wisconsin Crime Lab. Culhane proved Gregory Allen was Beerntsen's rapist, and Avery was freed.

Our message is: police forces and prosecutors worldwide have been setting-up or 'framing' people since Law enforcement began.

Human nature, right?

The laughable position of throwing one's hands up and crying that Law enforcement is beyond reproach, and, *'How dare they accuse good men, good family men, of planting evidence'*, is an absurd position, when this type of fraud is common across the globe, and had just been proven in Manitowoc County.

'We're beyond reproach', is an aggressive form of defense.

Wisconsin's holier than thou position is even more laughable when depositions hearings recently proved illegal and negligent fraudulence within the Manitowoc Sheriff's office, specifically for framing Steven Avery in the Beerntsen rape.

But what makes the fraud infinitely worse - as shown in *Making a Murderer* - is that the same Law enforcement system that framed Avery for rape in '85, should then investigate him for the murder of Teresa Halbach.

The developed western world outside of Wisconsin finds this utterly bizarre, and almost impossible to believe.

"I want to emphasize - that Manitowoc County's role (in the investigation of Avery) was to provide resources to us, as they were needed. Items on the property - to conduct searches they provided equipment, and that's their role - and their only role - in this investigation."

Sheriff Gerald Pagel of the neighboring Calumet County Sheriff's Dept made this statement for one reason. The Manitowoc Sheriff's dept had declared a conflict of interest in investigating Avery for Halbach's murder, because they had just been proven to have framed him once before, and a $36 million dollar civil rights suit against them was pending for Avery's framing conviction and 18 years of wrongful imprisonment.

But Pagel's statement was a lie.

Manitowoc Sheriff's Deputies were first on the scene when Teresa's RAV4 was found hidden at Avery Salvage. Manitowoc Sheriff's Deputies searched for, and found all of the chief trial evidence used to convict Avery, except the .22 caliber projectile holding Teresa's DNA.

Worse yet, two Manitowoc officers with conflicts of interest in the case were involved in every aspect of the investigation into Steven Avery, and were present at the time all conviction critical evidence (except the .22 projectile) was found or collected; Sergeant Andrew Colborn, and Lieutenant James Lenk.

These two men should not have been involved in the investigation at all. They should have stayed out of it. They should have been kept out of it.

They made Sheriff Pagel a liar.

They cast doubt over the validity of the crucial trial evidence.

If Steven Avery was Teresa's killer, their involvement gave the defense ammunition, put doubt in juror's minds, and jeopardized justice.

Did Sheriff Pagel know Manitowoc County Sheriff's Deputies were so deeply involved in the investigation?

Was Pagel attempting to cover-up their involvement?

The involvement of Manitowoc Deputies was entirely unnecessary, endangered the case, and put the MCSD under further damaging scrutiny.

Why did the MCSD not stand-down?

Why were they there?

Why did they keep returning?

It is certainly clear that you *cannot* set-up an innocent man for murder unless you have access to the crime scene.

Were Lenk and Colborn there to plant evidence, and frame Avery a second time?

II

TERESA'S RAV4

The finding of Teresa's vehicle, the metallic-blue-green 1999 model Toyota RAV4 SUV, on November 5th, 2005, was the break in the police investigation. Teresa had been missing for 5 days. The finding of the RAV4 on Avery salvage land allowed the police to gain search warrants, access, and then to seize the 44 acre property for 8 days - as one would expect in an urgent missing person's investigation.

Avery's Defense team claimed that Teresa's RAV4 was discovered under suspicious circumstances. The defense says Teresa's RAV4 was planted.

But was it?

(1) Lights, Camera, Action

Former PI Pam Sturm and her daughter found Teresa's RAV4 on November 5th, the 6th day of Teresa's disappearance. Teresa disappeared on October 31st, 2005,

Halloween, but was first reported missing by her mother on November 3rd - last seen on October 31st.

(a). On the 29.6 acres of the auto salvage lot, dubbed 'the pit', containing row upon row of over 4000 auto bodies, Sturm found Teresa's RAV4 within 20 minutes - it takes longer to find a part when you know where to look.

Avery's Defense says Sturm found Teresa's RAV4 impossibly fast because Sgt. Colborn had already found the car 2 days earlier, on November 3rd. A 'civilian' search team was then arranged by the MC Sheriff's department, and led to Avery Salvage by Teresa's ex-boyfriend, Ryan Hillegas; Sturm then went straight to Teresa's SUV.

Defense Attorney Jerry Buting says Sgt. Colborn had either found Teresa's RAV4 out in the County, or else he discovered it while illegally on the Avery property. As no search warrant had been obtained for Avery Salvage, Sturm (as a concerned civilian citizen) gained permission from Earl Avery to search the rows of cars. If the Sheriff's Department was exposed as being involved in a search for Teresa on private property, any evidence gained would be inadmissible in court; but it was obvious that the department was involved in organizing the search, and knew they would find Teresa's RAV4.

(b). Sturm looked suspect on the stand during Avery's Trial. She was nervous, flustered, and *non-verbally active.*

(c). When Avery's more aggressive attorney, Jerry Buting, produced a tape-recording of Sgt Colborn's November 3rd cell-phone call to dispatch, Colborn also became suspiciously uneasy on the stand. We've all heard Colborn's phone call, and it certainly appears that Sgt.

Andrew Colborn was physically looking at Teresa's RAV4 while calling in its license plates - 48 hours before the missing vehicle was officially found.

"Ninety-nine Toyota?"
"Yup!"

When grilled by Buting in court, Sgt. Colborn testified that he'd been given Teresa's license-plate number by a Calumet County Detective - the tag of a missing person to keep an eye out for - and Colborn was simply confirming the plate number was correct, and to whom it belonged.

(d). A tag check is such a short communication to MCSD dispatch, a radio message would usually be used. Why would Colborn use his private cell phone?

Well, if you are about to engage in evidence tampering in a murder investigation, you would start to get cautious, right? If you know Radio communications between officers and dispatchers are both recorded, and broadcast across the open airways, would you avoid self-incrimination over the radio? Of course. All sorts of people listen in on police channel scanners, including interested members of the public, and any-and-all members of the police force.

Maybe Colborn didn't realize that his cell phone call to dispatch would be recorded; or maybe he did, but thought the phone the more secure option of the two.

Avery Salvage

(2) Micro-Expression Analysis

On the stand during video-taped testimony, both Pam Sturm and Sgt. Colborn showed signatures of tension, deception, and lying; why?

Were they just nervous, or were they hiding details of Avery's second frame-up?

On Pam Sturm's testimony, our body language expert lists the following from the *full* trial video recordings.

(a). Sturm often, and at key times holds her chin/ nose up righteously, showing that she believes she is morally right. She does this during pauses, and after making a bold statement.

(b). Sturm's voice becomes softer and higher under cross-examination, which is a sign of lying. But when she is truthful, and less stressed, her voice returns to normal pitch and volume. "This 'tell' is a sub-conscious covering

technique that only very experienced liars or sociopaths can avoid." Lying can be very had to detect in the sociopathic; but conversely very easy to notice in a normal person.

(c). Sturm touches her nose with her index finger when pressured. 'This suggests lying.'

(d). Sturm wipes her brow with her hand. 'This repetitive action simulates wiping imaginary sweat from the brow, which is associated with 'honest' people lying under pressure.'

(e). Sturm clearly doesn't want to lie, but believes she serves a greater purpose in helping convict Teresa's killer. As far as Sturm knows, Teresa's RAV4 *was* found on Avery's property, and her lie of not having prior knowledge of this helps the 'good guys'.

(f). Under pressure in court, Sturm asserts God guided her to Teresa's RAV4, and that is how she found it in the impossibly fast time.

'This is in-fact, a common feature of deceit, where one will invoke God as justification,' our psychologist said.

(g) It was mentioned during a 'D group' debate that something was very wrong with Sturm's 'guidance by God' idea; and that is this:

Why would God allow the torturous rape and stabbing of a young woman to occur, but then guide Pam to her car?

Answers were:

God works in mysterious ways. Maybe Pam is a better worshipper than Teresa was. The Devil did it.

The inadequacy of these speculations is best covered like this:

If the 'Devil' commits all rapes and murders across the globe, then 'he' must be committing or provoking thousands of rapes simultaneously every hour, all without any intervention by God - yet God would 'guide' Pam Strum to one of the victim's cars?

If God guided Pam to Teresa's RAV4, why was she uncharacteristically nervous, and dreadfully suspicious on the stand?

Like Jerry Buting, the 'D Group' *all* felt that Pam Sturm's testimony was 'off'. However, the opinion of our expert was, and remains, that Pam Sturm was 'squirming on the stand because she knew lying in court is a crime.'

When we were all shown why our expert concluded this - the physical signs of deception, shame, and self-righteousness that Sturm displayed unconsciously, Sturm's lying became obvious. Of course, we have a strong idea why Sturm would lie and the reasons are limited:

(i) Sturm had alone decided Avery's guilt, and believed lying would help convict Teresa's killer.

(ii) Sturm is party to a common tactic used by law enforcement worldwide: The priming of witnesses to 'tell small lies' so as to bolster the police case. This happens when investigators have already decided who is guilty. Once Law Enforcement decides guilt, they stop investigating other suspects - what's the point, right? This witness-priming tactic directly involves another player in the RAV4 ruse, Sgt. Andrew Colborn.

Pam Sturm on testifying during Avery's trial

Here Sturm shows what micro-expression analysts call 'duping delight'. A quick smile or smirk whilst lying in court; in Sturm's case it may be because she is pleased the jury is buying her story.

Wiping non-existent sweat under the pressure of lying. Sturm displays the 'cross' of Jesus around her neck. Does this say: I am religious, so you can believe everything I say? Her body language fails to support any believability.

The private cellular-phone conversation shown in *Making a Murderer,* between Sgt. Colborn and the Manitowoc County Sheriff's Department dispatcher, was happened upon 'almost by fluke' according to Avery's attorney Jerry Buting. It was actually excellent 'lawyer-ing'.

Before and during pre-trial proceedings the State's Prosecution is *required by law* to provide the defense any discovered materials pertinent to the trial. Under pre-trial 'Discovery Materials', Buting had requested from the Prosecution *all* relevant taped voice recordings from the Manitowoc Sheriff's Department. Colborn's cell phone call recording to dispatch on November 3rd was *not* handed over by the Prosecution, who later claimed they didn't know about such recordings.

But a detective gave away the secret.

At a pre-trial hearing, Detective David Remiker stated under questioning that he had listened to a recording of a phone call between himself and Investigator Mark Wiegert, to confirm what exactly the two had said during a certain phone conversation.

Buting's ears pricked up. *'What? A recorded phone conversation.'*

In the massive archive of 'Discovery Materials' dumped on them by the prosecution, the defense had only found tapes of *radio* communications - not the department's *telephone* recordings.

Buting asked, *why*?

Buting requested the judge order the Prosecution to immediately disclose *all* telephone recordings, (being law under discovery materials), which he did.

In absorbing these tapes, Buting struck Sgt. Colborn's infamous call to dispatch, made not from his radio, but from Colborn's private cell phone.

It was a combination of luck and good lawyering that Colborn's telling conversation was unearthed at all.

When Buting turned the heat on Colborn during the Avery trial, some interesting things happened.

Sgt. Colborn on the stand

Our micro-expression and body-language expert conducted a lengthy video analysis of Andrew Colborn's direct, cross, and re-direct examinations; she found:

(a) Colborn was calm and maintained an even, deep voice when conversing with the prosecution.

(b) When pressured by the defense on calling in Teresa's tag on November 3rd, Colborn's voice becomes very quite, and higher-pitched. Colborn's voice becomes so quite, he has to be asked to speak up. This change in voice is akin to mouth covering when lying. Colborn was covering something. He was nervous about what might come. That however, may well be coming 13 years later.

If Colborn was lying in court, and was indeed looking at Teresa's RAV4 two days before it could *be* officially found, what does that mean?

There exist only two ways that Sgt. Colborn could've been looking at Teresa's vehicle on November 3rd.

(1). If Sgt. Colborn found Teresa's RAV4 somewhere out in the county; in which case the police would've had to have arranged her RAV4's transport to Avery's property, for it to be found 'officially' by Pam Sturm two days later. This however could also suggest that Teresa's remains were also found and moved. Or:

(2). Sgt. Colborn was on the Avery Salvage property without a search warrant or authorization, illegally snooping around on strong suspicion that he might find Teresa's RAV4. The obvious thing with this scenario is that it would take more than a drive-by one night to find her vehicle on the 44-acre property. It is therefore likely that police over-flew the Avery property during the day of November 3rd, saw a possible match for Teresa's RAV4, and sent Sgt. Colborn to covertly check it out that night. This ruse being necessary because no search warrant had been issued, and no legal grounds or probable cause existed for issuing a search warrant for Avery Salvage at that time. It's called getting creative.

Interestingly, Jerry Buting, in his book *Illusion of Justice,* states that Sgt. Colborn appears to have been calling in Teresa's RAV-4 tag *from the Avery property*.

This however, is a telling statement for those believing in Avery's guilt.

If Colborn was lying in court to conceal an illegal search, and not because he'd planted the RAV-4 at Avery Salvage, then someone on the Avery property was likely to be Teresa's killer - and Steven was the most likely, as he'd arranged to meet her that day. One must note that if Sgt. Colborn found the RAV4 somewhere other than Avery Salvage, and planted it there, then he must've known Teresa was dead on November 3rd, the day her mother reported her missing. It would not be a good look to plant the vehicle and then have Teresa turn up later alive and well. The summation of small facts regarding Colborn's strange actions suggests he found Teresa's car at Avery Salvage.

However, there is problem with the Defense insinuation that Colborn found Teresa's RAV4 on the 3rd and called in plates. The plates from Teresa's RAV4 were found crumpled up inside a Mercury wagon, just inside the salvage yard next to Avery's lane. They were found with a pair of woman's underwear.

The problem is, as always, Dassey.

Brendan told police that when he and Steven drove Teresa's jeep to the back of the yard, Steven went under the hood, and also took off the license plates. i.e. Steven didn't go back and remove the plates.

If Avery was the killer, Colborn couldn't have called in the plates themselves, because they were hidden near his trailer; but:

If Colborn found Teresa's RAV4 with no plates attached, and he had the VIN number (which police did have when Sturm called it in) then he could have compared the RAV's VIN (found in lower corner of driver's side windscreen) with the one he had, and then got on his cell phone to confirm the plate as 'Sam William Henry 582'. Colborn wanted to know the owner's name, and if it was a '99 Toyota.

(3) Cautious RAV4 Conclusions

(a) Teresa's RAV-4 *could have* been planted at Avery Salvage; either before Colborn found it there, or else by Colborn himself, or police, however;

(b) It appears most likely that Colborn found Teresa's RAV4 at the Avery Salvage location, and not elsewhere. This still allows a third-party killer to plant the car.

(c) However, Law Enforcement *were* acting very strangely indeed concerning Teresa's RAV4, and the Manitowoc County Sheriff's Department had a patent and proven history of framing Steven Avery, and were clearly not concerned if he rotted in jail, guilty of a crime or not.

(d) There was a clear and concerted effort by Manitowoc Law Enforcement to search Avery Salvage and find Teresa's vehicle there - before a search warrant was issued. The *D Group* believes that Law Enforcement had prior knowledge of the location of Teresa's RAV4 on the Avery property, and this knowledge confirmed Steven Avery's guilt for them (combined with other facts at that early stage of the investigation).
A 'possible RAV4' that looked similar to Teresa's was most likely identified during an aerial search by helicopter or fixed-wing aircraft, in a genuine attempt to rapidly locate the missing Teresa. However, in spotting the 'possible RAV4' on the Avery property meant an illegal aerial surveillance - *if* it proved to be Teresa's; this would destroy the find as usable evidence in court. Therefore Sgt. Colborn went in covertly to confirm the vehicle's identity. Once confirmed as Teresa Halbach's, "*'99 Toyota*", the 'Enhanced Civilian Search Party scheme was hatched.

(e) Analyzing the RAV4 in isolation of the other circumstantial evidence, raises two possibilities:

(i) Someone with access to the Avery Property such as someone that lives there put Teresa's RAV4 where Colborn and Sturm found it - Steven Avery, his brothers, or someone else; or,

(ii) A cunning third-party killer unknown to the Avery's set-up Steven to hide his crime, vis-à-vis the Ryan Hillegas, Ed Edwards, George Zipperer, Andres Martinez, or the 'German' scenarios. However, if this third-party set-up actually occurred, then the police *had to have planted* Avery's blood in Teresa's RAV4, and Teresa's DNA on the .22 caliber projectile taken from Avery's garage floor - as well as get Brendan Dassey to confess the exact story. This is clearly because a third-party killer like Ryan Hillegas would not have had access to Avery's blood; and it seems far-fetched indeed for him to have shot Teresa twice in her skull (2 bullet holes found in her recovered skull bones) only to dig out the bullets and plant them in Steven Avery's garage - the garage that Brendan Dassey cleaned with bleach the night Teresa disappeared, and the garage in which Brendan later said Steven shot Teresa twice in her head. Also remember that .22 long rifle ammunition can penetrate skull bone, but lacks the power to exit the cranium. This means the bullets recovered from Avery's garage, if un-doctored, were body shots.

(f) If this is what happened, the 'set-up killer' would have - or must have - planted Teresa's RAV4 on the Avery property, and; female bones, Teresa's jeans, and Teresa's shin bone in Steven's burn-pit using the drum found at Barb Janda's. (More on bones later, but tissue from the bone shin found and tested from the pit give a chance of 1 in 1billion that they were not Teresa's bones.)

(g) Who these third-party or 'other killers' could be was not put in front of Avery's jury by the defense; although Strang and Buting did have other suspects in mind (a list of 10), *The Denny Motion* meant the defense was limited as to how and when they could point the finger at any other killers; Judge Willis also hamstrung the defense when he required them to prove motive to the Judge of any 'third party' they wished to present as an alternative killer. It was indeed possible for the defense to do this, but time and resource limitations, Buting claimed, made third-party investigations problematic.

The Dionysus Group explored the Defense's 10 'other suspects' in detail, and reached conclusions about them - we also found other, more suspicious suspects that were never investigated.

(4) The New Theories

(i) The Crusher

Avery Auto Salvage's Hydraulic Car Crusher

Teresa's RAV4 was found near the crusher. Arguments as to why 'Avery the killer' did not crush Teresa's RAV4 have been raised by both 'guilters', and those professing Avery's innocence.

Attorneys Buting and Strang asked: why, if Steven were the killer, would he not have crushed the RAV4 immediately, making it easier to hide or dispose of?

We threw possible answers for this question randomly at one another around the table:

• The RAV4 was planted by the police or another killer, and Steven didn't know it was there. *This is what the Defense is alluding to.*

• On the night of Teresa's murder, the 31st October, Avery hid her RAV4 near the crusher and disconnected its battery, intending to crush it later - because he had to clean up the crime scene back at his garage and trailer home, and burn Teresa's body, electronics, and property in his burn pit. *This is what the prosecution suggests.*

• Earl and Chuck Avery had been round to Steven's trailer on Halloween around 5pm (where they smelled burning plastic). Steven would have known that operating the noisy car-crusher around that time of day would have been witnessed, and considered unusual by others on the property. Steven had been off work all that afternoon to meet the 'photographer', Teresa. He wasn't meant to be crushing her car.

• The RAV4's fuel tank, battery, rims and tires had to be removed before it could be crushed; the cleaning of the crime scene meant the crushing would have to wait.

• Maybe Steven could have crushed Teresa's RAV4 complete, but this would have made more noise, and been more unusual as the tires and gas tank popped under the crusher's hydraulic pressure. Maybe 'Avery the killer' was cautious of drawing attention to himself.

• If 'Steven the killer' planned to crush Teresa's RAV4 between October 31st and November 3rd, he had to find a moment when no one would see him crush a top condition, valuable auto. Maybe that window of opportunity didn't arrive. Or:

• Maybe he planned to strip Teresa's RAV4 for parts.

• Remember, the remains of a flattened and crushed vehicle are still reasonably easy to identify. The paint color, the make and model, and other features are still identifiable. Simply crushing Teresa's RAV4 does not make it go away.

• Maybe 'Avery the killer' planned to dispose of Teresa's RAV4 another way. Perhaps he didn't want the RAV4's crushed carcass on the property, tying him to Teresa's murder.

Dassey, in interviews rarely seen or known about, says early on in inquiries, that Steven wanted the RAV4 crushed, and 'the sooner the better.' But Dassey's reliability is problematic.

The beat drummed out by the prosecution is that Steven parked Teresa's RAV4 near the crusher so he could *drive* it to the crusher later. However, the Avery's car crusher is loaded by means of a large front-end-loader, as previously pictured. This front-end-loader can lift a car body from anywhere on the yard and load it into the crusher. 'Avery the killer' would not have needed to maintain the RAV4's drivability if he intended to crush it.

The car crusher's availability was, it seemed to us, an inconclusive line of thought. If Avery was Teresa's killer, we have no way of knowing his thought processes in regards to disposing of Teresa's RAV4. Other questions arise also:

Did the crusher work? Had it broken down? Did Steven have time? Was crushing it too out-of-the-ordinary?

Would you have crushed it, if you were the killer?

If not, driving Teresa's RAV4 to another location off the Salvage yard for disposal would have been highly problematic for 'Avery the killer':

• It could be seen by police or someone that knew Teresa.

• It could be remembered by witnesses.

• Chance could have it inadvertently caught by a random CCTV camera.

Disposing of Teresa's RAV4 on the Salvage yard seems the best option for 'Avery the killer', and the crusher certainly would reduce its profile and its ability to be easily seen or found by Law Enforcement.

But in our opinion, not using the crusher neither condemns nor vindicates Steven Avery, but it appears to us that Teresa's RAV4 *could* have been hidden in Steven's garage for several days, before being moved to its location near the crusher on November 3rd.

Further more; if Law Enforcement did not 'plant' Teresa's RAV4 at Avery Salvage, but instead spied it during an illegal surveillance operation, that returns us to our two possibilities of a third-party killer: an Avery family member, or a cunning unknown killer. Remember, if Teresa's killer was *anyone but* Steven Avery, then the police planted Steven's blood in Teresa's RAV4 -

But was it even Teresa's RAV4 at all?

(ii) The Switch

Internet sleuths have raised the question: was the RAV4 found and removed from Avery Auto a different vehicle from Teresa's altogether - a switch out?

Several photos are shown together in comparison with the photo of Teresa beside her RAV4, and a game of spot the difference begins. I'll insert the images, but they need to be viewed in color to grasp the theory.

The RAV4 found at Avery Auto, compared with Teresa's RAV4

The differences noted between the images in this 'swap-out theory' are:

Seized RAV4. Evidential Images	*Teresa beside her RAV4*
Indicator lens covers on the rear bumper appear orange	Indicator covers on rear bumper appear reddish
Door handles appear same as paint color	Door handles appear darker than paint color
No rub marks obvious	Rub marks on roof rail rear of B-pillar
No rub marks	Rub marks on rear door

No rub marks	Rub marks on rear panel, above bumper
Paint color appears a darker blue	Paint color appears a lighter teal

How do we explain these apparent differences?

The Dionysus Group reviewed and compared multiple images of the RAV4 Teresa is standing beside, with the evidential images captured during the vehicle's seizure from Avery Auto - and also images of the seized RAV4 inside the State's holding facility.

For paint color, and lens cover hue, the images of Teresa's RAV4 at the State's storage unit match the image of Teresa beside her RAV4.

Let me state that again: The RAV4 in storage matches the RAV4 in Teresa's photo.

The rear bumper indicators are the same color in these 2 images, suggesting that over-exposure has caused the indicator lens covers to appear orange in the evidential photos taken in the low light conditions at the salvage yard, illuminated artificially.

The door handle color issue is resolved in these 2 images also, suggesting that over exposure has lightened the evidential images of the seizure.

In photo comparison, we agreed that only photos taken during daylight should be compared, to ensure light consistency.

The next 'difference' to explain is the disappearance of the rub marks on the driver's side rear-door, rear guard, and above the rear driver's side door on the roof rail.

Teresa must have had these marks polished, buffed out, or repaired, otherwise the difference needs explaining.

Questions have been raised regarding each of the RAV4's image's overall paint color, suggesting there are two different RAV4's - each with its different shade of blue - Teresa's *teal,* and the plant *bright blue.*

It is true that for the 1999 model RAV4, Toyota offered several similar paint colors. In this theory, a RAV4 manufactured between 1996 and 2003 could have been used for the planted vehicle.

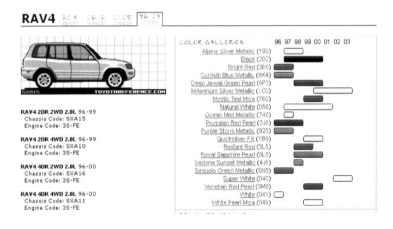

Toyota Owner's Manual, 1996 - 2003 RAV4 range

Of course the color chart image is useless in grayscale, but what I can inform you about Toyota's RAV4 paint color options for their '96 - '03 model is this:

● *Confetti Blue Metallic (8K4)* was not available on the '99 model, and is too light for both sets of images.

• *Deep Jewel Green Pearl (6P3)* is too green, not blue enough, and not the teal color of the RAV4 in any of the disputed images.

• *Royal Sapphire Pearl (8L5)* is blue, not greenish or teal. This tint was available for 1998, 99, and 2000 model RAV4s.

• *Mystic Teal Mica (760)* is the color we believe matches *Teresa's* 1999 RAV4, and the color of the RAV4 photographed inside the State's Crime facility. It appears that at night, and under bright artificial light, the *Mystic Teal Mica* becomes darker and more bluish. Toyota told us that this is because tiny metallic and aluminum particles in the base coats reflect different amounts of light through the clear coats under different light conditions.

Interestingly however, we could not all agree that the RAV4 photographed at Avery Auto on the evening of November 5th, 2005, was painted *Mystic Teal Mica*, and not *Royal Sapphire Pearl*.

However, the RAV4 in holding matches Teresa's RAV4, all except the absence of rub-marks on the bodywork.

When we used an extreme zoom close up of images of Teresa's RAV4, we noted a distinctive 'two pronged' mark on the rear driver's side window. We zoomed in on the same point on the image of the RAV4 in the holding facility, and identified a similar mark in the same place.

Online sleuths have also suggested that differences in interior trim coloring in passenger's seat comparisons is further proof of a RAV4 swap-out. We reviewed these images and agree that color saturation is the difference between the images, making one image appear more grey throughout.

We believe that all of the evidential images of Teresa's RAV4 are the same vehicle - the vehicle that Teresa is photographed standing beside.

Teresa's RAV4 at the Madison, Wisconsin, State Crime Lab

(iii) The Lay of the Land

Twelve years after Avery's conviction for Teresa's murder, myself and another D-Group member did a number of strange things:

• We flew to Mitchell International in Milwaukee, hired a vehicle, did some sight seeing, and then drove out to Avery Auto Salvage at Two Rivers. We bought parts for a 2005 Dodge Durango, but were not allowed access onto the lot. We stayed that night in Green Bay.

    ● The next day we over-flew the Avery property and surrounding quarries in a private Cessna that we had arranged earlier for a scenic flight.

This was an eye-opening expedition, giving us critical insights and understanding into:
● Teresa's RAV4's location on the yard.
● Access routes onto the Salvage yard from the main entrance at Avery rd, Kuss Rd, the rear access points, and the Quarry Rd.
● The topography of the land and quarry, and;
● The location of the buildings and dwellings in relationship to the access roads, fences, undulations and banks;
● But also other areas of interest to the investigation and trials, specifically what one could see from each key location, and the distances involved.

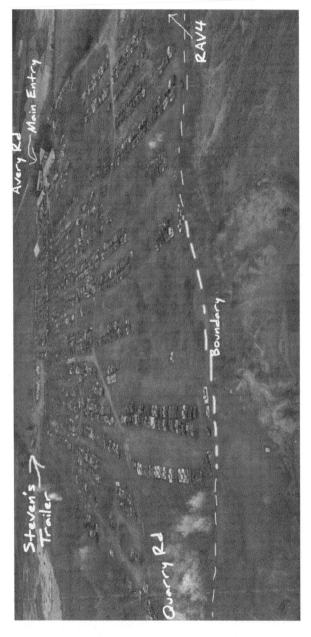

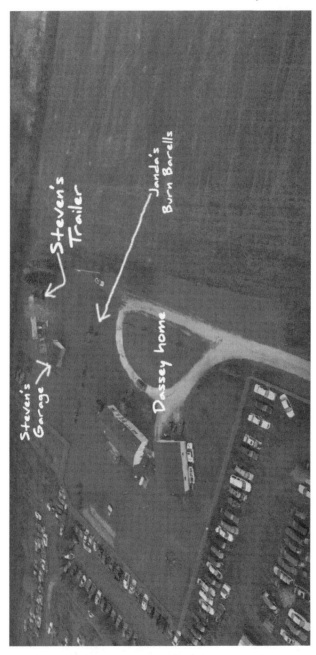

We discovered:

• Teresa's RAV4 was hidden at the furthest point on the property from Steven Avery's trailer.

• 3 ways exist for the killer to drive Teresa's RAV4 to where it was found;

(1) down Avery road, past the salvage business, past Delores and Allan's, and behind Earl Avery's house, straight down to the property boundary, which drops down steeply into the quarry; and

(2) through the private rear access road. A prison like hurricane wire fence runs behind Steven's and Barb's, preventing access to the Salvage yard from their properties. The road runs from Avery's to Kuss Road, and then around the Radandt Quarry to the rear of Avery Salvage, and;

(3) Down Jambo Creek Road, and into Quarry Rd.

• If you were the police stashing Teresa's RAV4 on the Avery property, via the rear quarry road, there are numerous spots to hide it that are handy to the rear entrance; to proceed further, down to the rear corner of the property where the RAV was found, would create undue risk, and would seem unnecessary and unlikely. Seeing gives perspective.

• When seen from the air, and on the ground, it appears that the odd and much debated 'camouflage', put up against Teresa's RAV4 (a hood, plywood, fence-posts, and branches etc) could have been used by 'Avery the killer' to prevent it being seen by those working in the salvage yard, prior to his later disposal by crushing.

Another idea is that the 'third-party killer' camouflaged Teresa's RAV4 to make it look like Avery was

hiding it. Note that a rusty car-hood, and a piece of board
had been purposely used to cover the RAV4's *alloy wheels*,
from the salvage yard side. Alloy wheels are something that
auto wreckers would notice in the yard as they collect and
smelter them into ingots to sell. This is clearly something
'Avery the killer' would do that no other third-party would.

• In Brendan Dassey's maligned confession, he said Steven's
first idea for disposing of Teresa's body was to put her in the
pond, but the water was too shallow. Dassey said Teresa's
dead body was put into the back of the RAV4 for
transportation to this pond, but then Uncle Steven decided
burning was the smarter option.
Let it be stated now that Dassey's confessions to police were
erratic and require full and through analysis to decide if any
of what he said can be taken seriously. Dassey's evidential
confession should certainly have been declared inadmissible
in his trial due to the methods use in its extraction. Here
however, it is mentioned in our discussion that Dassey was
not fed 'the pond' option by the inept investigators, and
Teresa's RAV4 was found beside the pond on the salvage
yard. However, whether reliable parts of Dassey's
confessions exist at all will be dissected in detail later in our
post mortem.

(iv) The Wilmer Sighting

In 2005, old Wilmer Seibert lived on the corner of the
Quarry Road (which leads to the rear of Avery Salvage), and
Jambo Creek Road, (which runs to the quarry from highway
147).

The 70 year old Wilmer *thinks* he saw Teresa's
RAV4, followed by a 'white Jeep', driving at 40 miles-an-

hour up the Quarry Rd, before Teresa's RAV4 was found on
the Avery property.

Wilmer says only the white jeep returned from the
quarry past his home.

Wilmer's late interjection may appear worthless, but
several points could be gleaned from it, and must be
analyzed.

• No small/ mid sized, blue/green 'jeeps' used this private
Quarry road. Or no vehicle fitting Teresa's RAV4's
description had business in the quarry.

• 'Jeep' is a term used by some to describe a short-wheel-
based four-wheel-drive vehicle, and not necessarily a vehicle
of the Jeep brand.

• Steven Avery drove a small, mid-grey Suzuki Samurai
4WD or 'Jeep', which could be the vehicle Wilmer Seibert
saw following the teal jeep in to the rear of the Salvage yard;
however its color could not be mistaken for white.

• From Wilmer's statement, nothing certain can be drawn;
but Teresa's RAV4 was a distinctive teal color, and the timeframe of November 3rd fits with the narrative of when the
murder and vehicle stashing occurred.

• Brendan Dassey, during one of his strange interviews by
Inv. Wiegert and Special Agent Fassbender, said that both
Brendan and Steven hid Teresa's RAV4, and that Steven
opened the hood. If 'Avery the killer' drove Teresa's RAV4
down Jambo Creek Rd, past Wilmer's house, and into
Quarry Rd to access the rear of the Salvage yard, would
Steven have gotten Brendan to follow in the Suzuki, to take
him back home, or would Avery have walked back across
the yard? Steven was teaching Brendan to drive at the time,
and promised Brendan to help find him a car if he did odd

jobs for Steven. However, Brendan stated that he and Steven took the RAV4 via Kuss Rd and the quarry, and after hiding Teresa's jeep, he and Steven walked home. This is backed up by the cadaver-dog track; both of which contradict Wilmer.

• If Avery was the killer, and did hide Teresa's RAV4 beside the pond at the rear of the salvage yard, would he drive it past all of the other houses and the main entrance on to H-147, and down to Jambo Creek Rd; or would he do what Brendan said? The only other way would have been to drive Teresa's distinctive and recognizable RAV4 through the main entrance to the salvage yard, where he would likely have been seen, past the window of Allen and Delores Avery, and then past Chuck Avery's house, risking being caught.

The Wilmer sighting appears to incriminate Steven Avery more so than any possible third-party, but let's be clear: Wilmer isn't sure if he saw Teresa's RAV4, and he isn't sure if the following 'jeep' was white or silver. He never saw the driver's faces. But he did see a blue-green SUV on Quarry Rd the day Colborn called in the plates.

    "Sam William Henry five-eight-two."

    But as has already been stated, *we* don't think 'Colborn' planted Teresa's RAV4 at Avery Auto, but instead found it without a search warrant.

    If a third-party killer had stashed Teresa's RAV4 this way - via the quarry - we don't think they would've taken the added risk of driving across the salvage yard to the pond where the RAV was found (not knowing who could see them going in and out). We have marked where we would have planted the RAV4 to set-up Avery, (were we the third-party killers), on this Google-Earth capture. The spot is close to the quarry entrance, but not so close as to raise suspicion;

it has a steep hilly mound and trees and bushes for cover; and it is out of sight of the main Salvage yard.

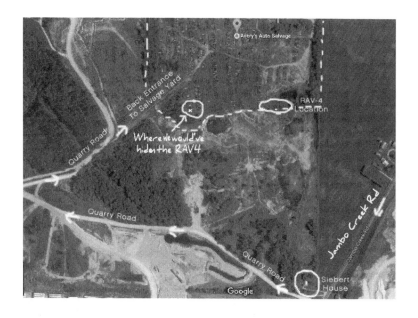

*The X shows a safer, easier spot for a third-party killer to hide
Teresa's RAV4.*

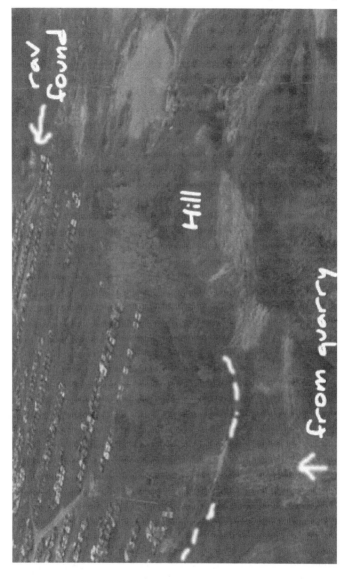

There are 3 explanations for how Teresa's RAV4 gets onto Avery Salvage land.

(1) Steven Avery put it there after murdering Teresa, planning to cover-up her murder (and possible rape).

(2) A member of the police planted it to frame Steven Avery for Teresa's murder. *This doesn't explain who murdered Teresa or how police knew she was dead on November 3rd. (Based on tens-of-thousands of case studies, we suggest it is common for law enforcement to plant evidence if they believe they must to convict someone they have decided or predetermined is guilty - it is very rare in western society for law enforcement to actually commit murder and set up a victim).*

(3) A third-party killer planted Teresa's RAV4 on Avery Salvage land, to frame Steven Avery for their murdering Teresa, and to evade suspicion.

At Avery Salvage, someone covered Teresa's RAV4 with items in a very odd way - a way that didn't conceal much of the vehicle. The items were a car hood, plywood, fence posts, and brush. The hood and the ply concealed the alloy rims from the salvage yard proper.

Evidential photograph of Teresa's RAV4, hidden on Avery Salvage property, Nov 5, 2005. Note that its alloy rims are covered.

'Planting' proponents suggest that Colborn hurriedly covered some of Teresa's RAV4 to make it look like Avery had tried to conceal her car. Or to conceal the RAV4 from the Averys.

As mentioned, 'Avery the killer' could have covered the alloys to stop them being salvaged, or to stop their presence raising suspicion, as the yard staff collect all alloy rims and stack them for smelting in the yard's on-site aluminum smelter. Equally, the 'cunning third-party killer' could have covered Teresa's alloy rims for the same reason - preventing the Averys from finding Teresa's RAV4 first.

A point of evidence against Wilmer's sighting being Teresa's RAV4 is that Cadaver-dogs, searching the area on November 5, did not indicate along this track - but they did indicate strongly on another track that leads to the rear of Avery Auto Salvage.

(5) Certainties

(1). Manitowoc Law Enforcement had prior knowledge of the exact location of Teresa's RAV4 on the Avery property on November 3rd, (two days before they were able to organize a civilian search of the property), and this knowledge confirmed Steven Avery's guilt for them (combined with other facts at that *early stage* of the investigation).

(2). Teresa's RAV4 was not swapped-out to frame Avery. One vehicle was found at Avery Salvage and photographed at night, under artificial lighting, and the same vehicle was put into storage at the Wisconsin Crime Lab in Madison.

(3). Teresa's RAV4 was driven into Avery Salvage via Kuss Rd and the quarry.

III

KEY EVIDENCE

The basics:

1. Teresa's RAV4 key was found in Avery's trailer on the 7th search of his home, by MCSD's Colborn and Lenk.

2. MCSD were, by their own admission, in conflict of interest with Avery due to the pending $30 plus million dollar civil suit, filed by Avery for his wrongful 1985 incarceration - and its intentional prolonging.

3. The key found in Avery's trailer was a 'spare key'; the RAV4 came with two keys, one main key, and a sub/valet key. The sub key did not open the glove-box or trunk.

4. The key was wiped clean. It held no finger prints. It held none of Teresa's DNA. It did however, hold a tiny amount of Avery's DNA. This implies that the key was cleaned, and then:

   (a) Avery put his skin-cell DNA back onto it, or;

   (b) Someone else cleaned the key when wiping the other fingerprint prone areas, and the police, or cunning Third-party killer, used Avery's toothbrush, or 'sink blood' to dope the key.

Keys

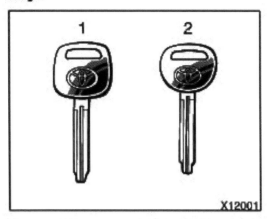

Your vehicle is supplied with two kinds of key.

1. Master key—This key works in every lock.

2. Sub key—This key will not work in the glove box.

To protect things locked in the glove box when you have your vehicle parked, leave the sub key with the attendant.

Since the side doors, back door (hardtop) and tailgate (soft-top) can be locked without a key, you should always carry a spare master key in case you accidentally lock your keys inside the vehicle.

From Toyota RAV4 Owner's Manual

It has been raised that because the key is the sub, and not the main, that this shows it was planted by police.

Why?

Which key was Teresa using?

Did she recently loose the main key, and start using the sub?

Fassbender retrieved underwear from Teresa's home for forensic testing; did he find the sub key there and think: *this could come in handy?*

This is what we noticed:

The sub key was not well worn.

However, it was attached to the ring and lanyard that Teresa's sister bought for Teresa as a gift from an agricultural show. The lanyard clips into a second section via a standard plastic clip. This second section was inside the RAV4, suggesting that Teresa was indeed using the sub key.

Was the second part of the lanyard planted in the RAV4?

We don't think so, because:

Teresa used this lanyard on her car-key. It would be found attached to the current key that Teresa was using to operate her RAV4.

If the lanyard was on the main-key, then police would've had to have the main key to have the ring side of the lanyard; and therefore would have simply planted the main-key.

Conclusions:

(a) The key pictured, is the key found in Avery's trailer, is the key Teresa was using.

(b) The person who parked the RAV4 where it was found on Avery Salvage locked the vehicle, and kept possession of the key. This could have been Colborn. It could have been a third-party killer.

(c) If Colborn was the 'planter', it explains how he and Lenk found the key in Avery's trailer; but it doesn't explain who killed Teresa, or how Colborn would know she was dead.

(d) If a third-party killer (and there are many possible 'other suspects'), then 'he' planted the RAV4, got out, locked it, and took the key with him. A third-party killer still has the key and needs to get it into Avery's trailer.

(e) Anyone of these planters had to also remove both the RAV4's license plates, crumple them, and put them in the Mercury wagon 130 yards from Avery's trailer.

But if Avery was the killer, then:

(a) He put the RAV4 by the pond and took the key back to his trailer, which seems totally stupid and unnecessary considering his intention to crush it later using the front-end-loader. Avery had no need for the key.

(b) If Avery wanted the RAV4 locked to prevent family, or Brendan looking inside, then why did he not throw the key into the Mercury along with the plates and panties; why keep the key?

However, (valid or not) Dassey corroborates the following:

(a) That he and Steven put Teresa's RAV4 by the pond, covered it with debris, and walked home.

(b) That Steven went under the RAV4's hood.

(c) That Steven put Teresa's key in a draw inside Steven's Trailer, after dropping it.

There are problems with Dassey seeing the *key*:

(a) Steven owned or operated at least 6 vehicles; the Monte Carlo, the Grand Am, the F-250, the Blazer, the Suzuki Samurai, and the snow-mobile. Brendan could have seen Steven put any one of these keys in his draw, cabinet, or drop any one of these keys on the floor.

(b) When investigators asked Brendan about seeing the key, his low IQ may have led him to agree with the key being Teresa's; or, investigators low IQ may have led them to think any key going in a draw must have been Teresa's. Brendan also said that Steven dropped the key and never picked it up. That's pretty careless if it was the key of the girl he made an appointment with and then murdered.

So how'd it get there?

In the May 13th interview, Wiegert says: Let's go back to this key again. Did you *really* see him drop it?

Teresa's key and lanyard - the same key that she started the RAV's engine with on October 31st, 2005 - was found in the Mercury Wagon along with the plates and panties - and was then transferred to Avery's trailer by Sergeant Colborn.

Why would Law Enforcement take this risk?

(a) When the key was planted or found, Dassey was not yet thought to be a part of events. They had no Dassey corroborations yet.

(b) The RAV4 on the property, the bones in the fire-pit, the untested blood in the RAV4, the plates and panties, the electronics - although convincing, none of these evidential items proved solidly that Steven actually killed Teresa. It could've been anyone.

Teresa's key was something the murder victim owned that is now in the main suspect's home.

It bolsters the case against Steven.

But the key plant was so badly executed,(in the way it was missed again and again, and then magically drops sideways and not down, from the cabinet lining, and was then found by MCSD) that it will eventually help destroy the case; and even if Avery was the killer, it will help set him free.

But what if the killer was Earl Avery, Chuck Avery, Bobby Dassey, Scott Tadych, or someone else looking for an *easy set-up*?

Police only had eyes for Steven.

They *believed* Steven killed Teresa.

But in planting Steven's blood and RAV4's key, police ended their ability to even consider anyone else - but they also trapped themselves in the lie, having to suppress other evidence to avoid getting caught.

* If not found in the Mercury Wagon, or the nearby trailer where the underwear was recovered, the sub-key could have been collected from Teresa's home; but that doesn't explain why Teresa's lanyard was on it. 'Avery the killer', or any other killer, could not have disposed of the main-key, only to have the lanyard turn up on the sub-key. Therefore the sub-key was the key Teresa was using, and the key that the killer used to lock the car.

IV

BLOOD

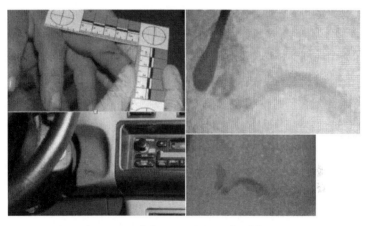

Avery's cut, and the suspicious ignition smear.

(1) Avery's Blood

Steven Avery had a cut on his right middle finger. His
blood, possibly from this cut, was found in several locations:

   a. The sink in his trailer.

   b. The floor by the sink.

   c. The lounge seat.

   d. A cushion.

   e. An internal door.

   f. The front door.

   g. The garage door.

   h. Multiple spots on the garage floor.

   i. The interior of his Pontiac, Grand Am.

   And;

   j. Teresa's RAV4.

The 6 daubs of Avery's blood, (5 inside the RAV4, and 1 on
the rear door-shut) don't add up in a number of ways,
making the defense position of Avery's blood planting
appear plausible enough to counter the prosecution.

  If Avery was bleeding from his cut finger, enough to
leave such daubs and smears, then his blood could also have
been:
    On the handbrake release.
    On the door handle.
    On the hood prop.

The rear vision mirror.
The gear shift.
Interior hood release.
Unless wiped down.

Blood should have been left on:
Interior trunk/ cargo door release.
The hood.
The hood latch.
The battery connection.
Unless Avery wore gloves when he drove the RAV4
to the pond.

Avery's clothing, through wiping.
The shovel used in the fire-pit.
The rake used in the fire-pit.
The bleach bottles.
Unless Avery put a plaster on the cut.

Possibly:
The driver's seat slide bar. (Although he would
likely use his left hand to slide the seat.)
His phone.
The Ford F-250 pick-up truck that Avery drove to
Patsy's gas station, around 5:10pm on Halloween.
And the fuel can that he filled there.

Blood from Avery's finger cut was found in Avery's sink, on
his front door, on a garage door, on a cushion in his trailer,
on his garage floor in multiple locations, and inside his
Pontiac Grand Am.

Zellner argues that if the prosecution were correct,
for Avery to drip blood in Teresa's RAV4, 'Avery the killer'
could not have been wearing gloves; so why were none of
his fingerprints found? The Zellner argument goes: if Avery
was the killer, why was his blood on some areas of the

RAV4 and not others? And why are others' fingerprints on Teresa's RAV4, but not Avery's or Dassey's?

Zellner taunts: 'Steven the idiot' leaves blood, whilst 'Steven the savant' cleans his prints.

One cannot leave blood, but no fingerprints.

But is this true?

What circumstances can lead to genuine blood transfer, and no fingerprints found in the RAV4?

1. Selective wiping is one answer; in the dark, 'Avery the killer' would not wipe the whole car down. 'Avery the killer' had to get back and clean the crime scene. If Avery did bleed in the RAV4, he must have quickly wiped-clean his fingerprints, and inadvertently his blood drips from:

Steering wheel.

Handbrake.

Gearshift.

Rear vision mirror.

Door handle.

Hood.

In this theory, he failed to wipe other areas because he didn't realize he'd bleed on them.

If Avery bleed in Teresa's car, he *did not* wear gloves.

But if this is true, there should be blood on the hood, and hood-latch, but there is not.

The issues here are in what parts of the RAV4 were 'wiped down' by the killer, and which were not.

The killer *did* touch the RAV4, because Teresa's blood was found in the rear cargo compartment.

Eight other sets of fingerprints were found on the vehicle, but not Avery's or Dassey's.

Even if the police or a third-party planted the RAV4, they would have needed to wipe-off the parts they touched;

the steering wheel, door handle, gear-shift, hand-brake etc, unless they wore gloves. In this theory, it appears that the real killer did only enough wiping to eliminate their own prints.

The Zellner theory aligns with the Buting theory; that Avery must have worn gloves to have eliminated his fingerprints, whilst leaving others; and therefore any blood in the RAV4 was planted by police.

Zellner is not saying she thinks Avery was in the RAV4, she is saying police simply planted his blood.

But remember, Brendan Dassey stated that Avery put a band-aid on Avery's cut finger. (A band-aid is a small, sticky first-aid plaster) Therefore, it is thought, if Avery bleed in the RAV4, it had to have seeped through the plaster, and any marks should carry this signature.

But, not so fast.

2. Either Avery did bleed in the RAV4, through the band-aid, and because it was dark, didn't realize and focused on wiping the *finger-print* surfaces, like steering wheel, gear-shift etc. He didn't realize he was bleeding, but knew fingerprints needed to be wiped; or:

3. Avery's blood was planted, but 'Avery the killer' had already wiped the surfaces he finger-printed before the police planted his blood; or:

4. Avery is innocent and police planted his blood. This is the third-party killer scenario; or:

5. Brendan says Avery did not put on the Band-aid until the garage phase of Teresa's abduction. Therefore, this opens up the possibility that Avery deposited his blood in the RAV4 whilst moving it from his driveway, into his garage, and not down in the salvage yard.

If Avery is the killer, he moved the RAV4 several times:

1.   From the driveway into his garage.

2.   From the garage to the pond.

3.   From the pond to the fire-pit.

4.   From the fire-pit back to the pond.

Between points 1 and 2, Avery dripped blood on the garage floor, and at several locations in his trailer; (front door, internal door, cushion.) This garage and trailer blood was tested and confirmed as Avery's, and is not considered to be planted. These were small amounts.

At point 2, Avery puts a Band-aid on the cut. 'Avery the killer' then puts on his gloves to lift Teresa's body into the trunk, and then drives the RAV4 down into the yard, leaving no fingerprints, but smears of blood. He wipes only the steering wheel, gearshift and handbrake. Avery's blood is deposited in the RAV4 before it is moved into the garage. The brief wiping is done in the salvage yard.

Therefore, it is *possible* to leave blood in Teresa's RAV4, but no fingerprints, whilst leaving historical fingerprints intact.

However, the defense alleges *blood planting*, and their position is strong enough to cancel out the blood evidence presented by the prosecution for one reason.

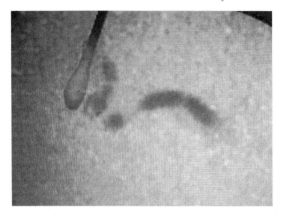

RAV4 ignition molding; Avery's blood

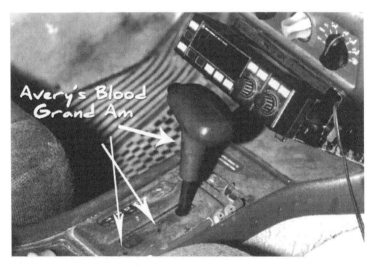

Trial Exhibit 305; Avery's Grand Am.

We think that *if* Avery's blood was planted in the RAV4, it had to be by Law Enforcement, because no one else had access to *enough* of Avery's blood.

The 'ignition bloodstain' in the RAV4 appears so obviously *painted* on with a swab, when viewed in the above image that we are forced to either:

1. Discount *Avery's* blood evidence found in the RAV4 because of inherent doubt, or;

2. Conclude that Avery's blood *was* planted by police.

When searching Avery's Pontiac Grand Am sports car, investigators found small droplets of Avery's blood on interior surfaces, which had presumably come from Avery's cut finger. This 'Grand Am blood' was deposited before 2:35pm - before Teresa arrived.

A witness testified that Avery had cut his right middle finger several days before. It appears that Avery re-opened the wound on Halloween, when unhooking a trailer.

We think the Grand Am blood droplets could have sparked the police idea to plant similar droplets in Teresa's RAV4.

However, the patterns *are* different. The RAV4 has smears, and the Pontiac has droplets.

Mr. Kratz was caught in a lie by youtuber Erekose. Kratz had claimed that the prosecution knew nothing of the 1996 blood vial, stored under seal at clerk of courts facility. But Kratz had mentioned the vial in an earlier email. Regards the vial, the nurse who drew Avery's blood and filled the vial stated that she had made the 'needle hole' in the rubber stopper whilst filling the tube. This hole could have been used by the planter to extract a few milliliters of blood. However, the blood from the RAV4 did not test positive for EDTA. But did they simply swap the swabs? Did Kratz give the FBI's Mark Le Beau Avery's 1996 vial, and blood swabs from someone else? The FBI only tested for presence of EDTA preservative, and did not confirm identity. It is possible that other vials of Avery's blood existed in storage elsewhere, that did not contain EDTA.

Back to the garage: Dassey said Avery cut the finger whilst attacking and restraining Teresa, or on glass, but Brendan could also have been *assuming* that was what had happened; anything could have re-opened Avery's old cut, and restarted the bleeding.

So what about the blood drips on Avery's garage floor?

Dassey said during an interview, that Steven had actually 'put a band-aid on his finger', at some point during the garage phase of Teresa's murder. If so, did Avery put the plaster on before or after they bleached the floor?

Here, Zellner raises a potent question: how does Avery clean all of Teresa's blood into a bleach smear that rendered blood testing inconclusive – but not destroy his own blood in the process?

Well firstly, beware the deception here:

Bleach *was* used on the floor, and Avery's blood *did* survive.

There is no doubt bleach was used on Avery's garage floor in a 3ft by 3ft area, co-incidentally on the same night Teresa vanishes.

The bleach appears to have been used to clean blood, but the smeared material was sufficiently broken-down so-as-to make testing inconclusive.

Dassey described the material to his mother, as 'reddish-black'.

But Zellner asks: If the bleach broke down Teresa's blood, how could it not have broken down Avery's blood too?

Brendan said that there was a lot of blood on the floor where he stabbed, and Steven shot Teresa. Brendan said they used bleach, thinner, and gas, along with clothing and rags to clean Teresa's blood.

For Avery's blood to remain when Teresa's dissolved, the following could have happened:

1. Avery dripped the blood before the bleaching, but his blood spots were found outside the bleached area; surely this is a given; or:

2. Avery may have dripped blood on the garage after he and Brendan had dried the bleach up with the rags, but by this stage, he should've had a plaster on the cut.

Our conclusion on Avery's blood is: all of Strang's, Buting's, and Zellner's questions have answers; all arguments, solutions. It is the ignition smear that casts doubt over the genuineness of the prosecution's blood evidence. If one smear of Avery's blood in the RAV4 is planted – then all Avery's blood in the RAV4 is planted.

(2) Teresa's Blood

If Teresa's blood was in the garage where Dassey said it was, her blood was destroyed by the bleach. Dassey drew a plan of the garage, indicating where the blood was, and this aligned with the bleach smear.

However, Teresa's blood was confirmed in only one location; the rear cargo area of her RAV4. A small patch in the rear cargo compartment, on the passengers' side wheel arch trim; and a 'pattern' on the inside of the cargo / trunk door.

Teresa's blood in the cargo area means that she was put inside.

Zellner has employed a blood pattern expert that analyzed the inside of the cargo door trim, and concluded differently to the original prosecution's expert.

We believe Zellner's expert will be correct.

Zellner's expert says that this blood pattern was cause by blunt trauma to the head, causing cast-off droplets to create the pattern.

I.e. Teresa opens her cargo door and her assailant hits her from behind with a hammer, or lug-wrench.

The other stain, the stain on the wheel arch trim inside the cargo hold, could have been created at this time, as Teresa's body was pushed inside. This is the Hillegas theory.

The Avery theory postulates that Steven hit Teresa with a hammer, breaking her skull - and then assisted the dazed Teresa into his trailer, and to the bed, where he restrained her whilst barely conscious.

The Avery theory also postulates that the 'impact stain' or 'hair contact stain' inside the car, was caused when Avery loaded Teresa into the cargo hold *after* shooting her in his garage.

Further bloodstain patterns were then created as Avery drove Teresa's body to the pond – his initial idea for disposing of her – and then back to the fire.

So why no blood pooling in the RAV4's rear?

The only answer in the Avery theory is a trunk or cargo liner, such as a tarpaulin, plastic sheeting, or blankets. There was clear plastic sheeting on a wall inside Avery's garage; as seen in photos.

The only thing Teresa's blood in the rear of the RAV4 proves, however, is that Teresa bludgeoned beside the open door; was put in the cargo area; and was then driven over rough ground.

(3) Unidentified Blood

A daub of male's *xy* blood, other than Steven Avery's, Brendan Dassey's, and Allen Avery's, was found in Teresa's RAV4.

What does this mean?

The defense says the presence of another male's blood excludes Steven and Brendan – but of course, it does not. What are the options?

a. The mystery blood could be historical; i.e. the unknown male dripped blood in Teresa's car before she drove to Avery Salvage on Halloween, 2005.

b. Or Avery and Dassey were assisted by a third male.

c. Or, like Zellner implies, a lone-wolf killed Teresa, and the police planted Avery's blood.

First, we must ask: Who was eliminated by blood sample?

Which males in the wider police investigation gave blood sample elimination exemplars?

Well, the answer is none.

This unidentified bloodstain will remain unidentified until blood samples are taken, and elimination protocols put in place. Elimination exemplars for blood were isolated to those on the Avery property at the time. Exemplars should have included: Scott Bloedorn, Ryan Hillegas, George

Zipperer, Andres Martinez, All Avery and Dassey males, All Halbach males, and all males in conflict of interest with the accused. New elimination testing should include all of these, and Edward Wayne Edwards.

The question from within the group is: Is the unidentified blood Charles Avery's? Did Chuck assist Steven and Brendan?

On November 5th, cadaver-dogs indicated in Chuck's bedroom, giving a 90% chance that human cadaver sent was brought in there.

Steven called Chuck at 5:57pm on Halloween. When investigators asked Brendan if Chuck 'saw anything', Brendan answered, 'probably'.

Chuck needs to be eliminated from the RAV4's unidentified bloodstain. This also casts doubt over the validity of Chuck Avery's statement to police; that at around 8:00pm on November 4th, Chuck saw headlights in the yard, near the area where the RAV4 would be found the next morning.

All Averys and all Dasseys except Bryan, gave buccal samples for DNA elimination purposes.

Can a DNA profile be drawn from the mystery blood, and compared to the collection of buccal DNA?

IV

SWEATING BULLETS

On March 1st the crime-lab discovered two small caliber bullet *entry* holes in (one side of) Teresa's recovered skull bones. The holes held trace lead and matched a small caliber consistent with a .22 rim-fire rifle, or 5.56mm center-fire rifle.

Steven wasn't talking, so investigators went for Brendan.

Wiegert and Fassbender clearly led Brendan to say Steven shot Teresa twice in the head. Brendan also offered 8 further shots to the body.

Brendan said Steven shot Teresa between 5 and 10 times in Steven's garage; the same garage that Brendan and Steven had bleached on that very same night.

The bleaching is not disputed. Brendan's Mom gave police Brendan's bleach stained jeans. Two empty bottles of

Bright 'n' Shine Bleach were found in Stevens' garage; and Brendan told his Mom about bleaching reddish black stuff from Steven's garage floor over the recorded prison phonelines.

Then police found their two .22 long rifle projectiles, one under a compressor, and one in a crack in the floor.

Let's assess:

(a) Steven had two .22 caliber rifles in his trailer, which police recovered and tested; one had been wiped clean of all prints and DNA, and one had not.

(b) Crime scene investigators though the reason for the bleach wipe-down of the firearm was to remove fine blood droplets from the fine blood droplet blow-back associated with close range shootings.

(c) In the later 'third-party' setup scenarios, we might ask: would any third-party killer break into Avery's trailer and wipe the gun down?

(d) The two shots to Teresa's skull entered the brain cavity and did not exit. These projectiles were burned with the body.

(e) If the two projectiles police recovered from Steven's garage floor were genuine, and not doctored evidence, they were from body-shots. These 'body-shots' were gained from Brendan by coercion; it was the two 'head-shots' that Fassbender did not fed to him. However, at this point, more study of the entire interview process and transcripts is clearly needed.

(f) A released former prison inmate told police that Avery had told him about Teresa's rape and murder. We put very little credence in prison informants. However, this informant should not have had any knowledge of what he did say. The informant said Steven told him that he had shot Teresa 10 or 11 times after she had died from strangulation inside the trailer, even before 'the stupid fuck' (Brendan) had sex with her dead body. It is the 'shooting part of this *narc* that interests us here. Why?

(g) If police thought only two shots went into Teresa's skull, and did not exit, then no projectiles would be in the garage. But after hearing about the 8 potential 'body-shots', they suddenly find two projectiles, matching Steven's DNA and fingerprint free twenty-two.

(h) Where were the other 6 projectiles? They did not exit the garage. However, Brendan also said Steven shot her outside, and inside the garage.

(i) The search for these other projectiles was very, very, very below par. Is that because they had already found what they needed? Or;

(j) They never found a projectile at all.

(k) Police test fired Steven's .22 for the purpose of forensic matching of ammunition to rifle.

(l) Did police simply use two of these test projectiles, and wipe Teresa's DNA onto one.

(m) Police had Teresa's pap smears, dirty panties, and toothbrush - all rich sources of DNA.

(o) Did police come up with the story of sample contamination on purpose? In court, the crime-lab's Sherry Culhane says she introduced her own DNA into the 'control sample', but not the 'main sample', of the bullet DNA. This usually voids the test. However, it also makes it look like only two projectiles were really found, and only one had a tiny amount of Teresa's DNA. This gives the bullet test a genuine appearance, whilst providing the *jury* with further scientific evidence.

We are sure prosecution saw this as a slam-dunk; DNA evidence recovered from the defendant's garage, corroborated by witness confession.

We can show that Avery's blood and the key were planted, but the bullet DNA is much harder. However, if one piece of evidence was planted, then a mistrial is the result. If one piece of evidence was planted, what is to say that other evidence was not also planted?

When Brendan told investigators that Avery when under the RAV4's hood, suddenly they found Avery's DNA on the hood latch. There appears to be 'too much' of Avery's DNA on this latch (1.9ng), when reconstructed tests suggest this type of contact transfer should leave less than 1.0ng. If the hood latch DNA was doctored, is the bullet find cast into doubt?

Of course.

Ms. Zellner dubs this bullet the 'magic bullet'. She says that once again, this magic bullet magically appeared after Brendan told investigators Teresa was shot in Steven's garage.

This bullet find came late in the piece; all other evidence had been either planted or found at this point.

The planted key puts Teresa's property inside Avery's home.

So why doctor this bullet, Evidential Item FL?

If this bullet was doctored, it's method was far different and far superior to any of the other sloppy evidence tampering.

The bullet projectile (FL) held minute trace material.

a. Red paint.

b. Wood.

c. Teresa's DNA.

When the crime lab test fires firearms and recovers the projectiles and casings for forensic testing, they fire the weapon into ballistics gel, which absorbs the projectile's energy slower than wood, or a hard painted surface. The Item FL projectile had hit a hard surface and as such, was highly deformed; this rules out Item FL from being recovered from the lab's test firing range.

The minute trace paint, and wood profiles on the projectile are from impacts whilst the bullet was flying at high speed. If doctored, the *minute* amounts of paint and wood used suggest a significant improvement in the doctoring techniques used.

The blood was poorly applied to the RAV4's dash; and the hood-latch DNA was over applied by twice the expected amount.

But was the bullet fired outside of the range? Was it fired inside Avery's garage by investigators, and then recovered?

It is possible; however, the amount of Teresa's DNA on the bullet was so minute that only one forensic test could be done. Could these bumbling keystone cops really screw up the other evidence tampering, and then nail this bullet so genuinely?

If Teresa's underwear, or her toothbrush was used to apply her DNA to that bullet, then more DNA would have been on the bullet than was found - just like the hood-latch swab. (This was explained to us by a scientist at the New York Crime lab, under the proviso that it was not quoted.)

If so, then the combination of these details suggests that the bullet, Item FL, could be the only *real* piece of *forensic* evidence that investigators found definitively linking Teresa to Avery's weapon and garage.

But there is more.

VI

CUTTING TO THE BONE

Someone *did* murder Teresa and someone *did* burn her body.

The bones found in Avery's fire-pit and burn-barrel were human female bones. One of the bones, a shinbone, held tissue from which a partial DNA profile was gained.

7 of the 16 loci were isolated. The calculated probability that the tissue is not Teresa's is, one-in-one billion; i.e. there is virtually no chance that the tissue recovered from Avery's pit was someone other that Teresa's.

If Culhane is presenting the truth, then Teresa's *actual tissue* was recovered from Avery's fire-pit.

Therefore, unless Teresa amputated her lower leg, and eloped to South Africa, we can at least assume her to be dead, and the cremains hers. Teresa was not human trafficked, unless her leg was surgically amputated.

So - how do Teresa's bones get into Avery's fire-pit, grass, and barrel? There are four possibilities:

(a) Avery killed Teresa as per the Dassey explanation.

(b) The police killed Teresa, burned her body, and planted the cremains there.

(c) A third-party killer burned Teresa's body elsewhere, and then planted the remains in Steven's pit and barrel without arousing suspicion, or being seen; which is not impossible.

(d) If a third-party did plant Teresa's cremains in Avery's pit, then they had to have pulled material out of the pit, where Avery and Brendan did burn a bonfire on Halloween, put the bones underneath, along with the steel-belting that Teresa's body was actually burned with. This could only have been done between Nov 2nd, and 3:30pm on Nov 5th. We will see why this is soon. Or;

(e) In an elaborate ruse, Teresa amputates her leg (her flesh and sinew were attached to the shinbone). Her accomplices somehow acquire a spare body to burn; maybe from a cemetery. They burn this body so as *all* DNA material is gone, and then plant the material in Avery's pit along with Teresa's amputated leg. Police test the bones and (luckily) only find Teresa's DNA. (Partial DNA profile, 7 of 16 loci. 1:1000,000,000). This theory of Teresa faking her own death are indeed circulating the internet; but leg amputation is non-negotiable if she did.

There are however, several disputed facts, and 'oddities' concerning the burned bones, dubbed cremains.

(1) A piece of 'possible human pelvis bone' was recovered from a site on County land, accessed by Radandt's quarry. This is near the rear entry to Avery Salvage. For some reason, this bone has not been firmly identified as human by the State. Did this bone chunk show signs of having been heated, or burned?

(2) Cadaver-dogs indicated the historical presence of a corpse in several locations both on and *off* the Avery property; locations which access the Radandt quarry, and Kuss Rd, which could (then, but not now) access Avery's trailer, via a vehicle track across a paddock.

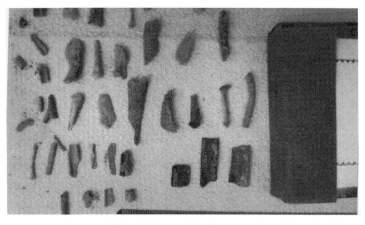

Exhibit of Teresa Halbach's cremains

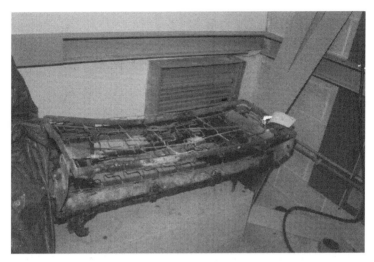

Exhibit 371, the van seat

(1) A Steely Argument

Questions regarding Teresa's bones and cremains have circulated the globe. The most significant are:

1. If Avery's fire-pit is Teresa's *original* burn site, why are 60% of her bones, and all but one of her teeth missing? This implies that some of her bones and 29 teeth are still at the 'original burn site'.

2. Why are bone fragments found in the grass, several feet from Avery's burn-pit? This implies that cremains were dropped by the killer whilst planting the bones in Avery's burn pit.

3. Why are the bones not 'melded' into the tire's steel-belts? This implies the cremains were not burned with the tires.

4. Why is Teresa's skeleton not in anatomical alignment? This implies the cremains were transported from another site.

We do know that Teresa's bones were enmeshed and inter-twined in some of the steel belting.

CSI's removing the cremains had to pull apart and cut the tires' steel wire-mesh to remove some of the bone. Bone was also entwined with the van seat.

This suggests that Teresa was burned **with** those tires and that van seat.

The six steel wheel-rims, and some of the steel-belting, was dragged out of that fire-pit (from the Halloween fire Avery denied having) on November 2nd, and stacked for Brendan to remove, says Earl Avery who witnessed this stacking and Brendan's subsequent removal.

This is the day before the police 'found' Teresa's RAV4 during their aerial search. If Avery had dragged the rims and the belting out of the Halloween fire-pit, and stacked them up for Brendan to remove, how did he forget having that fire?

The long, bench style van seat was on top of the wheel rims. To access the rims, Avery would have lifted out the seat. Teresa's bones were 'inter-twined' with this seat. This seat was in the pit before the property was seized.

Okay; Brendan said that he collected the tires and the van seat on Halloween (in a golf cart) for Steven to burn. Teresa was burned with the tires found in the pit, and the van seat, so was Teresa burned in that same pit? Does the bone inter-meshed with the steel belting and the seat mesh prove this pit was the original site?

It would seem so, but if so, why is 60% of her bone-mass missing?

The answer lies in thermodynamics.

Human bone will burn to ash at temperatures above 1400°F. To burn 60% of Teresa's bone mass, Avery's fire must reach temperatures above 1400°.

We know Avery's fire-pit reaches temperatures between 800° and 2500° Fahrenheit. Why?

Below 800°F the tires won't burn (the ignition point of automotive tire rubber); and above 2500°F, the steel wheel-rims would have started melting, but did not.

Teresa's bones however, were enmeshed in the steel belting, which had to be pried apart to remove the fragments.

In open pit fires, the fire will be at different temperatures at different parts of the fire-pit. Temperature distribution is not even like in an oven, and in-fact can fluctuate by hundreds of degrees.

So to answer the question: where is the missing 60% of Teresa's bone mass, we can say:

If burned in Steven's fire-pit, roughly, 60% of Teresa's bones reached 1400°F and burned to ash, but as some areas of the fire did not reach the required 1400°F, 40% of her bones survive intact. The steel rims would also act as shielding to certain bones.

Brendan said that Teresa was ***underneath*** the tires. Heat rises. Therefore, the full heat of the tires does not reach Teresa; enough heat is produced to cremate 60% of her body, but leaves 40% of her bones intact.

If she were put on top of the tires, a higher degree of burning would have occurred, and less bone would have remained.

So why is only one of Teresa's teeth found?

Even in a cremation oven, which reaches around 1800°F, the teeth remain intact, (and are later ground up).

Did the missing teeth get knocked by Avery's mixing and shoveling (as reported by Brendan, Kayla, and Blaine), into a hotter part of the fire-pit than the others, where they reached 2000°F and burned up. We find this unlikely, but possible. The entire jaw-structure is gone; burned to ash. This fact suggests the jaws reached a hot enough temperature to burn both the bone, and 29 of the teeth. The one tooth found, remained intact because it did not reach the ignition temperature of human tooth enamel. The Journal of Forensic Sciences says that at 600°C (1112°F):

(a) Teeth appeared charred and;

(b) Disintegrated completely during decalcification.

Information suggests that for Teresa's 29 teeth to burn to ash, they must have reached temperatures exceeding 1800°F. However, information also suggests that micro-particles would have remained in the fire-pit's ash layer, and *could* have been found had the correct techniques been used to excavate the pit. The microscopic damage incurred by the single surviving tooth's structure can also give an idea of the temperature that it reached.

For Avery's bonfire to burn the teeth, it had to reach unusually high temperatures for an open pit fire; but the combined kilowatts produced by the six gasoline soaked tires provides the needed heat for between 16 - 47 minutes, depending on the layout of the fuel. The conclusion is that it is clearly possible for the teeth to burn in Avery's fire.

Another big question is: why are Teresa's bones not melted, or melded into the steel-belting?

Well, bone is a funny thing.

Bone has an *ignition* point of around 1400°F, but bone's *melting* point is a whopping 3038°F. Bone has a much higher melting point than pure calcium; almost twice the temperature. This makes bone very hard to melt in fire; specifically, the fire must be at a temperature of 3038°F before the bone is inserted, or it will combust and burn before it can melt.

Bone in a cremation oven, at 1800°F, does not melt; it burns to dust, ash, fragments, and chunks.

Therefore, Teresa's bones could not have 'melded' into the steel-belting, because the fire did not reach bone's melting point.

The melting point of the automotive steel wheel rims is around 2550°F. If Avery's wheel rims did not melt in his fire, then Teresa's bone could not have melted.

Ms. Zellner raised the question: if Avery's burn-pit is where Teresa was *originally* burned, why are bone fragments found in the grass, several feet from the burn pit?

We had a range of possible answers:

a. Avery's German Sheppard dragged them out.

b. The bone fragments came out on November 2nd, when Steven dragged out the burned steel-belts, and the 6 wheel rims. Remember Earl Avery said that Steven had the 6 rims, and some of the steel belting stacked up out the front, ready for Brendan to take down to the yard. Steven had phoned Brendan and told him to remove the steel to the collection pile for recycling.

This is the most obvious way that a few fragments of Teresa's cremains get from the fire-pit, to the grass, but;

c. The bone fragments could have also dropped out when Steven transferred some of the larger bones to the burn barrel. 'Avery the killer' would transfer the bones to the barrel to hide un-burned bone from daylight viewing; or to continue burning them after the big fire was out.

Zellner's point is that a third-party killer could have used the burn drum to plant the cremains in Avery's pit, and dropped some in the grass in the process.

So why is Teresa's skeleton not in the normal anatomical position described at other open pit cremations? Does this mean her cremains were moved to Avery's pit from another site using the drum?

Well If so:

a. The tires and the van seat had to have been moved from this original site also, as Teresa's body was burned with them.

b. Movement; Brendan said Steven "*banged on the bones with the shovel*", and, "*mixed it around*", presumably to keep the parts burning hot. This agitation would move the bones and effect the alignment.

c. Un-burned Bones were taken out and put in the barrel, presumably to hide them from view; altering the alignment; and:

d. Steven pulled out the 6 steel rims, and some of the steel-belting for Brendan to take away. This would disturb the skeletal alignment the most.

All the defense want to achieve is juror doubt. They want to show that there is another explanation that nullifies the prosecution's theory. We can look at what is most likely. Surely, if Teresa was burned with Dassey's tires, then a microscopic amount of cremated bone chip would have remained within the belts that he took to the steel recycling pile. Were these ever examined?

For the police to have planted Teresa's burned, cremated corpse, they would've had to have known where her body was burned. This seems implausible.

A third-party could have planted the cremains, but would have done so whilst the salvage yard was under police lock down.

Interestingly, both Josh Radandt and Ryan Hillegas signed in to the property and went through the police cordon on November 7th.

Teresa's bones were found on November 8th.

(2) Cadaver Dogs

Research on cadaver-dogs shows that they are 90 – 100% reliable in Identifying scent from *human* corpses, whilst differentiating from other sources of decomposing material. A comprehensive pair-reviewed study showed an error rate ranging from 10% false positives, down to 0% false indications. The dogs track the strong smell of gases released by the body's cavities after death; these odors are unique to humans, and can be differentiated from other smells, just like drug-dogs can differentiate between narcotics.

However, when any evidence is proposed in a murder case, it *must* be corroborated by at least one other piece of evidence. Blood or a body is also needed to corroborate any cadaver dog indications.

But Cadaver dogs are still very useful.

The only corroborated cadaver-dog evidence in the Halbach case is: the rear cargo area of Teresa's RAV4.

The RAV4 contains Teresa's blood, and cadaver-dogs indicated the historical presence of a human corpse. From this, we can *'assume'* that Teresa's dead body was in the rear compartment of her RAV4.

We believe that this is a fair and correct assumption.

Cadaver-dogs did not go into Avery's burn pit area because Avery's guard-dog was tied up near the pit; the scent-dog teams focused on the 'track', which went from

Steven Avery's trailer, across the paddock to Kuss Rd, up through the quarry, and down to the pond where the RAV4 was found - then from the RAV4 to the quarry gate, and back up the berm between the Yard and the Quarry, to Steven's trailer.

Bear in mind, that this cadaver track could also have been made, by the killer, in reverse direction, as he transported the cremains in from the quarry.

A third-party killer could have:

(a) killed Teresa off site and brought her to the Kuss cul-de-sac.

(b) Stopped to collect a burn-drum from the deer camp.

(c) Driven into the quarry and burned her body where the pelvis is indicated.

(d) Taken the cremains back to Avery's in the barrel.

(e) Driven the RAV4 back to the Quarry, and into the salvage yard; carrying the cadaver's scent in the rear compartment.

One can see why police felt the need to plant the blood and the key. But this doesn't explain how a third-party killer left the quarry; and it doesn't explain the strong cadaver track from the salvage yard's rear gate, and along the berm, to Avery's trailer.

However, the 9 year-old cadaver-dog, Brutus, from Great Lakes Search & Rescue, started his scent work on the Avery property at 3:30pm on November 5th. Brutus indicated the cadaver-track shown in the later aerial photos; the very track Brendan said Avery and he drove Teresa's RAV4 to the pond.

Brutus indicated this track 3 days before Teresa's cremains were found, suggesting:

A cadaver was taken around that track, from the pond to Avery's trailer, *before* police found the bones in his pit. Another dog, Trace, indicated the same track independently. Why would a cadaver be on the property before the third-party killer planted the cremains?

A dead human corpse was on Avery land before November 5th, and before Hillegas and Radandt are said to have planted Teresa's cremains on the 7th.

Any planting of cremains had to have happened before 3:30pm on November 5th.

As Avery cleaned out his fire-pit on November 2nd, and reportedly saw no cremains, then one must conclude that any 'planting' of Teresa's cremains, and the creating of the cadaver track around the quarry and berm, happened between November 2nd, and November 5th.

Avery Salvage and Quarry from the Kuss Rd side, 2005.
The pins indicate the strong cadaver-dog indications; which are
different than just interest or winding.

The 'swirl track' shows the 'cadaver tracks' of independent cadaver-dogs, Brutus, and Trace, operated by Great Lakes Search & Rescue.

The theory developed by investigators was that whoever hid the RAV4 by the pond, carried cadaver scent as they walked back along the bank/ berm track, bordering the salvage yard and the quarry, toward Steven's trailer. This berm could be driven. The remaining 'cadaver tracks', were where the RAV4, holding Teresa's cadaver, was driven. Stronger indications are given at points where the RAV4 stopped.

Is this the track of a third-party killer?

When asked by which route Steven took the RAV4 to the yard/ pond, Brendan Dassey said they took it the exact way indicated by the cadaver-dog track; and that they walked home along the berm.

If they walked, there are two ways:

(1) Past the crusher and Chuck Avery's and out through the salvage yard's front entrance to the bus drop-off, and up the lane; where they would be surely seen; or:

(2) Along the berm and straight up to Steven's trailer, unseen. This is because the yard is set in a depression. The banks are steep from the yard's pit in the other directions, and are protected by hurricane-wire fencing. Although not impossible to negotiate, it is clearly easier to walk out of the salvage yard by the rear gate, and proceed unseen, along the berm, straight back to Steven's.

Cadaver dogs indicated a track along this berm, between Steven's, and the rear entry to the yard.

So why does the cadaver track go through the quarry as well as along Steven's berm? Why does the cadaver track lead down to the Kuss Road cul-de-sac? Why is there 'digging'

and a shovel in the trees off the road there? Why did Brutus
indicate at this digging? Why did Brutus indicate cadaver
scent in the gravel pit where the suspected pelvis fragment
was recovered?

Possibilities are wide and varied, but:

a. Brendan told police that, Steven said he put the 'pelvis'
bone in the gravel pit to "get rid of it". Maybe the bone was
too big to burn or break up. But why not get 'rid' of *all* of the
cremains? Why leave anything in the burn pit?

Brendan did say that Steven was going to bury it and
dig a new pit.

The thing we have found most odd regards this
'suspected pelvis piece' is that CSIs have never confirmed
whether or not it is human. Zellner will attempt this in her
latest round of high-tech forensic testing.

b. Did 'Avery the killer' take the hard chunk of pelvic bone
down to the Kuss Rd area first, and attempt to bury it? It is
closer to his trailer than the gravel pit. The 'digging'
indicated by Brutus and Trace was up off the road and deep
into trees.

c. Or did a third-party killer enter the game through Kuss Rd
cul-de-sac? Did they drive the RAV4 into the quarry via the
gravel road, laying the scent track that Brutus and Trace
located?

VII

Third Party
Suspects

In Teresa Halbach's case, the third-party suspects' list is mind-boggling.

We have one who may have seen Teresa on Halloween, after Steven Avery.

We have an abusive ex-boyfriend and possible stalker.

We have a rejected sexual partner and roommate who failed to report her missing.

We have pornographic photography and a lurid affair with a married couple.

We have at least *six* wife-beating sexual deviants.

We have an axe murderer.

We have America's most **un**known, most evil, and longest-lived serial killer of all time.

And we have Steven Avery, a known (but never charged) rapist of his young relatives, and a violent criminal; although this history was left out of *MaM* it nonetheless exists.

There is so much third-party action to assess here, that we must forgive Avery's initial defense team of Strang and Buting, the mammoth task of preparing for Avery's murder trial; working day-and-night, reading transcripts, building arguments, pulling together fragments, filtering lies, researching, organizing, and practicing cross examinations, and preparing defense witnesses - all on a strict budget.

The State of Wisconsin appears so loaded with wife-beaters, rapists, killers, and psychopaths that one's skin crawls.

In murder investigations detectives are taught to consider people known to the victim; partners and ex-partners, relatives, and acquaintances. And then to start their inquiries at the victim's last known location.

Teresa had very suspect acquaintances.

But her last know location was apparently Avery's trailer.

Bad luck if you're innocent.

(1) George Zipperer

In 2005, George Zipperer appeared crazy - in a paranoid-delusional sense.

Apparently, and according to Avery's prosecution lawyers, Teresa attended the Zipperer residence *before* driving to Barb Janda's (Steven Avery's sister and neighbor) at around 2:30pm on October 31st, 2005.

Although crazy, this removed George Zipperer from the prosecution's scrutiny. They say Avery was the last to see Teresa alive - and is therefore the most likely killer.

However, some believe that Teresa went back to the Zipperers' after meeting Avery. This is because Teresa had trouble finding the Zipperer home, and it is suggested, Teresa skipped the appointment so-as not to be late for Janda (Avery), and went back to Zipperer's afterwards.

George Zipperer was an angry man who thought people were trying to manipulate him. Zipperer's delusion culminated with *Auto-Trader Magazine. Auto-Trader* had found an ad that George Zipperer's son, Jason, had placed, advertising his Firebird with another company; *Auto-Trader* scan these adds and then cold-call the customers, offering advertising with Auto Trader. Auto Trader callers then began calling George Zipperer's home, asking him to list the Firebird with them.

Teresa, contracting to *Auto-Trader* as a photographer, the story goes, was unwittingly sent out to the Zipperers' to photograph their son's Firebird.

But the paranoid George Zipperer felt *Auto-Trader* was conning him, and that he was being manipulated. George's demeanor was so crazy, that he appeared a paranoid schizophrenic.

Delusional people are dangerous and can kill out of their delusional beliefs; but for the Manitowoc County Sheriff's Dept, Avery was the better fit, and Zipperer was not pursued.

Zipperer *could* have killed Teresa.

When questioned by police, George said that he wanted Teresa 'prosecuted for trespassing' on his property, and stated that 'she' was 'not allowed on his land'.

For this reason, most of Avery's proponents of innocence, have Zipperer as their number one, or number two suspect for Teresa's murder.

Teresa had it in her diary to go to Zipperer's home and photograph a Firebird; she was unaware of his opposition.

But note this: if George Zipperer killed Teresa, then he had to have shot her twice in the skull with a small caliber firearm, planted her RAV4 at Avery salvage and covered its rims; burned her body, and then planted her 'cremains' (including the rivets from her jeans) in Avery's burn pit, and her phone, PDA, and camera in Barb's barrel, all without being seen.

Evidently, Zipperer fits the description of a man who could kill through paranoid delusion - but could Zipperer set-up Avery so comprehensively for Teresa's murder?

For the set up, Zipperer could have asked Teresa when she arrived at his home: *'Where are you going after this?'*

'Oh, Avery Salvage.'

'Fantastic.'

However, in assessing the Zipperer third-party killer scenario, we must analyze the working timeline for the 31st of October, 2005 to understand how and if the fit is possible.

(2) The Timeline

The timeline is constructed by using witness statements that may vary in their accuracy. Court documents, affidavits, and Teresa's accurate cell phone records are also used.

October 31st 2005 (Halloween)

8:12am *exactly* — Steven Avery calls Auto Trader Magazine to arrange an appointment. He wants to list his sister, Barb Janda's maroon van, and needs a photographer. He asks for "that same girl who was here last time."

Although Steven knows her name, is familiar with Teresa, having met her five times, and had her cell phone number. If he wanted Teresa specifically, he could have called Teresa directly, but instead chose to go through Auto Trader. He makes the appointment for that afternoon under the name B Janda, and leaves Barb's home phone number as the contact. The prosecution suggested that Avery did this to conceal who Teresa was actually meeting at Barb's house. They suggest Avery couldn't call Teresa directly, as she would feel uncomfortable and turn him down; and this is why Avery didn't call Teresa directly, despite having her number, and why he concealed his caller ID with the *67 feature when calling Teresa.

The defense says Avery made the appointment under B Janda because the van for listing was Barb's. Avery wanted Barb to pay the bill for the listing.

We asked: why did Avery have to have Teresa? Couldn't any photographer do the job? And why did he ask for "that same girl who was here last time", when he knew her name?

10:30am *approx* — Andres Martinez enters Avery Salvage yard. Martinez often perused the yard, searching for auto parts. Later that day Martinez would violently attack his partner and her children with an axe, shouting "die you dirty bitch". All three suffered injuries, and the family dog was slain. They narrowly escaped murder because of the dog's actions.

11:43am *exactly* — Teresa calls Barb Janda's home phone landline which rings through to voice-mail. Teresa leaves B Janda a voice message, saying that she can be out to photograph the van after 2pm, or maybe later. She asks for the address. Barb Janda is at work all day, and Teresa is not expecting Steven Avery. Why did Avery give Barb's number when he knew she would not be home?

12:51pm *exactly* — Teresa phones a customer, Steven Schmitz.

1:30pm *approx* — Teresa Arrives at the Schmitz' home and photographs a vehicle for listing.

1:45pm - 2:12pm *approx* — Teresa drives to Zipperer's area and has difficulty finding the address.

2:12pm *exactly* — Teresa calls George Zipperer's home landline, looking for directions. The call is not answered and Teresa leaves a voice message. Joellen Zipperer (George Zipperer's wife) testified in court that Teresa arrived soon after this call, some time between 2pm and 2:30pm on October 31st *(from Witness Statement Exhibit 28)*. Just like Avery said, Joellen said Teresa left an invoice and a copy of Auto Trader.

2:13pm *exactly* — Teresa calls her voice mail, and checks messages. We can now say that if Teresa arrived at the Zipperers' it was between 2:14 and 2:20pm. A phone conversation at 2:27pm exactly, confirms Teresa had left the Zipperers'. Joellen also said that Teresa had spoken to George, and had permission to take pictures of their son Jason's, Firebird.

Why then, when police later came to George Zipperer's home investigating Teresa's disappearance, did he rant at police, demanding Teresa be 'prosecuted for trespassing' on his property?

This could have been a ploy by Zipperer to suggest he believed Teresa was still alive and could still be prosecuted.

Joellen's testimony is critical, as it suggests Teresa had completed her gig there, and would not go back after Avery's. Some suggest that Teresa couldn't find Zipperer's and proceeded to Avery's. However, Teresa never called the Zipperers' phone again, as she was accustom to do when running late or re-scheduling. Joellen could have been under pressure from her husband to lie; but if this were true, Teresa would have disappeared at 2:28pm, and should not have been seen later at both 2:35; and possibly again at 3:30pm at Avery Salvage.

If Teresa went back to the Zipperers' after Avery's, she would have phoned them, but did not.

2:24pm *exactly* — Avery calls Teresa's cell phone. He blocks his phone number by using the *67 feature. The call is recorded by Teresa's phone company, Cingular Wireless, as lasting 8sec, but it was not answered. We asked: is Avery really trying to conceal his ID? Because if Teresa answers, she will know it's Steven anyway.

2:27pm *exactly* — Auto Trader Magazine operator, Dawn Pliska, *calls* Teresa. Teresa answers and the call lasts 4min 45sec. Teresa tells Dawn that she is heading out to Avery Salvage now. Teresa has just left the Zipperers' area. It is a 10 minute drive from Zipperer's to Avery's. This would mean that Teresa left Zipperer's at 2:25pm. It usually took Teresa 10 minutes at each vehicle shoot, so we could say Teresa arrived at Zipperer's at 2:14pm, and left at 2:24pm. 3 minutes later she received a call that lasted 5 minutes - and 3 minutes after that she arrives at Avery's. 11 minutes from Zipperer's to Avery's.

2:35pm *exactly* — Avery calls Teresa's cell phone again, and again blocks his caller ID with the *67 feature. Teresa does not answer, probably because she is arriving at Avery Road.

2:36pm *approx* — Avery states to police (during a later interrogation), that Teresa arrives at his trailer soon after this unanswered call. We showed this is likely true. However, in initial police inquiries, whilst police were looking for Teresa as a missing person and trying to piece together her movements, Steven Avery said Teresa never showed up.

Later Avery said that she did show up, but that he never spoke to her.

Steven Avery's statements about Teresa's arrival changed 3 times. First, he said Teresa never arrived; then he said that she did arrive, but he never talked to her; and then he stated that she did arrive, and that he talked to her and paid her $40 and received a magazine. Steven also told his brothers that he never saw Teresa that day, and that she never arrived on the afternoon he specifically took off salvage work to meet her. However, Steven eventually changed his story to the version that is most accepted as accurate, and that of his affidavit.

> [M]r. Avery recalls that when he looked out of his trailer window, he saw Ms. Halbach snap one photograph of the Janda van. Mr. Avery put on his shoes and went outside. Ms. Halbach began walking towards Mr. Avery's trailer, but when she saw Mr. Avery, she waved and turned around to go to her car to get his magazine. When Mr. Avery approached the car, Ms. Halbach was in the driver's seat with the door open and the engine running. Mr. Avery approached the driver's door, which Ms. Halbach left open, and handed Ms. Halbach cash totaling $40.00. Ms. Halbach handed an AutoTrader magazine to Mr. Avery. Mr. Avery remembers there was no mud splattered on Ms. Halbach's car, or visible damage to the driver's side bumper or parking light of her vehicle, and the back seats were in the upright position. Ms. Halbach turned left on Highway 147 after

leaving the Avery property. (Affidavit of Steven Avery, P-C Exhibit 4).

2:36pm *approx* — Bobby Dassey, Brendan's older brother has been sleeping after a night-shift at Fisher Hamilton in Two Rivers. Bobby wakes, gets out of bed, looks out of his window, and sees Teresa. She takes two photos of Barb's van, and then walks toward Steven's trailer. Bobby doesn't stare at Teresa for ten minutes, as some suggest, he showers for 5-10 minutes before work. Bobby stated in a police interview that he got out of bed between 2pm and 2:30pm. It seems that Bobby didn't take note of accurate times on October 31st, which is clearly common, who does? Police ask witnesses to guess or offer times, but these can be inaccurate. We calculate that for Bobby to see Teresa walking toward Steven's trailer, the time must have been 2:36pm, as this is when Steven said she arrived, soon after not answering his call at 2:35pm exactly. Teresa didn't go to Janda's, because she did not have the address for the *B Janda* customer - but Teresa knew it was the Avery brothers, and approached Avery's familiar trailer to confirm the details. Just like that, in less than a minute, she had already photographed the van.

Two people, Bobby and Steven put Teresa at Steven's door at 2:36pm; as do our calculations based on phone records, and the 11 minute drive time from Zipperer's to Avery's.

Bobby Dassey

2:41pm *exactly* — Teresa's cell phone receives a call-forwarded-message and pings the Whitelaw cell phone tower, 13.1 miles from Avery Salvage. A voice message is left, and **this is the last activity from Teresa's cell phone handset**. Other activity was recorded on her account, which was not accessed by her handset; this was Ryan Hillegas, and later Mike Halbach deleting voice messages.

Avery's post conviction attorney, Kathleen Zellner, believes that the Whitelaw tower ping shows Teresa was not on Avery's property at 2:41pm. However, cell phones can connect to multiple towers and change adhoc as towers 'handoff' to each other. Teresa's cell phone could have been serviced by the Whitelaw cell tower while at Avery Salvage, if the closer tower handed off.

Nevertheless, at 2:41pm, Teresa has been at Steven Avery's for 5 minutes. She **is still** there because at:

2:45pm *approx* — Bobby Dassey exits his home by the front door, later stating to police that he was going bow hunting before work. Bobby remembers that Teresa's teal RAV4 was still parked in the driveway, but he did not see Teresa or Steven at this time. Teresa has now been at Steven's 10 minutes. Bobby is telling the truth and we see no reason to doubt him. Teresa is not outside or visible to Bobby at this time.

2:46pm- 2:50pm *approx* — Scott Tadych, Barb Janda's boyfriend, states that he drives up to, and parks outside the home where Barb and her four boys live. Tadych had been visiting his mother at a Green Bay Hospital. In Tadych's first statement to police, he said his arrival was about 3:15pm, but people don't always know the exact times that they carryout daily activities. However, Tadych must just miss seeing Bobby drive out; and: if Teresa leaves behind Bobby at 2:50pm, as Steven Avery claims, how does Tadych not see her?

Scott Tadych

2:50pm *approx* — Avery says Teresa drives away, and turns left on H-147.

3:00pm *approx* — Tadych gets hunting equipment, loads his vehicle, and then drives down Avery Road toward Highway-147.

3:10pm *approx* — Tadych and Bobby say they pass each other driving in opposite directions on H-147 near Mishicot; both say they are going hunting in different locations. Bobby and Tadych wave at each other as they pass. Bobby states in court that he noted the time, and expected that Tadych had too. At this point Tadych and Bobby alibi each other; but one might ask: how did they not drive past each other around 2:46pm when they were both at or near home?

3:30 - 3:35pm *approx* — At this time Scott Tadych says he arrives alone at his deer hunting stand.

3:35pm - 3:45pm *approx* — The school bus, driven by regular driver, Lisa Buchner, arrives at the drop-off point on Avery Rd, outside the main entrance to Avery Auto. At this point Lisa turns the bus around. Buchner states that she saw a woman resembling Teresa, and a vehicle resembling Teresa's teal RAV4.

The woman Buchner saw was photographing a vehicle, but which one?

Barb's Janda's maroon van was parked on the lane near Barb driveway. Barb's van was 332 yards from the bus drop-off point. Teresa had already photographed the van at 2:36pm, an hour earlier.

However, there was another vehicle for sale, which was parked at the bus turn-around point, a red and black Chevrolet Blazer.

Agreement as to which vehicle Lisa the bus driver saw the mystery woman photographing is problematic. If Lisa saw Teresa, this suggests she was on her way out, and stopped to photograph the red Blazer for sale, maybe so as she didn't have to return if Avery wanted it listed later.

We asked: If Bobby saw Teresa photograph Barb's van at 2:36pm, why would she be photographing it again 60 odd minutes later, at 3:40pm? Lisa said Teresa's RAV was still down by the Dassey house, so why would Teresa have left her car there and walked the 330yards to the Blazer?

'Redditors' suggest that it was not Teresa whom the bus driver saw, but it was someone interested in the Blazer -

but that person never came forward to say they were there taking photos on Halloween.

However, at this time, circa 3:40pm, Brendan Dassey and his older brother Blaine get off the bus and walk toward home.

In his initial statement to detectives, Brendan says he did not see Teresa or her vehicle, or any other woman taking photos, in direct contradiction to Lisa.

When confronted by Special Agent Sasse with Lisa's statement of seeing a female photographer and the RAV4, Brendan freezes, and then blurts out that he lied because he didn't want to go to jail.

This is important, because here Brendan admits that he did *initially* lie.

Brendan immediately changes his story, telling Sasse and Baldwin that he actually had to move off the road to let Teresa's jeep go past, toward Avery Road.

Is Brendan trying to fool police into thinking Teresa had driven away? Clearly, Brendan is smarter than he appears, and actually believes that he could face jail for whatever reason - As he said, Brendan does not want to go to jail. However, his 'driving away' statement is later contradicted by Brendan himself, and bus driver, Lisa Buchner.

Steven Avery said Teresa had already gone, 45 minutes before this, but Brendan and the bus driver place Teresa and her RAV4 as still there.

On the other hand, while walking from the bus to their home with Brendan, Blaine Dassey apparently saw none of this. Blaine saw no vehicle, no Teresa, no woman photographer, no Steven, no burn barrel fire, and no bonfire at any stage on Halloween. The fires were confirmed and corroborated by 10 other people, making Blaine's position curious.

But later, in court, Blaine changes some of his story. Under pressure, he now says that at 3:40pm, while walking from the bus to his home, he sees Steven throw a plastic bag into the burn barrel, which had smoke and flames coming from it. Blaine also recants, saying that at 11:00pm on Halloween night, he saw Steven, "Watching the fire, the bonfire." Blaine then stated the bonfire was behind Steven's garage.

Why did Blaine initially lie, and why did he maintain his lies for so long?

However, if the plastic bag that Blaine saw Steven burn contained Teresa's electronics, then she had been restrained in Steven's trailer for an hour; so the bus driver saw someone else taking photos, and Brendan was lying about seeing Teresa on Steven's porch at 3:40pm.

Either Brendan is lying, or Steven is lying, or both are lying.

Steven said Teresa left after Bobby at 2:50pm.

Because Teresa would not hang around on Avery's property for an hour before starting work, we believe the bus driver saw someone else. This is because Teresa should have already been gone for 45 minutes.

If Lisa did not see Teresa, then Teresa could have been restrained in Avery's trailer.

3:40 - 3:45pm *approx*— Brendan and Blaine Dassey arrive at their residence. In one statement to police, Brendan says he sees Teresa standing on Steven's porch. Blaine missed this, which seems unlikely.

Brendan makes multiple conflicting statements about what he did from this point on, between 3:40pm and 5:00pm, and this will be covered fully later. Brendan did state to police, and did tell his cousin Kayla, privately, that he collected mail from the mailbox. A letter was addressed to Steven, so he delivered Steven's mail before going home to play video-games. This is where the prosecution says Brendan heard Teresa's screams and cries for help; and that Steven answered his front door sweaty.

If Teresa was standing on Steven's porch, or if she was tied to Steven's bed, then Teresa's RAV4 would have been parked there, as the bus driver vaguely stated she saw (probably in the same position that Bobby stated it was at 2:45pm). How did Blaine Dassey miss Teresa's teal RAV4, parked in his driveway? Blaine also denied seeing any woman, in direct contradiction to Lisa Buchner.

Steven said he saw Teresa drive away around 2:50pm, after Bobby. (However, there was no active cell tower connections or pings from her cellular hand-piece after 2:41pm exactly).

Could Brendan and Lisa the bus driver have been wrong? Who was photographing the vehicle at 3:35pm? Despite worldwide attention, no one has ever come forward and said they were there between 3:35 and 3:45pm on October 31st, Halloween, photographing a vehicle.

Another point raised regarding this timeline is that it appears to destroy Ken Kratz much maligned opening pre-trial narrative. How could Lisa see Teresa taking photos one minute, and within 5 minutes she is tied up by her wrists, shackled by her ankles, already raped, and screaming by the time Brendan gets to Steven's front door with the mail? The court's criminal complaint provides the necessary missing time, stating that Brendan went home first, saw Teresa on Steven's porch, and then after some unspecified amount of time, got on his bike and rode back to the mailboxes, collected the mail, and then rode to Steven's where he heard Teresa calling for help.

This 'mail run' was later proved to be false – Brendan never collected mail.

We all think that if Teresa was restrained in Avery's trailer, it had to have happened around 2:40-2:45pm, and if so, Brendan Dassey could not have seen her on Steven's porch at 3:40pm. Was there anyone on Stevens's porch at all? Why would Brendan lie if not? Was this woman Brendan saw, the same woman that Steven was seen with later that day, at 5:10pm in Two Rivers?

4:35pm *exactly* — Avery calls Teresa's Cell. It registers as 13sec, but the phone company says it was not answered. Avery *did not use* the *67 caller ID blocking for this call. The prosecution suggests that Avery knew Teresa was dead, and no longer needed to conceal his identity. Further, they suggest that Avery was setting up an alibi with the 4:35pm call to Teresa. Avery said he wanted her to come back and photograph a front-end-loader; but she didn't answer and he left no message.

4:35pm *approx* — (The sun is going down). Neighboring Quarry owner, Josh Radandt tells police that he could see a fire in *a barrel* near Steven Avery's trailer, viewed from the deer camp across the quarry. Radandt saw the barrel, not the pit at this time.

4:45pm-5.00pm *approx* — (Twilight) Earl Avery and Robert Fabian, arrive out front of Steven's trailer in a golf cart. They both talk to Steven, who had just showered. They reported smelling burning plastic, and saw a fire in a barrel, which was in front of Avery's home. The charred remains of Teresa's cell phone, blackberry, camera, purse, and the purse's contents were later recovered from this barrel. This is the flaming barrel that Blaine saw Avery put a plastic bag into.

Steven confirmed by statement to police that he spoke with Earl around 5pm. Then he went by the Dassey residence looking for Bobby. But Steven must've gotten into his pickup, and driven straight to the fuel station.

5:13pm-5:25pm *approx, based on sunset and twilight times for Manitowoc on 10.31.05* — Steven Avery is seen by two witnesses, Dave and Sandra, at *Patsy's 42 Mobil* gas station, on 22nd Street, Two Rivers, filling a small fuel can. Dave and Sandra know it's Halloween because they were biking around Two Rivers specifically on Halloween. It is just on dusk, but they can't give an exact time. Dusk was 5:13pm. The drive time between Patsy's and Avery's is 12 minutes at regular speeds. Both Dave and Sandra recognize Avery from the news, and comment that Avery is doing ok, as he is driving a nice, dark Ford F-250, and is wearing the red and white jacket - like the one he wore in *MaM*.

Avery owned a dark F-250, which was parked in his drive when police seized the property. Avery could possibly have been buying diesel or gasoline for his intended fire, or it may have been to intensify the burning of Teresa's corpse - or clean the garage floor. These two witnesses say Steven was with a blonde-haired younger woman, who was riding in his front passenger seat. This witness statement is reliable. Was the young woman Steven's niece, Kayla? Kayla's written statements say she despised and feared Steven. Was it Teresa? The description does not fit Teresa's, as Teresa is a 25 year old woman with dark shoulder length hair.

5:30pm *approx* — (Nightfall) Bobby states he arrives home from hunting at approximately 5:30pm. Bobby goes straight back to bed, as he has a night-shift later.

5:30pm - 5:32pm *approx* — Brendan says his Mom, Barb arrives home. Barb said that when she got home, the three boys were there.

Barb thought she got home at 5:00pm, but her estimate must have been off by half an hour.

An interesting point (that will be covered later) now occurs. In a recorded prison phone conversation between Brendan and Barb, Barb says to Brendan: "What about when I got home at 5 O'Clock? You were here. When did you go over there?" (To Stevens)

Brendan says: "I went over there earlier, and then came home before you did."

Barb pontificates: "Why didn't you say something to me then? (Barb is directly referring to Teresa)

Brendan says: "I dunno. . . .I was too scared."

5:34pm *approx* — Tadych returns from hunting. He pulls up outside Barb's house and stays in the running vehicle. Tadych says, Steven Avery, Barb, and one of Barb's sons are standing outside talking. Barb got in and they drove to Green Bay.

It is possible that Avery drove to Two Rivers at 5:02pm approx, (or slightly earlier as Earl Avery's time of the 5pm conversation with Steven is approximate and could have been a few minutes earlier). Allow a few minutes to fill his fuel can and pay the cashier, and 10-12 minutes drive time back to his trailer, and Avery is back when Tadych arrives to see him standing outside Barbs with Brendan.

5:36pm *exactly* — Steven's fiancée / girlfriend, Jodi Stachowski, calls Avery from prison. Avery answers and the recorded call lasts 15 minutes. Avery sounded normal. Brendan Dassey says he was with Steven when Jodi rang.

5:38-5:45pm *approx* — Blaine Dassey's after school employer, Michael Kornley testifies that he called Dassey/ Janda's landline from his hotel, and talks to Brendan. Brendan was at his home.

5:57pm *exactly* — Steven phones Charles Avery (Chuck). Call lasts 5 minutes 23 seconds.

6:03pm - 7:00pm *approx, disputed* — Sometime between these times Brendan and Steven have contact.

Brendan's story changes a lot here. However, Brendan testifies that Steven called his home phone around 7pm, and asked him to come over to the bonfire.

Brendan says that he and Steven drove around the yard in golf-carts, collecting car seats, a cabinet, brush, and tires on steel rims to burn. This takes about 45 minutes.

Then they clean Steven's garage floor with bleach, gasoline, and paint thinner.

Brendan says the material they cleaned was reddish - black.

Brendan's Mom notes that Brendan's denim jeans are bleach stained on the knees. Brendan's bleach stained jeans are seized and are later entered into evidence.

7:30pm - 7:45pm *approx* — Tadych drops Barb home and he sees a bonfire behind Steven's garage. Barb also sees the fire, and two people standing beside it.

8:57pm *exactly* — Jodi calls Steven again from prison. Avery tells Jodi that Brendan is over, and has done some cleaning. The call lasts 15 minutes.

9:00pm *approx* — Avery states during his interrogation on November 9th, that he goes to bed and watches porn, until about 10:00-10:30pm. However, his recollection is proven incorrect.

9:00pm *approx* — Barb Janda calls Steven's phone. She checks if Brendan is wearing a jacket and is warm enough, and then tells Steven to make sure Brendan is home by 10pm.

9:20pm *exactly* — Steven phones Barb Janda. Not answered.

9:30pm *approx* — Bobby leaves the Janda/ Dassey home for work in Two Rivers. He sees a fire in Steven's pit, estimating the flames at about 5-6ft high.

10:00pm *approx* — Blaine Dassey arrives home. He states that his Mom Barb, and his brothers Bobby and Brendan were home. Blaine also states that he saw Steven tending a fire in Steven's burn pit. (Initially Blaine swore black-and-blue that there was no fire.)

10:05pm *approx* — Brendan goes to bed.

11:00pm *approx* — Kayla Avery, Brendan's 13-year-old cousin, tells investigators that she saw Steven stoking his fire with a shovel at this time.

Two statements from family living on the property, Blaine and Kayla, both contradict Steven Avery's Nov 9th statement to police by 2 full hours.

Avery said he went to bed at 9pm, but at 10pm he was still by the fire, and at 11pm was using a shovel in his burn pit. More will be said about Kayla's statements and court testimony, as her story is an important piece of the puzzle.

Summary of 10.31.2005

It's probable that Lisa the bus driver's accuracy in estimating the time of day is better that the others', as she arrives at this drop-off point on Avery Rd at the same time on school days.

Did Lisa see Teresa at 3:35pm?

We will never know.

Lisa's sighting was corroborated by Brendan's sighting of Teresa on Steven's front porch at around 3:40pm. However, if Lisa saw the mystery woman at the mailboxes where she turns the bus around, Brendan could not have seen this same woman on Steven's porch as he walked home - unless she ran past him.

This 3:40pm sighting of Teresa by Dassey makes no sense. Brendan also told several lies regarding this timeframe.

In direct contradiction, Steven never said Teresa was on his porch at 3:40pm; Steven said she had left at 2:50pm, and never returned.

Conclusion: the woman on Steven's deck was never there at 3:40pm, or, it was Kayla Avery. It was not someone enquiring about the Blazer, because they would have gone to Avery Auto's office.

However, Bobby and Steven, and our phone record calculations do have Teresa at Steven's trailer at 2:36pm, some 45-50 minutes earlier. Teresa photographed Barbs van at this time so *would not* have been photographing it an hour later.

The problem is, Teresa only needed a maximum of 10 minutes on the property to photograph Barb's Van, and if Avery's statements are true, Teresa should have been off the property by 2:50pm, as Steven swore she was.

If Lisa the bus driver did see Teresa, what was Teresa doing at Steven Avery's for the 50 minutes before she started taking photos of the red Blazer?

We conclude that Teresa was *not* who the bus driver saw at 3:35.

We also surmise that the woman who Lisa saw may not come forward out of fear. She may have summed up the situation and thought it better for her survival to not testify against the Averys. This is of course, pure speculation based on the Avery family's violent history.

We thought: if the mystery woman believed that Avery killed Teresa, then she may have thought that Avery may well kill her too. Better to keep out of it.

This doesn't mean we think Avery is the killer at this point, it is merely a speculation of how the mystery woman could have been thinking. Most people would come forward in this situation and say it was them taking the pictures at 3:45pm on Halloween, but no one has.

The big problem for Avery is that his statements about Teresa's arrival changed 3 times.

First, Avery told police Teresa never arrived. Then he said that Teresa did arrive, but he never talked to her. And then he stated that she did arrive, and that he talked to her, paid her $40 for work, and took a copy of Auto Trader.

Steven also told his brothers that he never saw Teresa, and that she never arrived on the afternoon he took off salvage work to meet her, on October 31st.

Why? Why did Steven lie 3 times?

Bobby and Brendan saw Teresa's RAV4, parked in lane opposite their home, near where Barb's maroon van sat. Teresa was there at 2:35pm and was still there at 2:45pm.

The problems police struck regarding the 70 minutes between 2:35pm and 3:45pm on October 31st were:

Steven Avery lied, changing his story 3 times.

Brendan Dassey lied, changing his story 3 times in interviews on November 5th and 6th, as part of the general inquiries before Wiegert and Fassbender got involved and actual interrogations started. The general inquiries simply asked who he saw and at what times on October 31st; nothing was fed to Brendan and no pressure was put on him during enquires - that happened later.

And later, Blaine changed his story, proving that he too had lied.

Why are they all lying about what happened in the 70 minutes between 2:35 and 3:45pm, the time Teresa arrived on their property?

When police formed their initial timeline and overlaid all of these inconsistencies with known facts, they shook their heads and said: "Something's wrong here."

As the stories changed, the picture began to align with the other information, including Bobby's observations, Brendan's confession, and Teresa's time accurate phone records.

This left Steven Avery looking like the only liar left standing.

This is why the police focused on Steven.

Nevertheless, when Police discovered that Brendan had spent that evening up until 10:00pm with Steven, they desperately wanted to know what Brendan knew, because if Steven was the killer, Brendan would know.

As for the bonfire; Bobby Dassey, Scott Tadych, Barb Janda, Kayla Avery, Kayla's mother, Candy, Josh Radandt, Blaine Dassey, Earl Avery, and Brendan all report details of the fire behind Steven's garage on Halloween.

This fire, as some suggest, was not an imaginary fire fed to Brendan by investigators. The bonfire was a real event. Blaine initially tried to deny it happened, while Tadych inflated its size.

The timeline is quite simple, it was the lying that made it difficult to align. The liars were Steven, Brendan, and Blaine - this is fact; all others seem to have told the truth as accurately as they could.

Why would Blaine adamantly deny there being a fire, whilst others confirmed it?

Why would Brendan spook, and attempt to alter the police perception of the crucial 70 minutes?

Brendan said he was scared of Steven on several occasions; he was genuinely frightened about what Steven would do if he got angry.

Did 'Avery the killer' scare Brendan into lying for him? Brendan was scared of going to jail for some reason, long before Wiegert stupidly threatened him with 90 years.

Was Blaine just plain scared of Steven?

Did Steven use fear to control the people around him?

So to answer the question: is George Zipperer the killer; based on the timeline, and the fact that Teresa never telephones the Zipperers again, suggests that she never went back to the Zipperers' home.

She would have called.

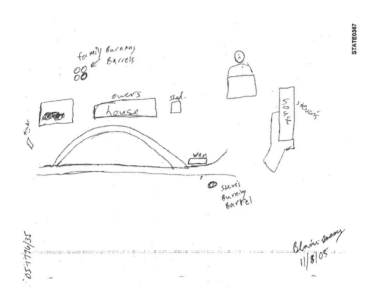

Blaine Dassey's drawing of his driveway where Barb's van was parked. The item marked 'Steven's burning barrel', is the flaming drum that Blaine saw Steven put a plastic bag into.

The school bus drop-off and turn-around point. It is 330 yards from here to the Dassey house.

(3) Andres Martinez

Earl Avery told police that an odd man named Andres
Martinez was on the salvage yard the day Teresa
disappeared. Martinez was on the yard several times a month
finding parts for his car; he had license to roam.

This Andres Martinez is the Same Andres Martinez
who, 5 days later on November 5th, drove to his ex-
girlfriend's house and attempted to murder her with an axe.

In front of her children, Martinez struck his ex-
partner in the side of her neck, opening a large, life-
threatening gash. She raised her hands in self-defense and he
chopped and broke her arm. The family dog tried to stop the
attack, delaying Martinez', and allowing her young children
a narrow chance to escape his murderous rampage. Martinez
threw off the dog and struck the fleeing children with
horrific axe blows. The injured dog tried again to stop
Martinez, and he hacked the animal to death. The woman
and her children escaped across the street, hid in a Tattoo
parlor, and called 911.

Martinez, a mentally disturbed psychopath, was
sentenced to 60 years for attempted murder, but was
extradited to his home country of Cuba.

Martinez was on the salvage yard the day Teresa
came to take photos, however:

Martinez arrived at 10:30am.

Teresa arrived four hours later at 2:36pm.

It is unlikely they were on the yard at the same time;
and it is unlikely they crossed paths.

Pam Sturm, when she arrived at Avery salvage on
November 5th, as part of the 'civilian search party', though
that she saw Martinez hunting for parts, and possibly
watching the search.

Although this proves nothing, it is known that
perpetrators of some crimes like to return to the scene and

watch. Was this what Martinez was doing? Why was he back at the yard? Maybe he got the wrong part, or needed something else, who knows?

Martinez felt comfortable on the yard, as he had permission to roam; this could mean that he was comfortable in hiding Teresa's RAV4 there, by the pond.

The scenario goes:

Martinez sees Teresa, waves her down, kidnaps, and kills her. Then he frames Avery by planting the RAV4, bones, and electronics.

The problems with this theory are:

(1). Steven Avery testifies that he saw Teresa drive away down Avery Road at around 2:50pm. When she gets to Highway 147, Steven says he saw Teresa turn left. If Martinez was to wave down and kidnap Teresa, under the guise of a hustle shot, it would have happened on Avery land; but Steven says Teresa drives away.

(2). The police still plant Avery's blood in the RAV4, as Martinez did not have Steven's blood. The police still plant the .22 projectile in Avery's garage.

(3). The police still plant the valet/ sub key in Avery's trailer.

(4). The Dassey confession to his mother.

A narrative for the Martinez theory:

Martinez sees Teresa and follows her down H-147. He gets her to stop and shoots her twice in the skull. He puts her in the RAV's cargo bay and drives into Kuss Road. Cadaver-dogs gave signals at the Kuss Road cul-de-sac. Martinez drives into the quarry and burns Teresa without Josh Radandt seeing him; Radandt was at the Kuss Rd Deer Camp on the 31st.

Martinez plants the RAV4. Later he uses the burn-barrel at the deer camp to collect the bones and transport them to Avery's fire pit. He leaves the Deer Camp drum, and takes Avery's drum back to the Deer Camp.

The police, believing Avery is Teresa's killer, do the rest.

(4) Josh Radandt

The theory put forward is that Radandt wanted the Averys' land to quarry, so he set to destroy the Avery salvage business by setting Steven up for murder.

Radandt (Badgerlands aggregates) owned all the land surrounding Avery salvage; Delores Avery's 44 acre plot sat bang in the middle.

However, setting up Steven for murder may destroy the salvage business, bankrupting the Averys; but it was unlikely that this would force the Averys from their land.

This seemed pretty thin to us.

The set-up here would be similar to the Martinez set-up. Teresa is killed in Kuss Rd, burned in the Quarry, and her bones are planted at Steven's using the burn-barrel swap.

The police do the rest.

The following passage is the statement of Josh Radandt:

> *I was told my DOJ agents that they believed that Teresa Halbach's vehicle was driven to the Kuss Rd cul-de-sac by driving west through an empty field, (from Steven's) then south down the gravel road past the hunting camp until reaching an intersection with a gravel road that ran northeast into the Avery property.*
>
> *They told me that they believed Halbach's vehicle turned northeast onto the gravel road and entered the Avery*

property at its southwest corner. It is my understanding that this theory was based on the work of scent tracking dogs.

I also read and heard it from others that law enforcement stated that they believed that Teresa Halbach's vehicle was stored somewhere on Radandt's property before it was moved to the southeast corner of Avery property.

Later that week I received a call from law enforcement on my cell phone. Law enforcement asked me to unlock my three hunting trailers so they could be searched. I left work and drove to the hunting camp. When I arrived there was nobody there. I unlocked my trailers and left.

It is my understanding that they were searched by law enforcement and scent tracking dogs. Later that day law enforcement called my phone again. They informed me they completed their search and I could use them again normally.

During the course of the conversation law enforcement informed me that they were going to collect the contents of the burn barrel at the hunting camp at a later time. When I returned to camp they had the area cordoned off surrounding the burn barrel and had officers to watch the burn barrel day and night on a rotating basis until its contents were collected.

A few days after November 5, 2005, I remember seeing light in the Manitowoc County sand and gravel pit to the south of Radandt's property. I remember that the lights appeared to illuminate the entire Manitowoc County pit.

I understand that there were suspected human pelvic bones recovered from a gravel pit property south of Avery's Auto Salvage. Upon reviewing a map showing the coordinates at which these bones were found, I believe they were found in the Manitowoc County sand and gravel pit.

Prior to November 5, 2005, the only permanent security measures in place to prevent access to the Radandt sand and gravel pit by trespassers were "Private Property" signs posted at all entrances. There were locking gates or cables at each access road, but they were rarely used.

Approximately one or two months before the start of Mr. Avery's criminal trial in 2007, I was summoned to the courthouse. At the courthouse, I was questioned again about my recollection of seeing a fire in the direction of the Avery property on October 31, 2005.

I was not called as a witness to testify at Mr. Avery's criminal trial in 2007.

In Zellner's 2016 motion, she writes that Joshua Radandt accessed the Avery property four times during evidence collection:

11/5/06 – In at 5:25 p.m. with Travis Groelle; Out at 5:35 p.m. with Travis Groelle
11/6/05 – In at 5:08 p.m.; Out at 5:28 p.m.
11/7/05 – In at 6:59 a.m.; Out at 7:10 a.m.
11/7/05 – In at 11:51 a.m.; Out at 12:29 p.m. ("Civilian Volunteers with DCI")

We have shown by cadaver-dog tracking, the sent dogs indicated the presence of human remains and or a corpse near Avery's trailer, and on the berm road at 3:30pm on November 5th, meaning Radandt did not plant cremains during Zellner's indicated timings.

(5) Ryan Hillegas

Teresa's abusive ex-boyfriend, Ryan Hillegas, is Kathleen Zellner's number one third-party suspect, in Avery's post conviction relief. The affidavit of Gregg McCrary is provided as evidence of verbal, physical, and mental abuse.

Remember going forward, that Zellner's third-party suspect, and a real third-party killer, need not be one and the same; Zellner only needs to create enough doubt to free her client. She is not trying to convict Hillegas.

However, Ryan lies in court several times; and lying creates suspicion.

Ryan told Deputy Bill Tyson and Special Agent Tom Fassbender that he was living at Teresa's residence short-term, and he let them into Teresa's home to collect DNA. We were led to believe that Ryan lived at another residence, nearby.

MaM viewers will know that Hillegas accessed Teresa's *computer* by 'guessing' her password. Hillegas also called Cingular Wireless *(from his phone records)*.

Oddly, at least 6 voice messages were *selectively* deleted (not in order) early in the investigation. Did Hillegas gain access to Teresa's voice mail and delete messages before the police investigation? If yes, surely he must be the killer.

However, Teresa's brother, Mike Halbach, testified that on November 3rd, after Teresa was reported missing, Mike listened to Teresa's voice messages, trying to figure out where she might have gone, and deleted at least 10; presumably because they were unhelpful in locating her. It was Hillegas however, that gained access to Teresa's password protected message box.

The point here is: Teresa went missing on October 31st; her cell phone handset's last cell tower connection was at 2:41pm. She was reported missing by Mom on November 3rd.

Therefore, any activity on Teresa's voice mail account on Oct 31st, Nov 1st, or Nov 2nd, could not have been Teresa.

As she was not considered missing, it could not have been concerned family.

If someone accessed her voicemail before Nov 3rd, the theory goes, then they killed Teresa.

Zellner, in her post conviction accusation says: the killer deleted messages on November 2nd, to give himself more time to plant evidence. Zellner says that if family called Teresa and discovered her voice-mail full, it would set off alarm bells; and this is exactly what happened on Nov 3rd.

We thought Hillegas may have been leaving Teresa abusive messages; someone had been. Hillegas may have had an un-healthy obsession with his ex Teresa. If Hillegas had left a nasty message, and he knew Teresa had disappeared and that police would be looking into her activity, then it makes sense that Hillegas would want this deleted. The message could have been of bad enough flavor to have him charged with harassment.

Hillegas could also have been leaving Teresa threatening messages anonymously, and then providing Teresa his shoulder to cry on. The police would soon inform Teresa that her stalker was none other than, Ryan.

This could be the reason Hillegas went into Teresa's account, and deleted messages.

But if Hillegas listened to messages or deleted messages on Nov 2nd, before Teresa was believed missing, then Hillegas is the killer, right?

He is assumed to be the killer because no one else knew Teresa was missing; and Avery did not have the ability to delete Teresa's voice messages; And Teresa couldn't do so because she was dead. But is this really the only alternative?

(Speculation) If Hillegas deleted messages on the 3rd, he knew Teresa had been reported missing, and needed to act fast to remove his evidence of abuse, before the police found out.

So were messages deleted before Teresa was 'missing', on Nov 2nd?

In Avery's trial, Strang and Buting were able to show that after Oct 31st and before Nov 2nd, 8 messages were listened to, but not saved, and at least 1 message was removed. (The unsaved messages remain in the mailbox).

Avery couldn't have done this. Who accessed Teresa's voicemail before it was known she was missing?

We thought: When Teresa didn't come home on Oct 31st, and then still didn't come home on Nov 1st, Hillegas may have though Teresa had discovered his stalking. If Hillegas though Teresa may go to the police, he would have immediately accessed her voice-mailbox, listened to the 8 messages, and deleted the 1 or more that were abusive. Ryan had called Cingular Wireless' password help desk. *(Proof from Hillegas' phone records)*

This idea shows that just because someone accessed Teresa's voice mail on Nov 2nd, that they were not necessarily her killer.

Zellner has now acquired phone records that Strang and Buting did not enter into evidence. Remember that Mr. Zimmerman from Cingular Wireless testified that other records that held the answers to Strang's question did exist. These records are part of Avery's 2016 post conviction motion. The motion states:

*Five voicemail deletions occurred on October 31, 2005
and eleven additional deletions were made prior to
7:12am, on November 2, 2005.*

These deletions are separate from Mike Halbach's 10
deletions on November 3rd, unless he is lying too. Teresa did
not make these deletions. Someone was accessing Teresa's
voice-mail post death.

This could only be Hillegas, or Mike Halbach.

Mike claimed that he knew Teresa's password
because he was helping her with a website. But if Mike
knew the password, why did Hillegas and *'a group of us'*
have to guess it.

Hillegas perjured himself when he denied knowledge
of the short sexual relationship with Teresa's roommate, and
Ryan's friend, Scott Bloedorn.

Hillegas lies again, perjuring himself when he denied
remembering the time of day, or even whether it was dark or
light, day or night when he last visited Teresa. (Was Hillegas
living short-term with her or not?)

Hillegas lies again, creating a false alibi by claiming
to be with Kelly Pitzen at Teresa's house on November 3rd,
'all afternoon until midnight or 1 a.m.' But Pitzen phones
Hillegas at 5:16pm; and then Ryan called Pitzen at 7:18pm.
What was Ryan doing between these times that required him
to fabricate an alibi?

Hillegas lies again, perjuring himself when he says
the damage to Teresa's RAV4's front left park-light/
indicator lens was several *months* old. Hillegas said Teresa
had claimed insurance for the damaged light, had received
payment, but had not repaired the lens; spending the money
on something else.

However, Teresa's insurance company never paid out
on the policy.

It was surmised that the killer caused this damage, hiding the RAV4 in the rough terrain at Avery Salvage, or Radandt's Quarry, or whilst driving the Kuss Rd track in the dark and striking an obscured metal post. We think that the lens *was* knocked out by the killer; it is likely the killer stopped after hitting whatever they hit, recovered the broken light assembly, and put on the rear seat.

Was Hillegas concealing the broken lens because he didn't want anyone to go looking for the broken fragments and learn where the damage occurred? If he planted the RAV4 on the Avery property, and damaged the light on the 'metal post', then why bother picking it up, right? It becomes just another piece of Teresa on Avery Salvage land. However, Avery would pick it up - and probably toss it out of sight.

If Hillegas is the killer and the planter, then he damaged the light somewhere else.

*The damage to Teresa's RAV4. Front Driver's side indicator light,
and bumper, above and below the light. Note the impact damage
to the underside of the bumper.*

If the damage didn't exist prior to October 31st, and Ryan knew about it, then Ryan is the killer.

I'll just restate that: if Teresa's car was undamaged on Halloween when she arrived at Avery's – and Ryan knows it was damaged – Ryan is the killer.

Hillegas gave no alibi for October 31st; nor parts of November 1st, 2nd, or 3rd, when Teresa's body was burned, and her bones potentially planted in Avery's fire-pit, but Ryan was never even asked by police to provide alibis, as by this time Law Enforcement's focus was purely on Avery.

Why would Ryan give investigators a *false story* about the parking light?

The possible reasons are:

a. Ryan is the killer.

b. Ryan was mistaken.

c. Teresa does not see the value in putting in a claim and paying excess on a $40 light, and leaves it damaged.

d. Was the light serviceable on Halloween?

e. Had Teresa recently hit something, broken the light, and put it on the RAV4's rear seat. The broken light assembly *was* found inside Teresa's RAV4 by Crime Scene Investigators. But if this was *old* damage, would Teresa still be carrying around the broken part?

f. When was her last vehicle fitness inspection? If recently, did it pass?

It does seem likely that whoever put the vehicle in the Avery salvage yard, broke the light. They must have stopped, got out, collected the light, and put on the rear seat.

Would 'Avery the killer' have taken this precaution, yet leave cremains in his fire-pit – and then go on holiday?

Avery's defense team of Buting and Strang couldn't raise Ryan Hillegas as a third-party suspect, as Judge Willis did not allow the lack of motive and connection under the Denny ruling.

We asked: were abusive, jealous ex-partner, and roommate not motive, and connection?

Under this theory, 'Hillegas the killer' waited for Teresa to return home. Teresa was due home around 3:50pm.

Teresa's day planner showed that she intended to: *get Sarah's stuff from Mom at 3pm,* and: *do biz paperwork at 4:30pm.*

But as Teresa never showed up at her Moms, Teresa would've arrived home around early, at around 3:15. She gets out, goes to the cargo door, opens it - and then from behind - Hillegas bludgeons her and pushes her inside. However, this means:

(a) Teresa's phone battery died, or she turned it off at 2:41pm, whilst at Avery's, and;

(b) Teresa failed to go to her Mom's, and get 'Sarah's stuff', as she intended.

Hillegas' phone records reveal a period of inactivity, from 7:47pm on Halloween, October 31st, until 1:31pm the next day. Hillegas either had his phone turned off, or did not answer calls.

What was he doing?

We don't know, because Law Enforcement never asked him.

Then Hillegas had a six-hour gap in phone activity on November 2nd, from 10:06am until 4:12pm; and a gap on November 3rd, from 7:30pm until 8:10pm - the time when Steven Avery reported seeing headlights or taillights near his trailer from H-147, whilst driving away from the yard. The only way in was past Avery, or from Kuss Rd.

Proponents of the Hillegas theory suggest these 'gaps' are at times when he could have been burning, transporting, or planting Teresa's body and possessions.

This aligns with the cadaver-dog information. If cremains were planted in Avery's fire-pit, they were planted between November 2nd, and November 5th.

But alone, gaps in one's phone activity prove nothing.

But then, on November 4th, in a short three hour period, between 4:15pm and 7:25pm, Hillegas received 21 phone calls from an unidentified, number; this is prior to the 'civilian search group' going out to Avery Salvage the following morning.

Remember, if the police organized that search group, then they were breaking the law by searching without a warrant, and anything found would be useless in court.

We asked: if Hillegas *was* staying with Teresa, as he told Fassbender and Tyson, why did he never report her missing on the 31st, the 1st, or the 2nd? Teresa's Mom called the police and reported Teresa missing on November 3rd.

How long would you wait for someone to come home?

We thought: If a roommate didn't come home one night when they were planning to, we would try to find out where they were; but if they didn't come home the next night too, we would be concerned.

In court, Hillegas perjures himself *again* when questioned about the quality of Teresa's relationship with Scott Bloedorn.

Hillegas knows full well that Teresa and Scott have had sexual relations, but can't bring himself to say it in court.

Hillegas instead lies, saying Bloedorn and Teresa were strictly plutonic.

Is Ryan avoiding the obvious line of questioning: how did you feel about that? Were you jealous?

Teresa had also recently engaged in an affair with Brad Czech, and possibly his wife, whom Teresa had photographed pornographically.

Did this sexual activity tip Hillegas over the edge?

Hillegas had plenty of theoretical motive; but not enough to satisfy Judge Willis in overriding the Deny motion.

It is inexplicable to us, that in a murder investigation, the victim's ex-boyfriend, who possibly deleted messages from the victim's voicemail, *before* the police investigation even started, with no alibi, and whom delayed reporting her missing, was not considered a possible suspect; and was not included in elimination exemplars for at least blood, saliva, and DNA.

Hillegas was called 21 times by someone, the day before the most 'suspect civilian search' in recent criminal justice history.

Hillegas led this 'search', he had the sheriff's phone numbers, and a camera to give to Pam Sturm. This implies that the 21 unknown calls Hillegas took on November 4th, were from someone in Law Enforcement, setting up the 'search'. The number was blocked in such a way, that no one has been able to discover the mystery caller's identity.

In discussion, we cannot and do not begrudge Law Enforcement giving their full effort in searching for Teresa; the laws around probable cause and obtaining search warrants hamstring searches for missing persons; the search for a missing woman should be unhindered, but alas, probable cause aids criminals nationwide.

Nevertheless, Hillegas should never have been allowed into the missing person's investigation, because the missing person was his ex-girlfriend.

Hillegas said he was rooming with Teresa, and he let detectives into her home, where Fassbender acquired dirty underwear that would contain Teresa's DNA profile - but at that point, police had no idea that Hillegas had corrupted their investigation by hacking into Teresa's phone records - the police focus was full tunnel vision on Avery, because of the lies Steven, Brendan, and Blaine told regarding the period between 2:35pm and 3:45pm on Halloween.

In our body-language analysis, Hillegas showed hallmark signs of lying in court; signs which innocent people should not. Hillegas gives the quick smirk, known as duping delight, when he tells of hacking Teresa's phone account with a 'group of friends'.

Many a murder on the stand has revealed this odd micro-expression.

Hillegas lies about his knowledge of Teresa's sexual relationships. Is this because he didn't want to reveal any motive, and he fully understood the Deny rule?

People know that simply becoming a suspect in a murder case can lead to conviction, innocent or not. One must at all costs, avoid become the police's number one suspect, because that person will usually go down.

As with the other third-party suspects, Hillegas would have had to have burned Teresa's body and plant the bones in Avery's pit; he would've planted the RAV4, and covered the rims; and he would've put Teresa's purse and electronic devices into the burn barrel.

Once again, the police do the rest. Hillegas did not have access to Avery's blood.

But what these third-party killers also must do is:

a. Remove and crumple the RAV4's license plates, and put them inside a car body 140ft from Avery's trailer, on the road that leads to the quarry via Kuss Rd. These plates were found by dog searches, crumpled inside a Mercury wagon.

b. Put a pair of purple woman's underwear in a nearby trailer (if Teresa's).

c. Shoot a small caliber firearm twice into Teresa's skull. Hillegas was not tested for gunshot reside.

d. Go into Avery's trailer and wipe his Marlin .22 rifle clean of all fingerprints and DNA.

Initially to us, Hillegas' lying and deceit seems built around concealing his stalking, and systematic abuse of Teresa.

Nevertheless, stalking and abuse often lead to murder; some men believe they own their ex-partners.

With what they had on Hillegas, the State could have built a plausible case against him; and by rote of the State's certainty, and the convincing unwavering confidence in the guilt of the people they charge, it is highly likely a jury would have 'bought in' and convicted Hillegas of Teresa's murder too.

Are we really to believe the State has gotten every charge they ever brought against someone for murder correct?

Kathleen Zellner, in her 2016 post conviction motion for Avery's acquittal, has employed a blood pattern expert that says Teresa's blood spatter, found on the underside of the RAV4's rear cargo door, is the result of bludgeoning.

Zellner says Teresa arrived home, opened the RAV4's cargo door, and Ryan bludgeoned her and pushed her into the compartment.

Zellner has the privilege of accusing anyone; she doesn't have to prove it, only create doubt. However, proving Hillegas is the killer comprehensively would bolster Avery's post conviction appeal.

Zellner's blood patter expert can of course be challenged and contradicted by a prosecution paid expert, and therefore be nullified. She would need more.

To counter Zellner, one could also surmise that Steven Avery hit Teresa in the back of her head at his property, and then dragged her into his trailer. I.e.: Teresa opens her hatch to get out a copy of the Auto Trader magazine, and while bent over, Avery bludgeons her, creating the stain pattern. This is pure speculation, but it shows the weakness of Zellner's expert in proving Hillegas was the only person who could have bludgeoned Teresa. This also explains how 'Avery the killer' was able to tie up and restrain Teresa alone, without her fighting or running.

The previously accepted means of how the blood spatter got onto the rear door, is that it flicked off Teresa's hair when Steven and Brendan loaded her dead body into the back, after shooting her, and in preparation to take her to the pond. Then Steven decides the pond is too shallow, and burning is the best option. This is the statement of Brendan Dassey.

We asked: how could Brendan fabricate that scenario. It rings true, and is backed-up by several pieces of evidence; Teresa's blood was in the rear of the RAV4. The pond idea was not fed or suggested to Brendan by Fassbender; so *is* this a piece of the worst confession in history that can be taken as fact?

We are not there yet.

Did Hillegas kill Teresa?

He was certainly up to something - but deleting a dead person's voice messages, a killer does not make.

Let's say Ryan was leaving Teresa nasty messages. Then Teresa doesn't show up home for two nights. Hillegas may have thought: she's going to the police; *I need to delete those messages before she does.*

Before we can say Hillegas is the killer, we need to look at all the other suspects, and all available evidence.

(6) Mastermind, or Master of Puppets?
Edward Wayne Edwards

If you are inclined to believe that such a 'set-up', as was
necessary to convict 'Avery the innocent', is too complex or
difficult, then a trip through the Set-up murders of
Wisconsin's worst serial killer is necessary.

Ex detective, John Cameron raised the theory that the
prolific serial-killer, Ed Edwards, killed Teresa, burned her
body, and planted it to set-up Avery.

Edwards murdered victims, and then framed
innocent people using elaborate schemes that are almost
unbelievable to the ordinary citizen.

Edwards was in the Manitowoc at the time Teresa
was murdered.

So many details of the Halbach murder fit Edwards'
MO and style, that it merits deeper investigation.

(i) By Rope, By Fire, By Gun

In Edwards' two-pronged schemes, he murdered his victims,
and then cunningly framed someone close to them, leading
police to his intended prey. He planned these set-ups over
long periods, and often had multiple murder-set-ups on the
go at any given time.

It is thought that up to 17 innocent men have been
wrongfully convicted, await death sentences, continue life
sentences, or have been put to death for Edwards' frame-up
murders.

Edwards was a remorseless, occult killer who
blended his own mix of satanic religion with the goal of
creating chaos across America. Edwards claimed that he was
killing to collect slaves for his afterlife, by rope, by fire, by
gun. The extent of Edwards' chaos is enormous, murdering

constantly from 1945 until 2008, before his eventual arrest in 2009. Edwards died naturally in prison in 2011, whilst seeking the death penalty.

Edwards *was* the infamous Zodiac Killer; The 'Lipstick Killer'; and 'The Sweet-Heart' murderer. Potentially hundreds of murders are attributed to Ed Edwards - many have convictions.

Edwards set up innocent men for his murders by planting evidence. He planted blood, DNA, and weapons leading to someone known, or close to the victim - he provided police with connection and motive. He would write to, or contact the police or the media, stating that the 'killer' had given him details of the current murder, and lead law enforcement to a false conclusion.

Edwards has highlighted how fast law enforcement are drawn into tunnel vision and false conclusions, honing their focus on a single suspect if a few details line up.

Creating a few co-incidences was all Ed needed; police would do the rest by way of confirmation bias.

A dark black past was Edwards' most valued possession.

But did Edwards kill Teresa?

Some points align:

(a) Edwards was living in Wisconsin at the time of Teresa's murder, near enough to Avery Salvage.

(b) Edwards killed multiple times in Wisconsin.

(c) Avery was high-profile. Edwards did follow the news coverage of Avery's wrongful imprisonment and pending 36 million dollar civil suit against the State, as everyone in Manitowoc did; Edwards was also seen at Avery's trial, and was photographed standing behind Ken Kratz in Chilton's courthouse foyer.

(d) When one studies the mind of a satanic, set-up serial killer like Edwards', the prospect of framing Avery would have more than piqued his interest.

Avery verses the State would've had Ed salivating, wondering how he could exploit such a ridiculous situation.

Edwards planned and committed so many murders that it seems he must have done little else, leaving one to wonder how Edwards supported his wife and 5 children; but nonetheless, this is how Edwards lived for 63 years, robbing and stealing for money, and murdering to collect slaves.

Edwards admitted to few murders, but he did admit killing his 21-year-old adopted son to collect $250,000 life insurance.

In March 2017, Wisconsin Detective Chad Garcia, who investigated the 'Sweetheart Murders', described how the murders of Hack and Drew were solved following a tip off from Edward Wayne Edwards' daughter. Garcia said he was confident Edwards committed at least five to seven more murders, and "who knows beyond that?" Garcia listed 15 confirmed and suspected murder victims, but said he was less sure Edwards was the Zodiac killer.

The problem is, many of Edwards' murders were 'solved'.

Innocent men were languishing in jail or awaiting execution.

Retired Detective, John Cameron, believes that Edwards, excited by Steven Avery's release from prison in 2003, waited and then 'surveilled' him, planning the two-year set-up murder that would destroy both Avery, and the State.

Some say Edwards was in too poorer health to kill Teresa; but despite being 80 years old, and grossly overweight, Edwards committed his last murder in 2008, shooting a young couple whilst asleep in their tent.

Edwards was in poor health, but the O$_2$ tube he wore may have been a disguise to make himself appear an invalid, as this is how he thought. Edwards wore a fake beard, glasses, and shoe-lifters when he conned his way into appearing in a documentary on the subject of one of his murders.

Edwards in 2009

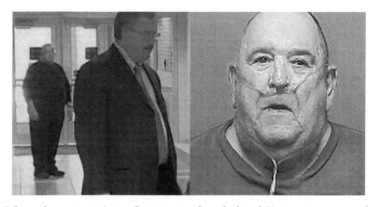

Edwards at Avery's trial, just standing behind Kratz, staring at the camera, 4 years before his eventual arrest in 2009. Edwards committed multiple murders across America between 2005 and 2008, despite his age and health. He was arrested after his daughter informed police. Edwards may have been the only killer Kratz saw all day.

Edwards disguised in the documentary about a murder that he committed.

(ii) The Plot Thickens: Edwards' MO

As the Zodiac killer, Ed Edwards sent letters, and coded written messages of various types to taunt police and the media. Edwards said that his name or identity was in the code.

However, when the code was finally broken in 2010, it revealed that one actually needed Ed Edwards name to crack the 'cipher'. Police of course did have this. Edwards created his Zodiac code, which he called a cipher, using symbols. But he also used intentional spelling mistakes, and irregular capitalization of words and letters, giving them double or multiple meanings. He also wrote some of his Es humped like an M, so the word ME stood for Ed Edwards or Edward Wayne Edwards. Hence the title of Cameron's book, *It's ME!*

Ed put his initials and name into capitalized words like, MEDIA; meaning Me Ed, and Ed Edwards. He also used and attacked the media and journalists, addressing letters to: 'Editor'.

But Ed's clues were just too vague for law enforcement at the time to detect. It wasn't until July 2010 that John Cameron and Neal Best looked into and cracked Edwards' Zodiac cipher. They then sent letters to Edwards in prison, employing the 'Zodiac cipher', and Ed responded back in code, proving that he was in-fact the cipher's creator, and the never caught Zodiac Killer.

Edwards had the gall, the balls, and the resources to pull off a set-up like Avery's; and he was hell-bent - he'd done this set-up hobby for 60years without being caught. Ed often shot his victims twice in the head at close range. Ed did weird things with planted evidence to confuse and embarrass police. But he always left a sign, usually a note or drawing; and if police were smart enough, Ed taunted, they could workout his identity.

Hello its me. Haven't you people figured out who is killing these little people yet I'll give you a hint, I used to be in San Fransisco. I used to stalk women, but I like to kill children now. At all my victims bodies I have left certain clues, but I guess it's too much for you Rebels to handle. So I guess I'll have to tell you. I'll to kill children because they are so easy to "pick off." Buy the way, if you still have letters from the other murders, I am not writing in the same hand writing.

Letter from the Zodiac Killer. In this letter he changes his handwriting style.

This brings us to the Avery case and the Sikikey letter. Edwards knew the Manitowoc County Sheriff's Department were pursuing Avery for Teresa's murder - everyone did. However, MCSD received 2 strange, handwritten letters; the first was the sikikey letter, received 5 days after Teresa's RAV4 was found, on November 10th. It read:

Manitowoc Sheriff
Avery

Body was burnt up in ~~alumaman~~ SMeLter, 3AM
Fridy Morn.
Sikikey

mamtavoc Shvag

A venx

E_x 497
(4)

M0S-2761

(KT) H-R.

12/1/06

Body Was burnt up in

aluminumSMeLter, 3 AM

Fridy Morn.

Si'kiKoy

Is the writing Ed's? The 'W's are pointy and crossed, but look at the 'double M' in Manitowoc. Now look at the following image of a 1967 letter by the Zodiac Killer.

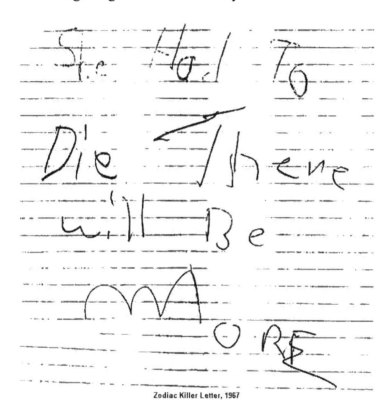

Zodiac Killer Letter, 1967

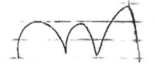

Zodiac 1967 on left. 2005 letter to MCSD on right. Ed did this as
the Zodiac to say, it's me, 'Edward Wayne Edwards'.

The sikikey letter suggests the 'body was 'burnt' in a smelter',
but does Avery Auto's smelter get hot enough? Aluminum
alloy's melting point is around 1220 degrees Fahrenheit
(660°C), which is far too low to burn bone. The main
problematic with Avery burning a body in the portable
furnace is that parts of the body would be trapped inside, and
would be hard to remove fully. If Ed wrote the sikikey letter,
the 'sikikey' will likely be the key to the code, and the letter
will reveal some hidden message.

The next letter MCSD investigators received was the
bizarre, CAROL letter, which read:

Dear Sir
Steven Avery never killed Teresa Halbach. She is a patient
at Winnebago Mental Health Institute.

CAROL
I seen her

Winnebago Mental Health Institute's logo

Is this Edwards saying: *I seen her*?

> *Ed Edwards hi?*

Clearly, Teresa was not a mental health patient. In several of his murders, Edwards posed as a psychiatrist. The Winnebago Mental Health Institute's logo is similar to Edwards' trademark rolled Ms and Es. Remember Ed's code would not be discovered for 5 more years. Edwards put spelling mistakes into his notes as a signature; he also crossed out some words; and he used incorrect grammar. Ed's signatures are in both letters to MCSD.

Edwards always left a sign for police.

As for Edwards handwriting styles and mistakes, in other letters, (not attached to murders), Ed used cursive script. Ed's script was aligned with the page and tidy; and contained no spelling errors or struck-through words; these were clues or parts of his code.

Cameron writes in, *It's Me*:

> *Edwards spends pages explaining the postcards - the placement of each individual letter, the letter size, tilt, every dot. From this he extracts codes and messages pertaining to the identity of the Black Dahlia murderer. He uses ladder codes and a code invented by Francis Bacon some 300 years ago based on binary system.*

Ed's Code

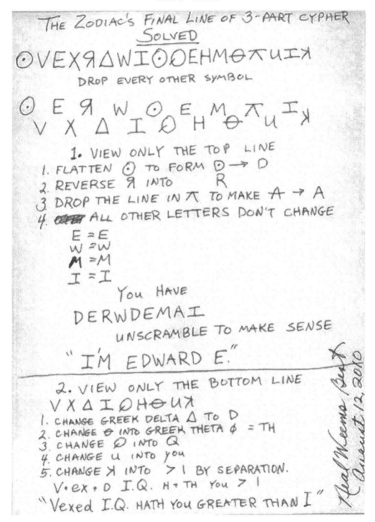

THE ZODIAC's FINAL LINE OF 3-PART CYPHER
<u>SOLVED</u>

⊙VEX9△WI⊙ΘEHMΘ⅄UI⅄

DROP EVERY OTHER SYMBOL

⊙ E 9 W ⊙ E M ⅄ I⅄
V X △ I Θ H Θ ⅄ u

1. VIEW ONLY THE TOP LINE
1. FLATTEN ⊙ TO FORM D → D
2. REVERSE 9 INTO R
3. DROP THE LINE IN ⅄ TO MAKE A → A
4. ~~OTHER~~ ALL OTHER LETTERS DON'T CHANGE

E = E
W = W
M = M
I = I

You HAVE

D E R W D E M A I

UNSCRAMBLE TO MAKE SENSE

" I'M EDWARD E."

2. VIEW ONLY THE BOTTOM LINE

V X △ I Θ H Θ u⅄

1. CHANGE GREEK DELTA △ TO D
2. CHANGE Θ INTO GREEK THETA φ = TH
3. CHANGE Θ INTO Q
4. CHANGE u INTO you
5. CHANGE ⅄ INTO > I BY SEPARATION.

V•ex•D I.Q. H+TH You > I

" Vexed I.Q. HATH You GREATER THAN I "

*Neal Weena Best
August 12, 2010*

This was the Zodiac's 3-part cipher, solved by Neal Best in 2010. "I'm Edward E", "Vexed IQ Hath you greater than I".

By giving Edward E, he is not quite giving his full name. Vexed refers to difficult, unresolved, and much debated - and Ed.

In times when psych-analysis was developing, Ed was diagnosed with antisocial disorder, and labeled a highly intelligent psychopath.

Ed the Zodiac Killer used Greek and Egyptian symbols, including the crossed circle of the Zodiac. However, Ed initially used this symbol because of the abuse he suffered as a child in a Catholic orphanage he was put into after his mother's death; the crossed circle of Catholicism and the sign of the Zodiac. He stamped this symbol into the skin of some victims, and used it on his notes to media, and police.

Ed killed lovers on lovers' lanes because his mother conceived him this way. When she died he was abandoned without a father to the cruel corridors of catholic orphanages.

An entire volume could be written on Edwards, and we cannot do so here, but Ed's 'clues' were often too vague or off track, or even too narcissistic for most to notice them. In examining the CAROL letter, to MCSD, post Avery we can say:

If from Ed, CAROL was capitalized for a reason. The letter held a grammatical error.

In the 1952 novel, *The Price of Salt*, set in the 1950s, aspiring photographer, Therese, starts a love affair with another woman. In 1990, the novel was re-published as, *Carol*. The same author wrote the psycho-murder thriller, *Strangers on a Train*.

The similarities are: Edwards was killing woman on lovers' lanes in the 1950's. Therese was a photographer in an affair with a woman. Theresa was a photographer in an affair with a woman (couple).

'I 'seen' her'.

'She is a patient of Ed Edwards'.

Vague but possible.

s-EE-n

When personal computers became common in the '90's and early '00's, Ed became more than just conversant. Ed blogged on websites leading Law Enforcement across the nation to false convictions. Ed also blogged on *Zodiackiller.com* using handles that reflected his previous murders. One of Ed's blog handles was, Zander_Kite.

The Zander Rd note found by police in Avery's desk, written on the back of a vehicle for-sale sign. The writing is not Avery's. The Phone number is Teresa Halbach's. Avery had Teresa's business card, with her number, and her number was in his phone's memory.

What Ed did throughout his 'career' of murder-set-ups, was plant clues at one murder, which alluded to his previous murders; some decades old, even going back to the 50s, 60s, 70s, 80s, and 90s.

Could the Zander Rd note have been Ed leaving a date and location: 3rd March, 2002, Zander Rd? Investigations into the address near Avery's at 3302 West Zander Rd, were fruitless.

But look at the '33' in the note. Is it Ed's, 'EE' or 'ME'?

Also, look at this image of an old abandoned, overgrown house at 3302 Zander Road, Two Creeks, Wisconsin. The abandoned dwelling is not far from Avery's. There is a new house near the dwelling now, that was not there in 2005.

This is spooky.

3302 Zander Road, Two Creeks, Wisconsin

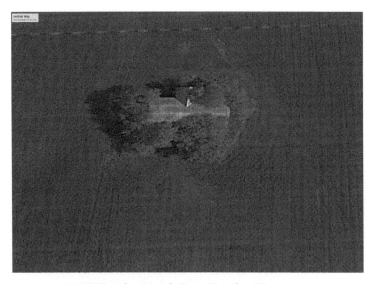

3302 Zander Road, Two Creeks, Wisconsin

The **Zander Road** address is near the Devil's Corner location, where the body of 32 year old Areerat Chuprevich was discovered in 2008.

The Thai woman had been missing since April 2003. Police found her vehicle near the Mariner Motel, where she had lived with her husband, Tom Chuprevich.

Areerat had a gunshot wound to the head.

The police pursued Karl McLeod for Areerat's murder, because McLeod knew Areerat. McLeod was married to Tom Chuprevich's stepdaughter; and 20 years earlier, had been convicted of sexual assault.

McLeod committed suicide in prison in 2006. There has been speculation that McLeod murdered the still missing, Amber Wilde, but;

Did Edwards lead police to McLeod after he murdered Areerat?

Did Edwards use the address at 3302 Zander Rd, Two Rivers?

Can evidence of Teresa be found at 3302 Zander Rd?

How did the 'Zander Rd note' get into the shelf of Avery's desk; poking out enough to be read?

We watched a *youtube* clip of investigators entering Avery's trailer, where his desk is clearly visible. The camera focuses on a letter on the desk, inviting Avery to a luncheon in two week's time; one can see the Auto Trader magazine, but no Zander Rd note. In this clip investigator Wendy Baldwin says: "I don't think he'll be able to make it." (to the luncheon). This shows at an early stage that they only had eyes for Avery. She also opens Avery's closet, and suggests they take Avery's shoes and compare them to unsolved burglaries where print impressions were taken.

Where was the Zander note?

If Ed came back and planted it, how'd he get in? How'd he slip the scene guards?

(iii) Did Edwards Kill Teresa?

Edwards was fully capable of murdering Teresa and setting up Avery; he had destroyed so many others by framing.

Analysis suggests that Edwards may have written the Sikikey letter; but the Winnebago Mental Health letter has Ed written all over it.

However, we would expect *more* from Ed - something more occult, religious, or Zodiac.

Some say Edwards' occult beliefs, based largely on Al Crowley's writings, meant that Ed may have specifically chosen Halloween to kill Teresa; but we doubt this, as Avery made the appointment randomly at 08:12am Halloween morning, and Ed had no way to know Teresa was going there. However, if Ed is the killer, he must've followed Teresa, and observed her for some period of time.

But did Ed kill Teresa and set-up Avery?

To do so Ed had to do the following:

(a) Wait for Teresa to leave Avery Salvage.

(b) Drive up behind Teresa, and get her to pull over.
Ed did exactly this in his 1970 abduction of 23-year-old Kathleen Johns in California.
A car rushed up behind hers flashing its headlights, indicating for her to pull over. The vehicle parked behind her's. Edwards got out and said that he had noticed one of her wheels wobbling, and offered to fix it. If Edwards used this ploy on Teresa, she could have gotten out of her car to get the lug-wrench from the rear cargo area. She hands the lug wrench to Edwards and he bludgeons her in the head; this explains her blood cast-off on the inside of the rear cargo door. Then in trademark fashion, Edwards would shoot her twice in the head. Ed was never a sexual predator, he often just killed on the spot; by gun, by rope, by fire.

(c) Push Teresa's body into the back of her RAV4 and drive to a predetermine location, possibly a hunting lodge in the nearby Drum forest, or 3302 Zander Rd.
Part of Zellner's new forensic testing includes Teresa's lug-wrench from her RAV4. Interestingly, a dark colored

*vehicle was reported as being parked on the roadside
near Avery's during the disappearance. Edwards drove a
dark colored van.*

(d) Burn Teresa's body.
*Ed is experienced at this, a multiple convicted arsonist
who previously referred to himself as Ed Burns. Ed kills
by rope, by gun, by fire.*
*He has planned the planting of the RAV4 and the bones,
but will purposefully leave evidence that confuses police.*

(e) Plant the RAV4.
*Ed enters Avery's property by the Kuss Rd track, hits the
post, damages the blinker-light, and puts it in the trunk.
To his delight, police later plant Avery's blood. Ed had
no access to Steven's blood. The small drops in Steven's
sink were not enough. Police appear to have gotten the
idea to plant blood from seeing Avery's cut finger, and
the blood daubs in Avery's Pontiac Grand Am.*

(f) Plant Teresa's cremains, purse, and electronics.
*Then Ed plants the bones, and the electronics; he plants
the crumpled plates and the underwear near Avery's
trailer, and then he turns around and drives back out to
Kuss Rd. The only thing is, Ed has to have known to burn
Teresa specifically with tires, and to transport the bone
inter-meshed with the burned steel-belting.*

(g) Ed creates the human cadaver track that the sent-dogs
Brutus and Trace followed, and Great Lakes Search &
Rescue mapped.

The problems are:

How can Edwards plant the RAV4 key, or the 'Zander note'
in Avery's trailer, or clean-down Avery's rifle, when police
are controlling the site and would see him? Remember, a

condition of this theory is that Edwards *has* the RAV4's key
in his possession. The RAV4 was found locked, with no key.

The vehicle planter had the key.

The key *was* the sub-key, complete with lanyard.

For the Edwards theory to hold, the police found
Teresa's sub-key - on the Avery property. Perhaps Ed tossed
it into the Mercury Wagon along with the plates and
underwear.

You know the rest.

So why would *Edwards* lock the RAV4 after
planting it? Why take the key? Why not leave the key
behind? Perhaps he planned to plant it in Avery's trailer.

> Remember what Josh Radandt said: *A few days after
> November 5, 2005, I remember seeing light in the Manitowoc
> County sand and gravel pit to the south of Radandt's
> property. I remember that the lights appeared to illuminate
> the entire Manitowoc County pit.*
>
> *I understand that there were suspected human pelvic
> bones recovered from a gravel pit property south of Avery's
> Auto Salvage. Upon reviewing a map showing the coordinates
> at which these bones were found, I believe they were found in
> the Manitowoc County sand and gravel pit.*

Avery was taken into custody on November 11th .

Even in the Ed Edwards scenario, the police must
also plant or fabricate the .22 projectile, holding Teresa's
DNA. The projectile *was* fired from the .22 rifle found in
Avery's room, and Edwards had no access to it. The police
however, took Avery's .22 and test fired it multiple times to
compare grooves and marks on the projectiles.

Kratz swore that Law Enforcement didn't have
access to Avery's gun; but this was false (a.k.a lies).
Fassbender, (the agent who ordered DNA expert Sherry
Culhane - in writing - to take 'the projectile' and put Teresa

in Avery's home or garage), had a projectile from Avery's .22 caliber firearm.

Culhane had Teresa's DNA from at least 5 pairs of dirty panties recovered by Fassbender and Hillegas - and Teresa's toothbrush.

Teresa's RAV4 was found with its battery cable disconnected. Would 'Edwards the killer' really have bothered?

It was surmised that 'Avery the killer' would have disconnected the battery, to isolate any GPS tracking device, but as Teresa's RAV4 had none, it was more likely that Avery disconnected the battery to disable the remote locking mechanism; this is because searchers could come through the yard, pushing the button on a spare door remote, and locate the car by its unlock feature.

These are not things that would concern Ed.

The cadaver track was created before 3:30pm on November 5th; If Ed was there, how was Ed not seen? There are no fences or trees between Steven's and the Dassey house. The houses are clearly visible from both Avery Rd and Highway-147; the land is flat and baron.

Avery kept a large German Shepard guard-dog at his trailer, how did Ed get past the barking dog without raising the suspicions of Bobby, Kayla, Brendan, Tadych, Barb, Blaine, Chuck, Earl, Candy, Allen, or Delores? Avery's dog stopped GLS&R from entering the fire-pit on November 5th.

The only answer to that question is that Ed planted the cremains and electronics after police seized the site, and the residents were forced to leave for the 8 days of investigation. But if so, the cadaver track around the quarry and Avery's berm, had to have been laid or formed by a dead body, before 3pm on November 5th – the day Sturm found the RAV4.

Nevertheless, Ed has been doing this a very long time.

This point raises the point: why would 'Edwards the killer' risk planting evidence so close to the Avery and Dassey homes? Would Ed plant in a location that would incriminate, but be safer or less visible? Or would he go for Avery's fire pit?

After researching Ed Edwards, we realized that if he did kill Teresa, regardless of who wrote the strange notes to MCSD, Ed *would* have left his signature *at the crime scene*.

Is the Zander note this signature? We think there would be something else; maybe something that police missed, or concealed.

We asked: did Ed simply send these letters to Law Enforcement for fun? Did Edwards wait for murders to happen and then send in cryptic letters to confuse, hinder, or distress police?

It appears that Edwards sent these letters to police, but only to humor himself.

(7) Griesbach's German

When prosecutor Michael Griesbach conducted an independent investigation into the Halbach murder, he uncovered a potential third-party suspect; a man that he had prosecuted before. Griesbach dubbed him Wolfgang Braun, to conceal his real name; others have dubbed him the German.

Brian McCorkle has written an interesting article on the German, so it is best to cite him in full:

> While the Search for Teresa Halbach was underway in November 2005, another series of events was beginning in

Bonduel, Wisconsin. A woman was moving from Bonduel, Wisconsin to Maribel. She had rented a house with the lease to start on 1 November, 2005. The house was on a property that included several outbuildings.

In Bonduel, her husband had exhibited bizarre behavior such as sleeping in their attic and sleeping in a fetal position.

She discovered that the labels had been cut from her clothing, and then her underwear was missing. Her husband denied any knowledge. During the week, he said he burned something at their new address and said it was a doll crib. There was a doll crib at the Maribel address, however, it was not burnt, however. During the marriage, the citizen found that her husband had attempted to burn himself in the past. He also had previously burnt her clothing. He was diagnosed with personality disorder, narcissistic disorder, depressive disorder, and psychosis, but he refused to take medication.

She found that on 31 October, 2005, he visited the Maribel area and had stopped at the rental before the lease began. He spoke of visiting an auto salvage yard. He commented that a woman wanted to take pictures of the rental property on 31 October while he was there, and he felt that the photographer was "stupid."

During the week, she observed that her husband had scratches on his back and a cut finger that bled intermittently. She was beginning the move while working in Green Bay.

She found her underwear stuffed in an attic closet at the Bonduel home. She also noted a boom-box along with cans of Cherry Pepsi Cola near the steps of the Maribel home. Her underwear disappeared again.

On the 5 of November, when they stopped for lunch in the Maribel area, the husband saw a missing person poster for Halbach and stated dogmatically, "She's dead."

The following evening, her husband's behavior turned worse. He refused to allow her into the Maribel rental. The citizen contacted the Manitowoc County Sheriff's department, and he was arrested on 6 November, 2005. He was charged with disorderly conduct and resisting an officer.

When she returned to the Bonduel home to continue the move, she checked the attic cupboard again for her missing underwear. Instead, she found a pair of yellow lace panties than were not hers. They were about her size and had stains consistent with menstruation. She placed the panties in a plastic bag to ask her husband about them.

About 10 November, 2005 she looked through the outbuildings in Maribel for her missing clothing. She found some of her clothing cut into pieces. She also discovered a can of lighter fluid with a bloody fingerprint.

Unbeknownst to the citizen, her husband had been placed in two separate psychiatric care facilities during his custody. He was released to an outside address in January, 2006. Court records show that address as Glen's Bar and Grill in Manitowoc. The County did not notify the woman that her husband was free and in the community.

Between November and the end of the year, a few odd things happened. Two explicit adult magazines were placed on the property. Also, her dogs found relatively fresh bones somewhere on the property. She discarded the bones.

While attempting to distract the dogs from the bones, the citizen dropped her husband's tool chest in one of the outbuildings. A masons' hammer and a pair of surgical gloves fell from the chest. The hammer had visible dark red flecks.

In January, she noticed a person staring at her home from the gas station/truck stop across the road. She then discovered that her husband had been released as well as his address. When she parked in the parking lot of the bar and grill, he approached her car and insisted that she take him to the Maribel residence and began searching the house. During the search, he struck her. She called the Sheriff's Department, and her husband was rearrested.

The new charges were burglary, intimidation of a witness, criminal trespass, resisting an officer, and bail jumping.

One night she noted a second floor balcony door was open. She entered the home and secured the door. After that she discovered an opened closet at the base of the stairs with a pair of women's jeans, a top, and a pillowcase stained with red stains.

She contacted the sheriff's department. When a deputy arrived, the citizen explained her findings and wondered if the clothing were connected with the Halbach case. She then discussed the other incidents with the deputy. The deputy stated that she believed the Halbach clothing had been recovered! She collected one magazine and the yellow panties.

If the Halbach clothing had been recovered, it was not information that was released at or after the trial of Steven Avery. If not, then the deputy was fabricating.

The citizen was contacted by Manitowoc County Detective Dennis Jacobs. Jacobs is the child sex investigator for Manitowoc County. He insisted that the panties were from a child despite the staining and size. He wanted the citizen to accuse her husband of pedophilia. He also volunteered that authorities had their suspect in the Halbach case.

She told Detective Jacobs of the cut clothing and a previous incident when her husband had burnt her clothing. His response was that was not a crime.

The woman left Wisconsin for a job in Oregon. On 2nd March, 2006 the Manitowoc County prosecutor dismissed the charges of burglary and intimidation against the husband. Charges of disorderly conduct, criminal trespass, and bail jumping were also dismissed. He pleaded no contest to the two resisting officer charges and was sentenced to time served.

She believes that the victim services office in Manitowoc County provided her husband with her new address. He was at her door soon after his release.

She considered the events of the week of 31 October, 2005, and her husband's behaviors and injuries. The citizen believes that there may be a connection with the Halbach disappearance. When she asked her husband about any possible connection, he simply laughed and said no one would believe her if she reported her suspicions.

But, she had developed a distrust of Manitowoc County law enforcement. Her husband was probably correct that the

Wisconsin authorities could not accept the concept that someone else did the crime.

State Prosecutor Griesbach thought the woman, (who he dubbed Sophie) was telling a true story, but knew more investigation was needed. The woman, 'Sophie' actually gave physical evidence to MCSD that could have been used to forensically eliminate the German from the Halbach inquiries, but MCSD did not follow up.

The German told his wife that he was at a salvage-yard the same day Teresa vanished; was it Avery Auto? They lived only 6 miles away.

The German told his wife that while at the wreckers he had spoken to a photographer about photographing their rental, and that she was 'stupid.' Was this Teresa?

Interestingly, Mr. Griesbach had acted as prosecutor against the 'German' before, and knew the pedigree of his character, and mental stability. Yet Griesbach pulled back from further consideration of the German in the Halbach case, because he claims he could not decide whether or not 'Sophie Braun' was being truthful.

Let's look at what we have:

a. The German had been in and out of four mental institutions, and had been diagnosed anti-social, narcissistic, and depressive.

b. He refused to take medication for his mental aliments.

c. His wife claimed that he had drugged her, and cleaned out her bank account. That he had beaten her; raped her; threatened to kill her; and had soaked himself in gasoline and threatened to kill himself.

d. He liked to collect women's underwear; and as many pairs were dirty, we can assume he was breaking in to homes to take them.

e. He was obsessed with fire and burning property.

f. He had previously burned his wife's clothing.

g. A day or two before Teresa Halbach's disappearance, he told his wife that he had burned a doll's crib, but had not.

h. In their shed, his wife found, surgical gloves, a bloody hammer, and a lighter fluid container with a bloody fingerprint.

i. When they saw a poster for the missing Teresa, the German said to his wife: 'She's dead.'

j. Possible connection; he may have encountered Teresa at the salvage yard.

k. When the wife approached police, they said they already had the killer; which was Avery.

Griesbach's German, Wolfgang Braun, looks like a prime third-party suspect. Did Griesbach drop the idea, so as to not supply future defense counsel with ammunition?

Probably not – the cat was out of the bag anyway.

The thing that goes against the German being the killer is: Avery said, that at around 2:50pm on Halloween, he watched Teresa get in her truck, and drive away. He said she turned left at Highway-147, and drove out of sight. (Did he really watch her all that way?)

If the German was the killer, he must've been waiting out on H-147, and flagged Teresa down.

Then he killed her by two shots to the head, and:

a. Planted the RAV4 on November 3rd; and Brendan just made a lucky guess that he'd put a car hood and branches up against it.

b. Drove the quarry track and the berm road by Steven's to lay the cadaver sent trail that Brutus and Trace indicated, on the 3rd

c. Planted the bones and the cremains that were inter-twined in five sets of burned steel-belted radial tires on November 3rd or 4th.

d. Planted the crumpled license plates, and purple thong, on the 3rd or 4th. And possibly the key, in the Mercury Wagon 140 yards from the Dassey home.

e. Went into Avery's home and wiped down the rifle above his bed, but not the other .22 in the trailer.

f. Therefore, the police plant Avery's blood and DNA on the RAV4; and the police find and plant Teresa's key.

If so, this panty sniffing nut-job seems to have killed with no motive, which departs from his MO. And then he goes to extraordinary lengths to frame Avery. He uses expert techniques like burning the body with tires and planting the steel-belts in Avery's pit unseen. Wiping down his rifle, etc, etc; it is a massive jump from his norm.

However, this doesn't explain why Brendan and Steven bleached a small section of Steven's garage floor on Halloween.

It doesn't explain why Steven, Brendan, and Blaine lied to police regarding Teresa's arrival, and actions at Avery's on Halloween.

It doesn't explain how Brendan knew a car hood and branches had been put against the RAV4; and that he had put it down the back by the pond.

It doesn't' explain the strong cadaver indications around Avery's garage; and along the berm track – that Brendan had said they had used to hide the RAV4.

And it certainly doesn't explain what's coming next.

VIII

Dassey's Confessions

(1) Indications

The feeling is strong that Wisconsin State investigators coerced Dassey's confessions.

Did they?

Four months after the murder, investigators grill Brendan: Teresa's car was found on your property. The remains of her burned body are found next-door at Uncle Steven's. Steven has been arrested - and the night Teresa was last seen, *you* were with your uncle.

Later two men come to Brendan's high school, remove him from class, and take him into the principle's office. They are Investigator Wiegert, and Special Agent Fassbender. They start by saying they are there to help Brendan, and to help relieve his anxiety. They say that authorities demand they charge him, because he is suspected to be involved - but they believe that's not the case. They have kids too and they're there to protect Brendan and help him. Then they proceed to continually tell Brendan that he saw something, and they know it.

From *MaM* we know that some of what Dassey confessed was fed to him during interrogation.

But, initially quite a bit wasn't. And later, in May, when Brendan changed his story, he produced an original narrative completely un-coerced.

But can any value or trust be placed in Brendan's confessions?

Why did Brendan lie, and what can we learn from his 'story' changes?

It only took me a day to read every available transcript of Dassey's recorded interviews and interrogations; but it has taken weeks to make sense of it all.

(a) November 5th, 2005: Brendan was "questioned" by police during initial inquiries. The RAV4 had been found and police were trying to piece together Teresa's movements, hoping she was still alive.

(b) November 6th, 2005: Brendan was questioned by Detectives Sasse and Baldwin.

(c) February 27th, 2006, 10:30am (almost 4 months after Teresa's murder): Official Interview at Mishicot High School. Inv Wiegert and SA Fassbender.

(d) The same day, February 27th, 2006, 3:21pm: Interview was continued at Two Rivers Police Station.

(e) March 1st, 2006: Brendan was questioned by investigators Sasse and Baldwin and in an unmarked car. (Only audio of this is available from stevenaverycase.org).

(f) March 1st, 2006: Interrogation at Manitowoc County Sheriff's Dept, Fassbender and Wiegert.

(g) Brendan is questioned at Fox Hills Resort.

(h) May 13th, 2006: Brendan requests an interview at Sheboygan County Jail.

Basic observations:

Along with Steven and Blaine, Brendan lied to police from the very first interaction on November 5th.

Police, looking for the missing Teresa, knew she had been at Steven Avery's at 2:35pm Halloween day, 4 days earlier, so they asked Brendan if he had seen Teresa or her RAV4.

Brendan said No, and that he had never seen her or her car.

Why?

However, Bobby Dassey *had* seen Teresa at 2:36pm, and he told this to police; Bobby also saw Teresa's RAV4 was still parked on their lane at 2:45pm. Brendan arrived home from school circa 3:40pm; but the bus drive told police at that time, that she saw a woman taking photos, and also - she saw a vehicle like Teresa's down the lane. Bear in mind that the court testimony was different. Lisa's sighting was presented to Brendan and he immediately froze up. Then Brendan changed his statements, and said that *he had* seen Teresa; and that her RAV4 was parked by Steven's when he walked home from the bus.

When asked why he didn't say so, Brendan said he lied because he did not want to go to jail.

There is a strong belief that Brendan's 'story' or confessions were wildly erratic; and were so because he was trying to guess and provide the answers that he thought investigators wanted. But over time his confession progressed to a coherent timeline. Dassey was led to some details, but not initially. Dassey also knew some specific details that only the person that planted the RAV4 would know.

(2) School's Out: February 27ᵗʰ, 2006

Points going in:

(1) Investigators are focused on Steven for the murder; taking no chances, they have planted evidence to strengthen their case from 'possible conviction', to 'slam-dunk'.

(2) Investigators know Brendan was with Steven on Halloween, the evening of October 31st.

(3) They know the RAV4 was stashed and covered, because they did not plant it, and didn't consider that someone else might have.

(4) They know Teresa was burned in Avery's fire-pit, because they didn't plant the bones, and didn't consider that someone else might have.

(5) They know Teresa was burned with the large, metal sprung van seat frame, as her bones were entwined with the metal lattice. They surmised the same for the steel-belted tires, which had bone in them also. If someone else planted the bones, they had to take the tires out of the pit, put in the bone, and load the tire back on top.

(6) Cadaver dogs tracked from the RAV4's location to Steven's house, along the back berm track, adding weight to there theory.

(7) Investigators conclude that Brendan must know *something.*

Some believe that police *targeted* Brendan because of his lack of intelligence; but police were clearly *duty-bound* to interview Brendan - if they didn't, they would have been derelict in their duties.

However, here the police make their first mistake. They know Brendan lied initially about seeing Teresa, and then again about Teresa's jeep going past him in the lane. Investigators think Brendan is likely being pressured to lie or cover for Steven. The result is Investigators interviewing Brendan without his mother, lawyer, or support person in the principle's office - two-on-one with a 16 year-old, slow youth.

Big fail.

This process could have led to a judge ruling the confession truthful, but unreliable. An unreliable confession is inadmissible in trial.

Investigators isolated Brendan because they did not think they could get Brendan to talk openly unless he was alone.

A kid is not going to talk about 'these things' in front of his Mom, and a lawyer would just shut them down and plead the 5th.

Then investigators though, even if Brendan's interview becomes inadmissible, it will still help us understand what happened, and explain the trail of genuine evidence.

However, right throughout this interview, Dassey lies about small details. Anyone engrossed in the case must read the transcripts. Here we can only summarize *our* findings.

F= Special Agent Fassbender

W= Inv. Wiegert

B= Brendan Dassey

Redacted -F: ...and if you were out there by the and stuff, and by your own words you went and got that seat out of a - the vehicle seat, remember that one? Brought it over and someone put it on the fire. Did you put that seat on the fire or him?

B: We both did.

F...What did you see in the fire?

B: Branches a cabinet and some tires.

F: Did you see any body parts?

B: (Silence; shrugs.)

F: ...Because Teresa's bones were inter-mingled in that seat. And the only way her bones were inter-mingled in that seat is if she was put on that seat or if the seat was put on top of her.

~ Brendan confirms Steven's bonfire, and Steven's invitation to attend it. Steven initially lied, and said there was no fire. Why? Blaine also said no fire, as if he had been intimidated into lying for Steven too.

Investigators asked Brendan if he saw body parts in the fire, but the first thing Brendan says he saw was *'clothes like a blue shirt - some pants.'*

The Reid interview technique is in use during this interview, albeit a softened version; Investigators are calm and quite, but say they already 'know', and have evidence. They coach Brendan on seeing body parts, by suggesting he may have seen a foot.

Brendan says Steven had a shovel and poked in the fire with it, corroborating Kayla's observation.

In this interview Brendan's 'tactic' (and he does have one) is to tell Investigators that Steven *told* him details of what happened to Teresa; as if Brendan wasn't there and did not see anything; Brendan separates and distances himself from events.

This is *before* the investigators employ interrogation tactics on the 16 year-old. Brendan confirms Stevens's interaction and involvement in Teresa's death, but says he was only *told* about it.

Because timings and genuine evidence failed to align with Brendan's accounts, Investigators were drawn in to interrogation mode, and made the mistake of leading on some details.

But on page 459, Brendan reveals specific details of the RAV4's hiding.

W: Her jeep, he tried to cover it with what?

B: Branches. . . a car hood.

The innocent Avery should *not* have known branches and a hood were used to cover Teresa's car. Brendan says Steven *told* him this.

The inconsistencies and lies from interview one are confused with Brendan trying to please Investigators:

a. That Steven stabbed Teresa in her RAV4.

b. That Steven hid the knife under the Driver's seat.

c. That Steven drove the RAV4 to the pit / pond past Chuck's house.

d. That Steven cut himself whilst stabbing Teresa.

e. Several other small details.

These untruths were not fed to Brendan. Brendan simply answered straight questions with false information. Why?

Brendan lied because he was told not to talk.

W: What did he tell you?

B: That I should keep my mouth shut, they where hers.

W: Did he threaten you?

B: Sort of.

F. What'd he say?

B.(silence) . . . . stab me too.

W: Or else he would stab you too?

B: Yeah.

Wiegert says: *Brendan you remember you are not under arrest, right? You can stop answering questions at any time, right? Yes? You can walk out anytime you want, right?*

When asked : Why did you lie? Brendan says: I was startin' to get the mind's thoughts.

F: Tell me about those.

B: That people are tellin' me not to say anything and that.

At the end of the interview Investigators set to make a written statement of what Brendan has said so far. This statement will include the inconsistencies and lies Brendan has used to try to fulfill the orders from family or Steven.

Wiegert reads back Brendan's 1st written statement: *I got off the bus at 3:45 and seen her jeep down at Steven's house. Then I went in my house and played playstation2 for 3 hours, and then I eat at 8 and I watch TV. And then I got a call from Steven, if I wanted to come over to have a fire, and I did, and he told me to bring the golf-cart, and I did. So then we went driving around the yard and got to pick up the stuff around the house. Then we dropped the seats by the fire*

*and went to get wood and the cabinet and then went back to
throw the seat on the fire and then we waited for it to go
down and throw on the wood and cabinet. Then I seen the
toes before we throw the wood and cabinet on the fire. When
we did that he seen me that I seen the toes. He told me not to
say anything and he told me that he stabbed her in the
stomach in the pit and he took the knife and put it under the
seat in her jeep.*

Brendan filled this statement with lies. Why?

(a) Our psychologist believes that Brendan was
distancing himself from Teresa's murder, by saying Steven
told him about it.

(b) Brendan was obfuscating because Steven had
threatened him with stabbing, or 'ending up like her', if he
'talked'. However, Brendan doesn't believe that Steven will
'get out' at this point.

(c) Brendan was mixing details, because family such
as Allan Avery (Grandpa) and Steven's brothers had
pressured Brendan and Blaine to 'not drop Steven in it'.

Another point is: people lie when they don't trust.
Brendan did not buy-into Wiegert and Fassbender promises.

Brendan had anticipated what would happen if he
told the truth - if he told Teresa's story.

Brendan did not want to go to jail.

The idea that Brendan had no idea what was
happening is purely a tactic of Avery's defense team. When
Brendan asked if he would go back to class, he said this to
show the investigators that he believed that he had done
nothing wrong.

Remember Brendan initially, on Nov 5, said that lied because about not seeing Teresa because he did not want to go to jail.

Brendan then employs tactics that distance him from the crime; but Brendan wasn't smart enough to close all the holes.

Brendan's detail had holes that Investigators picked. They knew what evidence was planted, and what wasn't. They knew the dog track. They knew the timelines.

After writing the statement incriminating Steven, but distancing himself from the crime, Brendan was then taken in to Two Rivers police Station and re-interviewed. The questions were the same; some answers were different.

(3) Two Rivers Two Stories: February 27th, 2006

Once again Investigators isolate Brendan. They don't employ interrogation tactics straight away, but ask him the same questions.

Brendan answers the same way, but adds some detail, like Steven had brought out some gas (petrol) to intensify the burning.

Brendan repeats his initial version, and confirms that Steven would stab him if he talked.

Brendan says Steven drove the RAV4 to the pit (salvage yard) past Chucks house.

Brendan maintains that Steven had *'just' told* him the details. Brendan portrays that was not there.

F: Did he tell you where? (Where Steven hid theRAV4)

B: Behind in the woods area. Down in the pit by the lake or pond.

F. Did he tell you what he did to try'n hide it?

B: He put branches over it and a car hood.

Once again: only the people who hid the RAV4 would know these specifics.

Then, coached by the Investigators, Brendan says he saw toes in the fire. Whether this was true or not, Investigators' tactics made this initial admission *unreliable*. Unreliable confessions are inadmissible, whether corroborated by other evidence or not.

W: Were you scared when you saw what you saw? (Body in fire)

B: Yeah.

W: Why didn't you tell anybody?

B: I was scared to.

W: What were you scared about?

B: That they would think I helped him.

Brendan shows earlier that he was not overly bothered by Teresa's murder and burning; but he is scared of being caught.

In between the two February 27th interviews, police had called the Madison crime-lab where Teresa's RAV4 was held in storage, and had them check under the RAV4's seats - but no knife was found.

Brendan now says he lied about the knife under the seat because he was nervous.

In this interview, Brendan says Steven *told* him that he'd used the sled, (and later the creeper), to drag Teresa's body to the fire from the garage alone. Brendan later admits neither was true. Police find no forensic evidence on either the creeper or sled.

Did Brendan say this to once again distance himself from the crime? Using the sled would allow Steven to drag Teresa himself; but Brendan later says that he helped Steven carry her from the RAV4's rear. Brendan had her feet.

(4) Head-Shot: March 1st, 2006

In this interview, investigators Wiegert and Fassbender have information from the crime-lab that Teresa was shot twice into the skull.

F: Who shot her in the head?

B: He did.

F: Then why didn't you tell us that?

B: Cos I couldn't think of it.

It is suggested that Brendan couldn't 'think of it' because it never happened, and he was coached to say it.

However, an important detail here is that Brendan also said that he could not, and did not watch when Steven shoot Teresa. Brendan may not have known Steven shot her in the head. Brendan also still believed he had a chance of getting off if he kept distancing himself from the crime, and steering investigators toward Steven.

In addition, the low powered .22 projectiles penetrated Teresa's skull, but did not exit. With little blood or damage from the .22, Brendan may not have noticed the headshots. Contradicting that however, Brendan does say that Steven shot Teresa *twice* in the head. This number was not fed to Brendan, but it was correct.

At the end of this interview, when only Brendan and his Mom are in the room, Barb says:

> *Barb: Did you?(do it) Huh?*
>
> *Brendan: Not really.*
>
> *Barb: What do you mean, not really?*
>
> *Brendan: They got to my head.*

Some think that 'they got to my head' means Brendan didn't do what he said; that he had been led by the investigators.

Author Shun Attwood goes this far:

> "They got to my head" is Brendan's explanation for why he had falsely confessed. The psychological pressure from his tormentors had overwhelmed him. To alleviate that pressure, he had regurgitated details fed to him by the investigators.

Firstly: what does 'not really' mean?

Did you kill her?

Not really.

If one is innocent, this answer should be, NO.

They got to my head, very likely means that the investigators got him to give more information than he was supposed to.

But more importantly, this was only the beginning of Brendan's confession; there was much more to come.

(5) May Day: May 13th, 2006

For over two months, Brendan has been locked-up based on his flawed evidential 'throat cutting confession'; but now Brendan's story changes dramatically.

Fassbender reads Brendan his rights and tells him that he is being recorded.

F: Go ahead and tell us what you wanted to tell us.

*B: Starting with **that day**?*

B: ...At 7 O'clock I got a phone call from Steven to see if I wanted to come over to the bonfire . . . so I went over there. We went to pick up some stuff around the yard then after that we - he asked me to come in the house cos he wanted to show me somethin'.

This is the first time in the investigation that Brendan admits going into Stevens' trailer on Halloween; he had previously denied going inside *(Distancing)*.

*B, cont: And he showed **me** that she was laying on the bed ta - her hands were roped up to the bed, and that her legs were cuffed.*

    *And then he told me to have sex with her, and so **I** did, because I thought I was not gonna get away from him, cos he was too strong; so I did what he said, and then after that he untied her, and un-cuffed her, and then brought her outside, and before he went outside he told me to grab her clothes and shoes. So we went inta the garage, and before she went out, when before he took her outside, he tie - had tied up her hands and feet, an then was in the garage and he stabbed her and then he told me to. And after that he wanted to make sure she was dead or somthin' - so he shot her 5 times, and while he was doing that I wasn't looking, because I can't watch that stuff. So I was standing by the big door in the garage and then after that, he took her outside, and **we** put her on the fire, and **we** used her clothes to clean up the - some of the blood.*

And then we put her in the fire, and her clothes. We were standin' right by the garage, to wait for it to get down, so we threw some of that stuff on it after it went down.

And then about 9 O'clock my Mom came home and she called Steven on his cell phone to tell him that I was supposed to be home at 10 O'clock, and she asked Steven if I had a sweater on.

So while we waited for the fire to go down, by the time it did get down, it was probably close to 10 O'clock, so he told me to go home. So I did, and then got in the house and I talked to my Mom for a little bit - then I went to bed.

True parts are corroborated, like phone calls and times. There is truth in here.

Brendan admits to helping Steven hide Teresa's car. Investigators believed that Steven took Teresa's RAV4 at night, down the berm track beside his house, and down into the yard; they believed this because cadaver-dogs tracked and indicated this path. The dogs had tracked the strong smell of the gases released by the body's openings after death; these odors are unique to humans, and can be differentiated from other smells, like drug dogs can differentiate narcotics.

F: So did you go down to the pit with him that night? (Salvage yard, not fire pit)

B: Yeah.

F: Tell me about that.

B: Well the way we got down there was the back way, where behind this cabin, and cos there's a field right behind there. There's trees behind them. There's a field there. There's a way back there.

F: Yeah?

B: So that's the way we took it, and then went down in the pit and put it right by the lake, so it wouldn't take long to crush it.

F: Ok. And what else?

B: And he took the plates off.

No leading. No coaching. Teresa's license plates were found 140 yards from Steven's trailer in a Mercury wagon, along with purple woman's underwear. If Steven put the plates there, then Colborn could not have called them in straight from the car. Steven is the only person in the list of suspects would take the plates off. But critically, if Brendan wasn't there, he would not know the plates were removed.

B: Then we started walkin' up to the house. And by the time we got back it was 10 O'clock.

F: Right.

B: Then I went home, and talked to Mom a little bit, and went to bed.

Brendan rapes Teresa, helps burn her corpse, and then goes home, say's hi Mom, and pops off to bed.

Some suggest that this doesn't add up.

Our psychologist disagrees.

The physical causes of psychopathic traits and/ or remorselessness can be genetic, neural, developmental, or environmental – psychopathy can befall any developing brain. Brendan is remorseless.

During this interview, Brendan says they burnt the bedding on which Teresa was raped.

Brendan gives specific details of his raping Teresa.

F: Did you have an erection? Was your penis hard?

B: Yeah.

F: Did it stay hard while you were having sex with her, or did it get soft?

B: No.

F: No what?

B: It stayed hard.

Now we can really start to pry apart the steel-belting of Brendan's confessions.

IX

A BLOODLESS COUP

(1) Cutting to the Facts

Where is the blood?

Even Kathleen Zellner is still asking, where is the blood in Avery's bedroom?

Ken Kratz and the prosecution team used Dassey's early statement, that Brendan had cut Teresa's throat, as confession evidence to secure his murder conviction.

However, on May 13th, Brendan admits that he did not cut Teresa's throat.

The throat cutting never happened.

a. No blood equals no throat cutting.

b. The only way Brendan could have cut Teresa's throat on Steven's bed and have no blood soak into the mattress, is if Teresa was already dead, and her blood had pooled in her abdomen.

c. Brendan maintained that Teresa was still alive when they carried her out to Steven's garage.

d. None of Teresa's blood is found in Steven's trailer.

e. Blood was discovered in Steven's garage, but as it had been heavily bleached, the blood could not be typed or identified, as bleach can break down blood's structure.

[May 13th, 2006, pg821]

W: Did you cut her throat?

B: No.

The issue of Teresa's cut hair was puzzling for all. But it should have been obvious to such experienced investigators, that no hair found, equals no hair cut.

The hair cutting Brendan admitted to on March 1st did not happen; none of Teresa's hair was found.

During the May 13th interview, Brendan confirms that Teresa's hair *was not* cut.

W: What about her hair? Did you cut off the hair like you said earlier, or is that a lie?

B: A lie.

W: Why? Why did you lie about that?

B: Cos I was nervous.

W: Are you nervous now?

B: No

W: So you didn't cut any hair off?

B: (Shakes his head) No.

Brendan says 4 times that he *did not* cut Teresa's hair. So what's going on here?

We think Brendan said that he cut Teresa's hair on March 1st to *avoid* the question: What happened to her head?

When Brendan tells Wiegert that he lied about the hair because he was nervous, nervous means that he was afraid of the truth, and started looking for ways to avoid the question. Brendan also says that when Steven shot the very much alive Teresa in the garage, Brendan had to look away.

Interestingly, in this May 13th interview, Brendan does not want to talk about what he told 14 year-old Kayla Avery about seeing Teresa 'pinned up' in Stevens' trailer. We think Brendan is trying to protect Kayla from retribution; but with Steven in jail, retribution from whom?

But then Dassey drops the bombshell of bombshells.

W: So a couple days prior . . . you said there was this lady he knows. Or tell me how he says that. I don't wanna put words in your mouth. Tell me how he says it to you.

B: That he had a girl comin' over to take a picture of the van . . . That he would kill her.

W: When was the first time he had mentioned killing somebody?

B: A few days before October 31st.

W: And how did that get brought up?

B: Cos we were watchin' TV, and on the news there was someone that killed someone.

W: Okay. And what did he say when he saw that?

B: That he was gonna plan to kill someone, and.

W: And who did he say he was gonna plan to kill?

B: The girl that takes the pictures of the cars for the magazine.

W: And he told you that while he was sitting at his house watching TV?

B: Yeah.

W: Did you say anything to him - like you shouldn't do that, or?

B: No.

W: Did he ask you to help him?

B: Yeah.

When one reads the full section of this interview, a bell is rung that can never be silenced. Brendan explains how Steven had chosen Teresa.

When Brendan came home from school at 3:40pm and walked with Blaine towards home, Brendan saw Teresa's RAV4 parked on the lane, and knew Steven had her.

Brendan explains how their plan was to have sex with Teresa. Moreover, Brendan wanted to, because he wanted to know what sex was like.

On May 13th Brendan recanted his testimony, that he rode his bike to the mailboxes, collected mail, and then dropped it to Steven's.

The mail drop to Steven's never happened.

Brendan made this up to provide a reason, *justifying* his going to Steven's trailer in the first place.

Brendan already knew Teresa was in there.

All of the small lies or statements that Brendan recants in this interview - all of them - are statements that distanced him from the crime.

W: We heard you were crying a lot. Is that true? Its' okay. If you were, It's okay. I understand that.

B: Yah.

W: Why were you crying a lot?

B: Cos after a while, I was thinkin', that I did the wrong thing.

W: How long did it take you to think that way?

B: Like two weeks.

W: So the day after, you were okay? A couple days after you were okay?

B: Yah.

The Mercury Wagon on Avery's lane. Teresa's license plates were found in this vehicle.

(2) Kayla

In December, 2005, Brendan told Kayla that he had seen Teresa Halbach 'pinned up' in Steven's trailer; and that he'd seen Teresa's bones in Steven's fire.

Brendan did not tell the 14-year-old Kayla the parts that he played.

Remember that at 11pm on Halloween, Kayla had seen Steven prodding the fire with a shovel.

Now Kayla truly believes that her angry uncle restrained a woman, killed her, and burned her in his fire - a fire she saw.

Kayla's fear is visceral.

Her uncle is a killer.

He had also tried to touch *her*.

He had held Kayla's arms and pinned her to a wall and told her that she had "Big boobies."

Kayla thought: *How long before I'm in Uncle Stevens' fire?*

Kayla did not want to upset Uncle Steven.

Steven was dangerous, unpredictable, and a murderer with no respect for any law.

In January, Kayla went to her school counselor. Kayla talked about Brendan and Teresa.

Kayla's counselor went to police.

On March 7th, 2006, investigators Wiegert and Fassbender interviewed Kayla at 3:36pm. However, Kayla broke down in tears and said she couldn't *remember* any of it.

We think this was a reaction born of fear; fear that Steven may get out, and seek revenge.

But then Kayla told the investigators about Brendan's confession to her, and that Steven had made the threat - that if anyone told, the same thing would happen to them.

Kayla made a written statement (Exhibit 163, Dassey v Wisconsin), but when she came to testify in Brendan's trial, the fear prevailed, and she couldn't go through with the testimony against Steven.

Kayla knew details of Teresa's murder that evidence corroborated.

Brendan had confessed Steven's role to her; but Kayla pulled out, saying that she had lied. There was no other way that she could withdraw her testimony in any believable way.

Who coached Kayla to withdraw her testimony?

Did someone intimidate her?

We thought: Why would Kayla go to her school counselors, shaken and fearful, if her statement was false?

Was fear a factor? Who did she fear? Was it only Steven?

Allen Avery was actively pressuring Brendan to not take a plea bargain, and to not testify against Steven. Did he also pressure Kayla?

A teacher who was with the counselor testified in Brendan's trial:

Teacher: Kayla came into the office and she was asked by Ms. Baumgartner if she minded that I was there. And Kayla said no; and she said she was there because she was feeling scared.

Q: All right. Let me stop you there first, and ask who else, if anyone, was present for this conversation?

Teacher: No one else.

Q: All right. So there's just the tree of you?

Teacher: Correct.

Q: All right. And did Kayla reveal to the two of you why she was feeling scared, and why she wanted to talk?

Teacher: Yes. She told us that she was scared because her uncle, Steven Avery, had asked one of her cousins to help move a body. She also said she was scared about going to the shop, and she specifically asked if blood can come up through concrete.

Q: Describe for us, if you will, Kayla's demeanor, her affect, during these revelations.

Teacher: She . . .She was scared!

Q: Did she seem at all confused?

Teacher: No.

14-year-old Kayla Avery's official statement:

Statement of Kayla Avery

3/7/06

Brendan told me that he saw the body parts of Teresa in the fire pit behind Steven's grown.[SIC](garage)
Brendan got the mail and brought it to him and he sat in a chair in Steven's bedroom. Then Brendan walked out of the house and he heard skremins[SIC] (Screams) in Steven's house. When I tried to talk to him at Ashle's B-day party and I asked him to talk to me and he did not want to talk to me about it. I think Steven should stay in jail or prison. I do NOT like him at all I really think that Brendan did something and he got forst.[SIC] (forced)
I hate Steven a lot.

P.S. Teresa was pind up[SIC]
P.P.S. I hope he rots in hell
Love
Kayla Avery

When Kayla backed out of her testimony, stating that she had lied about talking to Brendan, people took her at face value. But this is a terrified 14 year old girl with a murderous uncle and God only knows what else in her family.

Many did not consider that Kayla was scared to her core, unsure of her future if she testified, and was intimidated and alone.

Kayla believed that, "*If anyone told, the same thing would happen to them*".

Whilst Avery was locked-up awaiting trial, another family member, Steven's niece, went to CCSD's Wendy Baldwin, and said that Steven had raped her.

a. She was Seventeen in 2003, when Avery was released.

b. She explained how Avery had systematically convinced her that her parents hated her.

c. She told Ms. Baldwin that Steven raped her on her cousin's bed.

d. She told him to stop; but he did not.

e. Steven told her that he would set her house on fire if she told. And that he would hurt her Mom and Dad.

f. When she heard Avery may be released on bail, she feared for her life, and the lives of her family.

This case was assembled into a statement, and was prepared for use at Avery's trial under 'other acts'.

Judge Willis let none of Avery's other acts go before the jury, as they were far too prejudicial. This 19 year old niece's statement, Judge Willis ordered sealed. The official other act statement is available.

Then another woman came forward, in 2006, and reported that Avery had also raped her when she was 17. This rape happened in 1981, before the 'cat burning', and before Avery was wrongly imprisoned for Penny Beernstein's rape. Avery told her whilst raping her, that if she screamed, there would be trouble.

Every *Avery* male alive at the time in 2005, had been a wife beater, and sexually violent. Steven Avery was accused of both with ex-wife Lori. At the time of his 2005 trial, he was also being investigated for violence against girlfriend, Jodi.

(3) Dassey Talks

There are several recorded prison phone conversations between Brendan Dassey and his mother, Barb Janda. The following is a transcript of the recording taken of Brendan and his mother on May 13th 2006. Throughout the transcript, I'll note speculations and conclusions drawn from the Dionysus Group, that are agreed upon. An original facsimile of the Defense copy is also included. I will add detail at certain points; this detail is our opinion.

Phone Call Brendan & Mom: 5/13/06
Track #6 on CD

Phone ringing

Mother:..........Hello

Operator:........Hello, this is a collect call from Brendan, an inmate at the Sheboygan County Jail. To accept the charges press zero. This call is subject to monitoring and recording. Thank you for using...

Brendan::::::::::::Hello

Mother:............Yah

Brendan::::::::::::Did you talk to anybody?

Mother:............No

Brendan::::::::::::Oh

Mother:............What do you mean talk to anybody?

Brendan::::::::::::Cos Mark and Fassbender are gonna talk to you

Mother:............About what?

Brendan::::::::::::About the case

Mother:............When did you talk to them?

Brendan::::::::::::::Today

Mother:............When are they gonna talk to me?

Brendan::::::::::::I dunno

Mother:..........What do you mean?

B:::::::::::::::::::Well. . . . I guess yesterday that Mike guy came up here and talked to me about my results

['That Mike guy,' is the private investigator used by Wiegert and Fassbender on the Dassey investigation. Here Fassbender has used the threat of telling Brendan's mother that he raped and murdered Teresa, hoping to get Brendan to admit his role in Teresa's death. For the benefit of the investigating team, Mike had taken a polygraph recording of Brendan, which Mike says proves deception. These are the 'results' that Brendan is referring to.]

M:........Yah

B:::::::::And

M:........Yah

B:::::::::What?

M:........I haven't talked to nobody. I told you, nobody calls me and lets me know nothin'

B:::::::::Yah. ... Do you feel bad if I say it today?

M:........You don't even have to say it, Brendan

B:::::::::Why?

M:........Because just by the way you're acting I know what it is

B:::::::::What?

M:........I don't want to say it over the phone

B:::::::::About what happened?

M:........Huh?

B:::::::::About what all happened

M:........What all happened? What are you talking about?

B:::::::::About what me and Steven did that day

[n.b: Here Brendan is asking his Mom, Barb Janda, if she will feel bad if he admits to Teresa's rape and murder. Barb tells Brendan that he doesn't have to. Barb also knows the conversation is being recorded, so she feels uncomfortable talking about this on the prison phone. Here Brendan says: 'About what *me* and Steven did that day.' Is this a confession to his mother? It also appears that she already knows Brendan's involvement, and therefore, guilt.]

M:........What about it?

B:::::::::Well Mike and Mark and Matt came up one day and took another interview with me and said because they think I was lying but so, they said if I come out with it that I would have to go to jail for 90 years

M:........What?

B:::::::::Yah. But if I came out with it I would probably get like 20 or less. After the interview they told me if I wanted to say something to her family and I said that I was sorry for what I did

M:........Then Steven did do it

B:::::::::Yah

M:........Crying. . . . Why didn't you tell me about this?

[A lot is happening here that needs unpacking. In most cases of false confession, the investigators back the suspect into a corner by giving them two options that both lead to an admission of guilt: here the first is the threat of 90 years in prison if he doesn't confess; the second is, if Brendan admits to Teresa's murder, he will be treated leniently, with only 20 years in prison or less. The question for an innocent suspect that the police have decided is guilty is: does Brendan feel that his innocence is not enough to save him? But then Brendan says that he was 'sorry for what I did' in the second statement of complicity in the telephone conversation with his Mom. Barb then states: 'then Steven did do it', referring to the rape, murder, and mutilation; and Brendan says, 'yah.']

B:::::::::Yah. But they came out with somethin' that was untrue with me

M:........What's that?

B:::::::::They said that I sold crack

M:........What?

B:::::::::Yah

M:........That you what?

B:::::::::That I sold crack

M:........Really?

B:::::::::Yah. They said that they heard that from someone

M:........Who said that to you?

B:::::::::Both of them

[Here Brendan says, 'but they came out with somethin' that wasn't true with me.' He says this as if the murder charge *was* true, but the crack selling was not. The investigators know that Brendan, an intellectually challenged kid, is not selling crack cocaine. They have shocked Brendan with this so as to see how he reacts to hearing an untrue charge. They want to compare his reaction to the one he had when questioned about Teresa.]

M:........Really?

B:::::::::Yah

M:........I don't think so

B:::::::::No I didn't. And they asked me if I smoked a cigarette and I said I did once, but I didn't like it. Then they said that Travis said I was always talkin' about over by him

[We think the investigators are still keen to see how Brendan gives a truthful denial. Here Brendan shows a clear answer of 'No' to the question of selling crack. He can answer a question from his Mom decisively. However, after the second interview by Fassbender and Wiegert, when Brendan's Mom asked him if he 'did it?' Brendan mumbles: 'Not really.']

M:........Really?

B:::::::::Yah. Then someone came out with me trying to commit suicide

M:.........Why did you even go over there, Brendan? [to Steven Avery's Trailer]

B:::::::::I dunno. I don't even know how I'm gonna do it in court though

M:........What do you mean?

B:::::::::I ain't gonna face them

M:........Face who?

B:::::::::Steven

M:........You know what, Brendan

B:::::::::What?

M:.........I'm gonna tell you somethin'. He did it, and you do what you gotta do. Okay?

B:::::::::What'll happen if he gets pissed off?

M:.........What makes a difference? He ain't goin nowhere now, is he?

B:::::::::No

[Here Barb Dassey confirms Brendan's confession with the words: 'He (Steven) did it.' Brendan shows his fear of Steven's anger, something the other younger members of the wider Avery family have expressed. Barb believes Brendan's confession, but believes that Steven's guilt will mean his incarceration, and this will keep Brendan safe from his rage, *'He aint goin' nowhere now, is he?'* Remember that during Dassey's evidential confession, he said Steven threatened him with the same as Teresa got - presumably stabbing and shooting, as the burning hadn't happened at that point.]

M:........Okay then. . . .Why didn't you tell me bout this earlier?(Barb Crying) Huh?

B:::::::::(Indistinguishable. Brendan's voice breaks up)

M:........(Speaking to someone else in the background) Hello, I'll talk to you later. I'm talking to Brendan. Okay. Alright. Anything else?

B:::::::::What?

M:........So did you talk to her family?

B:::::::::No

M:........Huh

B:::::::::They just asked me if I wanted to say somethin to them, on tape

M:........Did you?

B:::::::::Just that I was sorry for what I did

M:........Did he make you do this?

B:::::::::Yah

M:........Then why didn't you tell him that?

B:::::::::Tell him what?

M:........That Steven made you do it. You know, he made you do a lot of things.

B:::::::::Yah. I told them that. I even told them about Steven touching me and that . . . .

M:........I wish you would've told me, okay

B:::::::::Yah

M:........How'd you answer the phone at 6 O'Clock, when Mike called then? (Referring back to October 31st 2005, the night Teresa disappeared)

B:::::::::They told me they looked at the records and he didn't call

M:........Huh?

B:::::::::They said they had the record and-

M:........What about when I got home at 5 O'Clock? You were here (Barbs home, next to Steven Avery's)

B:::::::::Yah

M:........Yah. When did you go over there? (To Stevens)

B:::::::::I went over there earlier, and then came home before you did

M:........Why didn't you say something to me then? (Barb is directly referring to Teresa being restrained in Avery's trailer or burning in the fire)

B:::::::::I dunno. . . .I was too scared (Whether Brendan was scared of Steven Avery, or scared because a rape and murder had occurred in which he had played a part, is unknown.)

M:........You wouldn't have had to been scared, because I would've called 911, and you wouldn't be going back over there. If you would've been here, maybe she would have been alive yet. . . . .

So, in those statements . . . you did all that to her, too? (referring to rape and throat slitting)

B:::::::::Some of it

M:........Did he make you do it?

B:::::::::Yah, so who's all home?

> [Is Brendan trying to avoid talking gory details with his Mom by changing the subject? He's admitted his involvement to his Mom, and is happy she's buying the 'Steven made me do it' out clause, but clearly it is too early for Brendan to talk about specific details like sexual intercourse and throat cutting with his Mom. Another possibility for Brendan's glib admission to rape and murder, and then saying: 'so who's all home', it was suggested, could be that he is completely remorseless, possessing a sociopathic mind. 'Yeah I did rape Teresa and cut her throat, so who's all home?']

M:........Just me and Blaine (Brendan's older brother)

Op:::::::::You have one minute left

With that telling conversation over, what can we learn about Brendan Dassey's previous confessions? Confessions it was claimed in Making a Murderer, that were coerced.

The group began to debate. The only defense against this taped self incrimination and confession to his mother that has been raised, is that of prior brainwashing by the investigation team of Wiegert, Fassbender, and Mike.

Does this justification hold water? Was Brendan
brainwashed into giving this confession to his Mom over the
prison phone line? Was this a false confession, planted in
Brendan's mind over the weeks and days prior?

Mom:. . . you did all that to her, too? (referring to Teresa)

B:::::::::Some of it

While our psychologist believes that Brendan was telling the
truth to his mother during this 13/5/06 call, we all agreed
that the technique used by his interrogators at the Fox Hills
resort was problematic. Threatening Brendan with 90 years
in prison, and then offering a reduced sentence to confess is
the hallmark trait of false confessions, leading to wrongful
convictions the world over. Special Agent Thomas
Fassbender also told Brendan that Fassbender would tell
Brendan's Mom what happened to Teresa, but it would be
better coming from Brendan. Fassbender prompted him to
'tell her tonight'. Hence this is the first question Brendan
asks his Mom when she answers the phone: 'Did you talk to
anybody?'
    Brendan is worried what his Mom will think. And it
was news to most of us that this is a common trait of
psychopathic killers that one may not realize. It seems too
normal.
    But at every turn the investigators' aggressive
techniques cast doubt over every piece of useable knowledge
and evidence that they gain from Brendan. However, during
this prison phone conversation, Brendan was under no
pressure from his Mom, and appeared to be truthful with his
answers, confessing to his Mom no less than three times
during the recorded conversation. Brendan's Mom appears to
know that Brendan is guilty, but if we move to the next

recorded phone conversation between Barb and Brendan, there is a noticeable shift in both Barb's demeanor, and tactics.

Brendan Dassey & Mom, Barb, Phone conversation from 5/13/06 (Defense copy)

Mom:...Hello

B:::::::::Yah

M:........You heard me, huh?

B:::::::::Yah

M:........Was you attorney there when Mark and those guys were?

B:::::::::No

M:........Don't talk to them no more

B:::::::::Yah

M:........They're puttin' you in places where you're not-

B:::::::::Yah

M:........You know the reason they're talking to you is to get more information out of you and what your attorney should be doing is putting an order on all of them that they cannot interfere with you or your family members unless your attorney is present

B:::::::::Yah

M:........Cause they're all investigators for the Halbach case

B:::::::::Yah

M:........Not the Dassey case. It's the Halbach case

B:::::::::Yah

M:........Cause the only thing that they're putting out there is bad stuff for you and if you weren't *there at the time, if you didn't slice her throat. You did not have sexual contact with her-*

B:::::::::No

[It appears that Barb has instructed Brendan to change his tune. From the initial shock of the previous call, and her wanting to learn what really happened between Steven, Brendan, and Teresa on October 31st, Barb decides to do what most mothers do - to protect her son.]

M:........That's the reason that they're sayin'. Yah, that's all in the report here that Mom's got

B:::::::::Yah. So if I was in the garage cleaning up that stuff on the floor, how much time will I get though for that?

M:........What was it?

B:::::::::I don't know. It was reddish black stuff

[Brendan refers to a true statement corroborated by evidence, namely that he and Steven cleaned the floor of Steven's garage on the night of October 31st, using three products: paint thinner, gasoline (petrol), and bleach. The question raised by the Dionysus group here is important: Steven's garage was a mess, and had clearly never been cleaned, let alone had its floor scrubbed. So why did Steven pick this night to get Brendan to help him clean the floor with solvents, gasoline, and bleach? Is it just co-incidence that they chose to do this never before attempted cleaning task, the very same night that Teresa disappears and Brendan coughs up a story of rape, murder, and mutilation? Steven hadn't specifically brought cleaning products for the job, he appears to have hastily grabbed what was readily available, suggesting the clean-up was impromptu. Why was it so important to clean the central floor area then, but not the rest of the floor, around the edges? Was it because, like Brendan said, they were cleaning up Teresa's blood after her murder? Was the stuff Brendan describes 'reddish-black' because blood had mixed with the oily grime of a workshop floor? Later luminal testing showed that bleach was used on the floor - Brendan was in-fact, correct.]

B::::::::::I don't know. It was reddish black stuff

M:........See, what they're probably going to do is turn around and have it that Steven said this, Steven is saying you were here. If you say 'Yah' - not meaning Yah it's true - just Yah, they're going to say okay, Brendan was there. Brendan did that. And then they're going by Steven and saying, well Brendan said this and Brendan said that. (Barb wants Brendan to stop admitting culpability)

B::::::::::But what does Steven say about it? (Brendan wants to know what Steven's story is so he can follow the narrative)

M:........Steven just says that you're a dumb shit

B::::::::::Yah. Well last time I talked to Mark and that, they said that Steven was trying to pin me and Bobby for it. (Brendan's older brother. Also another tactic used by law enforcement that leads to false confession.)

M:........Yah. They came to our house wondering what Steven said, right over the phone to Chucky, mind you, that he goin set it up with his attorney that he blames it on me and Earl

B::::::::::Yah

M:........And I looked at Mark and Tom (Wiegert & Fassbender) and told them that well if he tries doin' that he's going to be one sorry son-of-a-bitch

B::::::::::Yah

M:........I told them it is pretty pathetic he has to go fricking kill somebody an take an innocent kid down with him

B:::::::::Yah. And plus if he didn't do it then why would - was he trying to hide up north that day?

M:........But see, they got that on camera, that you were sitting right across the table from Steven smiling at him

B:::::::::I had my head down

M:........Yah

B:::::::::That's cos they said act normal

M:........Mm-huh

B:::::::::Yah

M:........It is normal, Brendan, to sit down all the time. So did you see the body in the fire?

B:::::::::No

M:........Steven says that you seen the body in the fire

B:::::::::No

M:........You know if he killed her?

B:::::::::Not that I know of

[It appears to us here that after instructing Brendan to deny involvement in Teresa's murder, that Barb is coaching and testing Brendan with the type of questions that she believes the investigators will ask. Brendan starts well with 'no', 'no', but then in response to the question: You know if he killed her? Brendan says, 'Not that I know of.' Psychology tells us that this is usually the response of a liar; he should have said no, like he did with the other questions, and like he did when Wiegert falsely but intentionally accused him of selling crack.]

M:........So then how do you know that there was bullet shells outside of the garage?

B:::::::::Cos when Mike came up here he had pictures of it.

[Whether the .22 caliber projectile with Teresa's DNA on it was planted or not, it is a clear fact that investigators did not know to search Steven Avery's garage for firearm projectiles until Brendan's confession on March 1st of 2006, over 2 months before these phone conversations with his mother were recorded. Luminal testing uncovered the bleach clean-up, and two .22-long caliber projectiles were either found or planted. Mike had pictures of the .22-long caliber ejected brass shell casings, not the projectiles, because investigators had gone to Avery's garage and conducted in-depth forensic searches based on Brendan's statement. Further, the projectile marked Item FL, held the genetic profile for wood, red paint, and Teresa's DNA. It would seem, if the projectile was 'doctored' and Teresa's DNA applied to a test-fired bullet, that it would not carry paint and wood; test-fired bullets are fired into ballistics gel for recovery, so the bullet would be clean before Teresa's DNA was applied.]

M:........They told everybody that you told them that there was bullet shells inside the garage

B:::::::::No

M:........That Steven shot her 10 times

B:::::::::No. In the picture they had a bullet right by a crack or something cement

M:........Ah. Don't believe those guys - what they say

B:::::::::Yah

Conversation continues

M:........You go into court, you look down at the table

B::::::::::Yah

M:........The Judge says somethin, all you say is, Yah

After deep individual assessments and group discussion, what we concluded from these prison phone conversations was:

(1) Brendan Dassey clearly and un-coerced, admits involvement in Teresa's murder, to his mother.

(2) Brendan corroborates parts of his March 1st confession; showing the key parts of his earlier and much disputed confession to be correct, and not seeded, fed, or coerced from him by Law Enforcement.

(3) Despite periodically using interrogation techniques on Brendan Dassey that should be inadmissible in a court of law, true statements about the events before, during, and after Teresa's murder can clearly be taken from these interrogation sessions, video-taped by Mark Wiegert and Thomas Fassbender. Specifically, the bullets and casings found in Avery's garage; the cleaning of the reddish material or blood from Avery's garage floor on the night of Teresa's disappearance; and that Steven Avery murdered Teresa.

(4) It shows a clear attempt by Barb Dassey, Brendan's Mom, to enter denial and protect her son (even if guilty of rape, murder, and mutilation of a woman) by coaching him to deny, and 'just say Yah', to the judge.

PHONE CALL BRENDAN & MOM   5/13/06
                           TRACK #6 ON CD 5-10-06
                                                  TO
                                            5-13-06

Phone ringing

M: Hello
B.   Hello this is a collect call from Brendan and inmate at the Sheboygan County Jail. To
      accept charges press 0. This call is subject to monitoring and recording. Thank you for
      using
B.   Hello

M: Ya
B: Did you talk to anybody?

M: No
B: Oh

M.   What do you mean? Talk to anybody?
B.   Cause Mark & Fassbender are gonna talk to you.

M.   About what?
B.   About the case

M.   When did you talk to them?
B.   Today.

M.   When are they gonna talk to me?
B.   I dunno

M.   What do you mean?
B.   Well, I guess yesterday that Mike guy came up here and talked to me about my results

M.   Ya.
B.   And

M.   Ya.
B.   What?

M.   I haven't talked to nobody. I told you nobody calls me and lets me know nothing.
B.   Ya., Do you feel bad if I say it today?

M.   You don't even have to say it Brendan
B.   Why?

1

M.   Because just by the way you are acting I know what it is?
B.   What

M.   I don't want to say it over the phone
B.   About what all happened?

M.   Huh
B.   About what all happened?

M.   What all happened, what are you talking about?
B.   About what Me & Steven did that day.

M.   What about it?
B.   Well, Mike & Mark & Matt came up one day and took another interview with me and said because they think I was lying but so, they said if I come out with it that I would have to go to jail for 90 years.

M.   What?
B.   Ya. But if I came out with it I would probably get I dunno about like 20 or less. After the interview they told me if I wanted to say something to her family and said that I was sorry for what I did.

M.   Then Steven did do it.
B.   Ya

M.   (Mom Crying) Why didn't you tell me about this?
B.   Ya, but they came out with something that was untrue with me

M.   What's that
B.   They said that I sold crack.

M.   What
B.   Ya.

M.   That you what?
B.   That I sold crack.

M.   Really.
B.   Ya, They said that they heard that from someone.

M.   Who said that to you?
B.   Both of them.

2

M.   Really.
B.   Ya.

M.   I don't think so
B.   No, I didn't and they asked me if I smoked a cigarette and I said I did once but I didn't like it. Then they said that Travis said that I was always talking about it over by him.

M.   Really.
B.   Ya. Then someone came out with me trying to commit suicide

M.   Why did you even go over there Brendan?
B.   I dunno, I don't even know how I am gonna do it in court though.

M.   What do you mean?
B.   I ain't gonna face them.

M.   Face who?
B.   Steven

M.   You know what Brendan
B.   What

M.   I am gonna tell you something. He did it and you do what you gotta do. Okay.
B.   What will happen if he gets pissed off.

M.   What makes a difference, he ain't going no where now, is he?
B.   No.

M.   Okay then. Why didn't you tell me about this earlier? (Mom Crying) Huh?
B.   [   ] (Brendan's voice breaking up) *Music in background*

M.   Hello, I'll talk to you later. I'm talking to Brendan. Okay, alright. Anything else?
B.   What?

M.   So did you talk to her family?
B.   No

M.   Huh
B.   They just asked me if I wanted to say something to them, on the tape.

M.   Did you?
B.   Just that I was sorry for what I did.

3

M.   Did he make you do this?
B.   Ya.

M.   Then why didn't you tell him that.
B.   Tell him what/

M.   That Steven made you do it. You know he made you do a lot of things.
B.   Ya, I told them that. I even told them about Steven touching me and that.

M.   What do you mean touching you?
B.   He would grab me somewhere where I was uncomfortable.

M.   Brendan I am your mother.
B.   Ya.

M.   Why didn't you come to me? Why didn't you tell me? Was this all before this
     happened?
B.   What do you mean?

M.   All before this happened, did he touch you before all this stuff happened to you.
B.   Ya.

M.   Why didn't you come to me, because then he would have been gone then and this
     wouldn't have happened.
B.   Ya

M.   Yes, and you would still be here with me.
B.   Yes, Well you know I did it.

M.   Huh
B.   You know he always touched us and that.

M.   I didn't think there. He used to horse around with you guys.
B.   Ya, but you remember he would always do stuff to Brian and that.

M.   What do you mean.
B.   Well he would like fake pumping him

M.   Goofing around
B.   Ya but, like that one time when he was going with what's her name Jessica's sister.

M.   Teresa?
B.   Ya. That one day when she was over, Steven and Blaine and Brian and I was downstairs
     and Steven was touching her and that.

4

M.   Really
B.   Ya.

M.   Oh, he makes me so sick (Heavy Breathing) What did they say to you?
B.   What do you mean?

M.   How many years are you gonna get?
B.   I dunno

M.   Well what did you just say to me
B.   That they, Teresa's family might ask the judge to be lenient or whatever. They asked me
      if I wanted to be out to have a family later on.

M.   I don't hate you Brendan, I hate Steven, alright.
B.   Ya

M.   I wish you would of told me, okay.
B.   Ya

M.   How did you answer the phone at 6 O'Clock when Mike called then?
B.   They told me that they looked at the records and that he didn't call.

M.   Huh
B.   They said that they had the record and

M.   What about when I got home at 5:00 you were here.
B.   Ya

M.   Ya. When did you go over there?
B.   I went over there earlier and then came home before you did.

M.   Why didn't you say something to me then?
B.   I dunno, I was to scared.

M.   You wouldn't have had to been scared because I would have called 911 and you wouldn't
      be going back over there. If you would have been here maybe she would have been alive
      yet. So in those statements you did all that to her too?
B.   Some of it.

M.   Did he make you do it?
B.   Ya. So whose all home?

M.   Just me and Blaine.

5

04/03/2007 14:42   2335252   WMSELSTEIN   PAGE 07/07

You have one minute left.

M.   Blaine & Brad are coming up tomorrow okay.
B.   Daddy

M.   Huh
B.   Is dad?

M.   He might me ya.
B.   Okay

M.   I call him and ask mom, can't Mom has to take her truck in
B.   So you aren't coming up

M.   I can't honey I gotta take my truck in tomorrow.
B.   For what?

M.   It's gonna take at least 2 - 2 ½ hours and that's in the morning
B.   Ya.

M.   I'll be up Wednesday.
B.   Okay

M.   Okay, alright
B.   Okay.

M.   Just remember I love you okay
B.   Ya.

M.   And don't do nothing stupid
B.   I won't

M.   See if you can talk to them.
B.   Ya.

M.   Okay, see you still come up to see

Thank you for using evercom

M.   Love you bye.
B.   Bye

6

5/13/06   *Tape #3*

Brendan Dassey & Mom, Barb, phone conversation from 5/13/06 (Defense copy)

Barb: Hello

Brendan: Yeah

Barb: You heard me, huh?

Brendan: Yeah

Barb: Was your attorney there when Mark and those guys were?

Brendan: No

Barb: Don't talk to them no more

Brendan: Yeah

Barb: They are putting you in places where you're not.

Brendan: Yeah

Barb: You know the the reason they're talking to you is to get more information out of you and what your attorney should be doing is putting an order on all of them that they can not interfere with you or your family members unless your attorney is present.

Brendan: Yeah

Barb: Cause they're all investigators for the Halbach case.

Brendan: Yeah

Barb: Not the Dassey case, it's the Halbach case.

Brendan: Yeah

Barb: Cause the only thing that they're putting out there is bad stuff about you and if you weren't there at the time if you didn't slice her throat. You did not have sexual contact with her

Brendan: No

Barb: That's the reason that they're saying. Yeah, that's all in the report here that Mom's got.

Brendan: Yeah. So if I was in the garage cleaning up that stuff on the floor, how much time will I get though for that?

Barb: What was it?

Brendan: I don't know. It was this reddish-black stuff

Barb: See what they're probably going to do is turn around and have it that "Steven said this, Steven is saying you were here". If you say "Yeah" not meaning "Yeah it's true" just "Yeah", they're going to say OK, Brendan was there. Brendan did that. And then they're going by Steven and saying well Brendan said this and Brendan said that.

Brendan: But what does Steven say about it?

Barb: Steven just says that you're a "dumb shit".

Brendan: Yeah. Well last time I talked to Mark and that they said that Steven was trying pin me and Bobby for it.

Barb: Yeah, they come to our house wondering what Steven said, right over the phone, to Chuckie, mind you, that he going to set it up with his attorney that he blames it on me and Earl

Brendan: Yeah

Barb: And I looked at Mark and Tom and told them that well if he tries doing that he is going to be one sorry son-of-a-bitch.

Brendan: Yeah

Barb: I told them it is pretty pathetic he has to go "fricking" kill somebody and take an innocent kid down with him

Brendan: Yeah and plus if he didn't do it then why would was he trying to hide up north that one day

Barb: But see they got that on camera that you were sitting right across the table from Steven smiling at him.

Brendan: I had my head down

Brendan: Yeah

Barb: They never called me on that Monday

Brendan: But I wished I had listened to someone before I went there.

Barb: Oh

Brendan: Yeah. You know who that was Mom?

Barb: Yeah

Brendan: Who?

Barb: I know who that was.

Brendan: Who?

Barb: Uh?

Brendan: Who?

Barb: Starts with a "T"

Brendan: Yeah. How do you know?

Barb: I know, you told me right.

Brendan: Yeah. Well, so who's all coming up here on Sunday Mom?

Barb: Probably me and your dad again.

Brendan: Dad said that he was going to try to get Brad though.

Barb: We're going to try to get your clothes –

Brendan: Yeah. Well, when I talked to that Mike and that 1 girl that comes up here to see how I'm doing, she wrote something down about Manitowoc juvenile sentencing. Yeah. I don't know if she's going to try to get me closer or what.

Barb: Who, Wendy?

Brendan: I don't know. No, I think it's Jackie.

Barb: Uh?

Brendan: Jackie

Barb: Jackie?

Brendan: Yeah. In the paper did they say anything about me losing weight and that?

Barb: Yeah along time ago

Brendan: Yeah but they think that I lost that and I was depressed because of what happened. But that ain't the reason.

Barb: Why did you lose so much weight?

Brendan: Mom Mom knows. Because I was trying to impress a girl

Barb: Oh

Brendan: But then she dumped me the day I was going to meet her, so I was depressed because I thought I wasn't going to get another one.

Barb: Oh

Brendan: But then Travis got me another one and then they arrested me like 2 weeks after she broke up with me

Barb: Well, do you blame her?

Brendan: No

Barb: This is a big stink. Nobody ever hurt your pride. Nobody. The only thing that they hear is what people print

Brendan: Yeah

Barb: And never once was it dead – they heard Brendan.

Brendan: Yeah

Barb: You go into Court, you look down at the table.

Brendan: Yeah

Barb: The Judge says something all you say is "Yeah"

Brendan: So does my Mom know if they have been selling my picture or something?

Barb: I don't' yet. Selling your picture on the Internet. 10 x 30 for $90. Who's selling that? I called down there and will file a lawsuit against them.

Brendan: Yeah

Barb: They can't sell your picture

Brendan: No. I was trying to figure out who said Mark and Thomas and me and they asked me if I ever smoked crack and that.

Barb: They said that they took a blood test from you when they hauled you in. They took a blood test from you and said you were on crack

Brendan: No. They never took my blood and that. They only thing they took was my fingerprints.

Barb: Oh yeah

Brendan: Yeah

Barb: Oh those liars. Cause they looked that up you was on crack. I said "no". I didn't know he was on crack. I didn't know he was on anything.

Brendan: I ain't

Barb: I told them that the only thing I knew you was on was an attendance freak.

Brendan: Yeah. I wonder if there is something that had to do with that 1 doctor when he gave me 1 thing in my arm

Barb: What did he do to your arm?

Brendan: Something about, I don't know.

Barb: Something for TB

Brendan: Something like that. Yeah, TB. He said that after 3 or 4 days he was going to come back up and where there was a lump he put the needle in. He check me and there was no bump there.

Barb: Yeah, there would be a bump there because of your muscle.

Brendan: Yeah

Barb: But TB. TB shots that's for tuberculosis. Didn't you get all your shots?

Brendan: Yeah

Barb: So why would they give you a TB shot?

Brendan: I don't know

Barb: You should be for tuberculosis.

Brendan: Yeah

Barb: I'll have to look it up on the Internet now. But they didn't draw no blood from you

Brendan: No

Barb: Did they take a piss urine from you?

Brendan: No. They took one of them cotton things and went on the side of my mouth

Barb: Yeah

Brendan: Yeah, that's it.

Barb: I don't know if that would show up on that in your saliva

Brendan: No

Barb: I don't know too much about it. I could look it up on the Internet though. Cause they told us that it was inside your blood

Brendan: No. Could it be in your blood if someone's around you and smoking it or something?

Barb: I don't know. I don't think so.

Brendan: Only because the 1 time when I was with Travis babysitting his dogs and that

Barb: Um-mm

Brendan: Because that 1 guy that used to live with him had that stuff and he was trying to make me do it and I said I wouldn't because this one mask thing. Yeah with these tubes on it

Barb: A bong

Brendan: I don't know it was like a mask with a tube in it

Barb: Yeah, a bong

Brendan: Yeah. Then he had this one bottle where this

Barb: Bowl

Brendan: Yeah

Barb: Was he smoking that?

Brendan: Yeah

Barb: Was it pot or was it crack?

Brendan: I don't know

Barb: That was a long time ago.

Brendan: Yeah

Barb: It wouldn't even been inside your system.

Brendan: No

Barb: Um

Brendan: But I really hate it when they put them leg cuffs on my legs because there's marks on my legs

X

ZELLNER'S ONE HUNDRED

Kathleen Zellner, Avery's Post Conviction attorney, has offered $10,000 to anyone who can answer her 100 questions to prove Steven Avery's guilt; so it is pertinent for us to examine them. However, Zellner has set questions that are not all able to be answered with specifics. Some questions will never be answered. Nonetheless, these questions seal the deal.

The Steven Avery Proof of Guilt Challenge

The Proof of Guilt Challenge: We are so convinced that you will fail at answering the following 100 questions that we will offer an award of $10,000 to anyone who fully answers all 100 questions based upon credible evidence that establishes Mr. Avery's guilt beyond a reasonable doubt.

Over the last 19 months, we have heard and read numerous claims that Steven Avery is guilty of the murder of Teresa Halbach. Without exception, the authors of these claims simply do not know the facts of the case nor do they address the most blatant discrepancies in the State's case against Mr. Avery. The Proof of Guilt Challenge is specifically designed to elicit from these commentators credible evidentiary support for their opinion that Mr. Avery is guilty beyond a reasonable doubt.

Before the Dionysus Group answers Kathleen's questions, we want to acknowledge her as an American hero. Her efforts in exonerating innocent murder convicts are so important, and we give her our full respect.

However, we cannot watch Ms. Zellner use her reputation and her skills to free guilty psychopaths. This would destroy the innocence project's reputation; a reputation that must be maintained to continue their important work.

Before we start, we have a question: How could Brendan have had nothing to do with Teresa's murder, if (as he told his Mom) he did *'some of it'*?

Mom: So, in those statements . . . you did all that to her, too?

Brendan: Some of it.

(Recorded phone call, May 13th, 2006 Sheboygan County Jail)

The proof of Guilt Challenge

Q1. Explain why, if Mr. Avery was "actively bleeding" from his finger, as Mr. Kratz told the jury, there are only 6 spots of his **blood** in the RAV-4?

A1. Planting and wiping combined to produce the odd evidence, because:

a. Someone from Law Enforcement planted all 6 daubs of Avery's blood in Teresa's RAV4.

Q2. Explain why Mr. Avery's **blood** is not on any of the objects in the car that he would have grasped with his hands, which would have also resulted in him leaving his **fingerprints**?

A2. Depends if Avery wore gloves or not, so:

a. Avery wore gloves and the police planted his blood; or;

b. Avery did not wear gloves, but because he had a 'Band-Aid' on the cut, wasn't bleeding through it. The car was hidden at night. If Avery did not wear gloves, he wiped the touchable surfaces such as steering wheel, gearshift, handbrake, rear-vision mirror.

c. The under side of the interior hood release was not tested.

d. Merely touching something does not always mean a usable finger or palm print will be left, or can be obtained.

***e.* He and Brendan hid the RAV4, both wore gloves, and police planted all of Avery's blood, is our preferred answer.**

Q3. Explain why Mr. Avery's **blood** was not present on the following items:

a. The key to the RAV-4;

b. The driver's door handle;

c. The rear passenger door handle;

d. The steering wheel;

e. The gear shift;

f. The hood prop;

g. The brake release; and

h. The driver's seat release bar.

A3. Because the police didn't put any of Avery's blood on those parts.

Q4. Explain why there are no **fingerprints** of Mr. Avery in or on the RAV-4, but, according to the prosecution, there is **blood** from his actively bleeding finger present in 6 spots, 5 of which are in the front of the vehicle and 1 on the rear passenger door jamb. *Note that Ms. Halbach's fingerprints are on the driver's door handle and 8 latent prints are identified on the vehicle, none of which matched Mr. Avery, thereby ruling out that the car was wiped clean of fingerprints.

A4. There are no fingerprints because:

a. Avery wore gloves, or:

b. He did not wear gloves and wiped certain surfaces, but not the door handle - this is unlikely, as we think both he and Brendan wore gloves.

There is blood because:

c. The police planted Avery's blood.

Q5. Why were the fingerprints of Lt. Lenk, Sgt. Colborn, and other potential suspects never compared to the 8 latent fingerprints in the following places: two on the rear passenger windows (TT:3/7/07:142-144), three on the pillar to the left side of the rear window above the taillight assembly (TT:3/7/07:143), one on the side of the wheel cover (TT:3/7/07:143), one next to where the key is inserted into the cargo gate (TT:3/7/07:143), one on the hood which would be left by someone trying to open the hood (TT:3/7/07:144). Note: Mr. Avery is ruled out from all the fingerprints in and on the vehicle.

A5. Bad police work, tunnel vision, assumption of guilt, confirmation bias, and evidence planting, because:

a. The police only had eyes for Avery.

b. No other suspects were considered, because once evidence was planted, Law Enforcement were committed to Steven Avery. To do anything else would bring attention to their planting Avery's blood, and Teresa's key in Avery's trailer.

c. Colborn and Lenk were not eliminated from the vehicle just in case they left prints somewhere they should not have.

Q6. Explain why repeatedly putting the key (10 times) in the ignition with a bloody middle finger on the right hand failed to produce any blood smear similar to the one noted by the ignition, but applying blood with an applicator produced exactly the same bloodstain pattern as that noted by the ignition. (Trial Exhibit 291). Note that the blood smear was 2.25 inches to the right of the ignition, making it impossible to deposit blood on the dash where the blood smear was deposited. (Crime Scene Photo with Ruler).

A6: Because the blood smear was wiped on with a Q-tip applicator. The force of the tip creates the strong blob, and the smear is from the paint-brush motion.

Q7. If Mr. Avery was planning to kill Ms. Halbach, why would he schedule an appointment with AutoTrader that could be traced to him (and was traced to him (SAO2486)) because the Janda and Avery AutoTrader accounts were linked by phone number and address.

A7. No one can say what goes on in another's mind, but we can speculate:

a. He is over-confident.

b. On May 13th, Brendan says Steven had targeted Teresa at least 4 days before Halloween, and always planned to kill her.

c. Related question: why did Steven tell Earl, Chuck, and police that Teresa never showed up - when she did? She did arrive because Steven later said she arrived at 2:36pm. And Bobby saw her, and her RAV4 circa 2:40pm. Why did Brendan, Blaine and Steven all start lying about the 70 minutes between 2:35pm and 3:45pm? We never saw her. Oh, yeah, we did see her, but she left. There was no fire. Oh, yeah, that fire.

d. Like many psychopaths, Avery assumed he could simply talk his way out of it. He felt bulletproof. We had a case recently where a man stabbed his girlfriend to death 58 times with a pair of pair of scissors. Her mother came into the bedroom and saw him stabbing her daughter. Yet this man pleaded not guilty, believing he could talk his way out of it. When he realized he couldn't, he pleaded self defense.

Q8. If Mr. Avery was planning to kill Ms. Halbach, why wouldn't Mr. Avery have called Ms. Halbach's cell phone, which she had given him, and arranged a meeting with her at a different location that couldn't be traced to him. *Note that at that time, Ms. Halbach's cell phone records did not show the phone numbers for incoming calls so Mr. Avery's incoming call would not have been identified in Ms. Halbach's cell phone records.

A.8. See Answer 7. Also, Steven had planned this. He wanted to tie Teresa to his bed and have Brendan rape her.

Q.9. Why would Ms. Halbach have given Mr. Avery her cell phone number and called him on October 10 (as her cell phone records indicate) if she was afraid of him?

A.9. We can't know Teresa's thoughts here, but:

a. She needs to for business, and people are reluctant to refuse business on the grounds of a bad feeling.

b. She wasn't *afraid* of Steven, she was creeped out by him.

c. She wasn't afraid or creeped out.

d. It was apparently after this October 10 appointment, when Steven came out in his towel, that Teresa felt a little weird. Did Avery see this as rejection and plan to get revenge?

Q.10. Why would Ms. Halbach have returned to the Avery property on October 31 if she was afraid of Mr. Avery as the prosecution claimed?

A.10. See answer 9.

Q.11. Why is there no forensic evidence (e.g., blood, hair, skin cells, fingerprints) **of Ms. Halbach** in Mr. Avery's trailer if she was raped and stabbed there?

A.11. Multiple reasons:

a. Teresa was not stabbed in Avery's trailer; Brendan recanted and corrected this false statement on May 13th,

2006. Teresa was stabbed and shot in Avery's garage. The throat cutting never happened; Brendan recanted this on May 13th also. Contrary to popular belief, Brendan was not coerced to recant these details on May 13th, he called the meeting with Wiegert and Fassbender, and did so without coaching. These points were not 'suggested' to Brendan in the earlier interviews, 2 months prior.

b. Surfaces were wiped down, along with the .22 rifle, knife, and leg restraints. Steven and Brendan were bleaching the garage floor on Halloween night when they had a bonfire going; they had the tools necessary to wipe the bedposts, drawers, etc. But Teresa's fingerprints must have been on the Auto Trader magazine on Avery's desk, right?

c. The hair cutting did not happen. Brendan said this in a childish attempt to avoid Fassbender's question: what happened to her head?

d. As Brendan stated on May 13th, he and Steven burned the blankets, sheets, and pillows in the fire.

e. Steven may have used a condom.

f. Dassey stated that he did not ejaculate.

g. All of theses things combined to control the forensic evidence.

Q.12. Explain why not even a fragment of Ms. Halbach's hair was found in Mr. Avery's trailer or garage, when Brendan Dassey described cutting her hair.

A.12. Brendan *never* cut Teresa's hair.

a. On March 1st, Brendan may have said this to Fassbender to *avoid* answering the question he was being pressured to answer: *What happened to her head?*

Something with the head? We know something happened to her head, you've just gotta tell us.

Brendan did not want to tell them, because Steven said if he did, he would suffer the same fate as Teresa. Rule and control by fear. Brendan knew and believed that Steven would follow through with his threats - if Brendan 'dobbed him in'. Kayla Avery pulled out of her testimony of Brendan's admission to her, because she too feared Steven; and Blaine denied the sky was blue trying to avoid Steven's wrath.

b. Any other cast off hair was contained in and on the bedding, which was folded into a pile, and burned.

Q.13. If you believe that Ms. Halbach was killed in the trailer and that Mr. Avery and Brendan Dassey cleaned up the trailer so thoroughly as to remove any forensic trace of Ms. Halbach, identify the specific cleaning products and chemicals that could have been used to remove all traces of forensic evidence (blood, hair, skin cells, etc.)

A.13. 'Trick question'; the following is how the clean up was achieved:

a. We do not believe Teresa was killed in Steven's trailer.

b. Bleach was used in the garage, not the trailer. The rape occurred in the trailer, so why no congealed liquid evidence? Bleach would have showed up in luminal testing; so bleach was not used.

b. As for the **forensic evidence**; there is a series of things that **had** to occur that **do not involve chemicals**, and they are:

c. Steven had hit Teresa in the head hard enough to get Teresa's blood to create a 'cast-off' pattern on the RAV4's rear cargo door; we believe that if he used a builder's hammer, this would have fractured her skull. Avery also strangled Teresa to near death before Brendan was invited to rape her. Some blood would have stained the blanket, and pillow on Avery's bed.

d. The stabbing happened in the garage, not the trailer. This blood, Brendan said on May 13th, was 'quite a lot', and was cleaned up with clothes, rags, bleach, paint thinner, and gasoline. The rags and clothes were burned in the fire; as evidenced by rivets from Teresa's jeans amongst the bones and ash.

e. Brendan did not cut Teresa's throat in Steven's trailer. He recanted this lie in final confession on May 13th.

f. When Teresa is moved to the garage, Brendan states that Teresa was alive.

g. At this point, they strip the bedding, blankets, sheets, and pillows, and burn them in the fire. This would take care of trace blood from Teresa's head wound, and Stevens' semen, unless condoms were used. Brendan said that he never ejaculated, but that his penis stayed hard.

h. But would there be enough blood to soak through the blanket, and into the mattress? Not if the stabbing occurred in the garage as described by Brendan. Any blood on the wood-work could be cleaned by standard house-hold spray products, but it appears that all blood from the possible head wound was contained on the bedding - as she was not stabbed in the trailer - and her throat was never cut.

i. On May 13th, Brendan confirmed that Steven premeditated Teresa's rape and murder. Perhaps Steven brought the 'van seat' into his trailer specifically for the rape; and later burned it along with the bedding. Remember, the bedroom lay-out was changed around for some reason.

Trial Exhibit 371, Avery v Wisconsin; a folding seat, burned by Avery. Was this the 'rape bed'? Teresa's bones were intermeshed with the van seat.

j. This 'rape-bed' idea was not mentioned by Dassey. It is more likely that Steven's wooden bed was used, and the bedding burned, as per Brendan's statement; but it is possible.

k. However, the answer to this 'trick question', is bleach right? - Because if anyone says bleach, and no reside is found in Avery's trailer under luminal testing, then: ah-ha, gotcha.

l. Despite being killed in the garage and not the trailer, the answer is rapid oxidation - fire.

Q.14. What proof is there that Mr. Avery **owned** or **purchased** any of the specific **cleaning products** that you identified in question 13 at any time before the murder? (Receipts, bottles, etc.).

A.14. We identified that bleach was used in Avery's garage - not the trailer; *but this is not entirely true.*

Note: Firstly one (not none) of us in the group can produce a 'receipt' for cleaning products. The other 8 cannot produce a single receipt for any cleaning products that we own, despite have cupboards full - so that is unreasonable; however, evidence does exist to answer this question:

> *a.* Photographs of the bleach bottles in Avery's garage; but we agree, police *could* have planted the bleach bottles.

Avery's garage. This is bleach; is reads 'brightens and shines'.
2005,

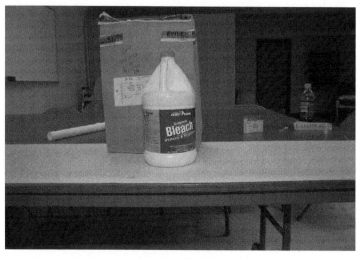

This is a different bleach bottle. Exhibit 183 of Avery's murder
trial. This bottle is empty.

b. The fact that Brendan had the bleach on his jeans; the
stained jeans were handed to police by Brendan's mother,
showing that his jeans were not doctored by the corrupt

cops of Manitowoc. Brendan's bleach stained jeans were then entered into trial evidence. It is likely that Brendan had never used bleach before that night, and did not realize its latent effect of color removal on denim. Let me make it clear: to get bleach stained jeans, you must have access to the bleach.

Sheboygan Jail, May 13, 2006:

Fassbender: When he came back from the fire – he had put her on the fire – now you come back from the fire, or he does; what do you guys do?

Brendan: We start to clean up the blood.

Fassbender: The jeep's still in the garage? Her jeep?

Brendan: Yeah.

Fassbender: Okay. What do ya use to clean up the blood?

Brendan: Her clothes.

Fassbender: Anything else?

Brendan: Bleach, gas, and paint thinner.

Fassbender: Was there a lot of blood on the floor?

Brendan: Yeah.

c. The luminal testing of the garage floor revealed bleach use; which *could* have been planted, but with two bottles of bleach in the garage, Brendan's stained jeans, and Brendan's confessions, it is doubtful.

Why did the luminal reveal bleach? Well the luminal revealed a 'wiped smear', 3ft by 3ft; and if not caused by bleach, then it could only be blood, as only blood and bleach activate luminal. The blood mixed with the bleach, was not able to be typed, because bleach destroys its structure, and DNA. The blood it is argued, could have been deer blood. But why would one bleach deer blood on Halloween, when one should be having fun around the fire? Deer blood should have been cleaned at the time of butchering; also deer are usually bleed by the neck, and gut, out where they are shot. When deer are butchered - (the cuts of muscle groups are removed) - little if any blood pools on the floor.

d. However, the Marlin .22 rifle above Avery's bed was wiped down - possibly with bleach, because no fingerprints or DNA remain on any part of it. A second .22 rifle in Avery's trailer, that was not wiped down, held fingerprints and DNA, like any well handled item would and should.

e. Avery was witnessed at Patsy's 42 Highway Mobile gas station, 12 minutes drive away in Two Rivers. Avery was seen at dusk (5:10pm - 5:20pm) on Halloween, 2005, filling a 'gas-can' and driving his dark F-250 pick-up.

Q.15. What specific evidence was there of a clean up in the trailer or the garage (e.g., chemical residue, wipe marks, diluted stains)?

A,15. For garage see Answer 14 (luminal reveals bleach); however for Avery's Trailer:

a. The .22 rifle above Avery's bed had no prints and no DNA, as it had been wiped. A second .22 rifle held both prints, and DNA, as it was never wiped.

b. Bleached blood and even semen would have left deposits detectable by luminal testing; but none was found in the trailer. Bleach was not used, except on tools and utensils. Bleach on the carpet or bedding would show up under black-light. But Avery's room was rearranged - why?

c. Any blood and semen from the bedding was collected in the blankets and on the pillow, and burned.

d. A 3ft by 3ft smear of bleached blood on Avery's garage floor. The blood's structure was destroyed, proving bleach was used and was triggering the faint luminal reaction.

Q16. If Ms. Halbach was handcuffed to the bed with Mr. Avery's **handcuffs**, why is her DNA not present on the handcuffs, but other individuals' DNA was on the **handcuffs**?

A16. As it turns out, Teresa's *hands* were tied with <u>rope</u>. Dassey stated rope for the hands, leg-irons for the legs. The <u>handcuffs</u> were not used on Teresa. Dassey described the rope specifically as yellow nylon rope. Yellow nylon rope is hard synthetic material, resistant to delaminating or leaving fiber behind.

The following image is a drawing made by Brendan Dassey, albeit under very strange circumstances that should have rendered it inadmissible in a court of law. However, it matches his May Day confession of rope, leg irons, and burned bedding.

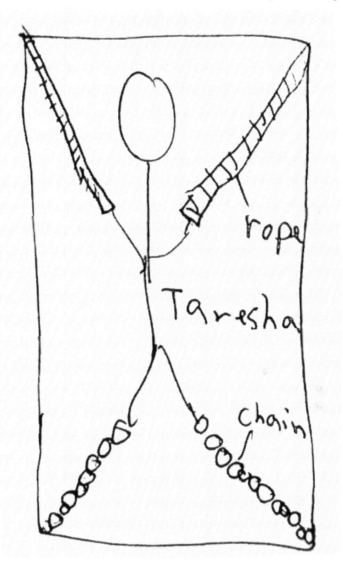

Q17. Describe any forensic process (known anywhere in the world) which would remove one person's DNA from an object (such as the handcuffs) but leave someone else's DNA on the object.

A17. There is none. But the prosecution did claim this during the trial.

a. Nevertheless, Steven did not specifically *handcuff* Teresa; he tied her hands with yellow nylon chord.

b. However, when an item is cleaned, and all DNA removed, it can and will acquire new DNA from that point on.

c. Items can also be partially cleaned; there is no law of physics that states if an object is cleaned, then the entire object is therefore clean.

Q18. Why, if Ms. Halbach was handcuffed to the bed and brutally raped, were there no striations on the post mounted 2.5 feet above the mattress on the headboard?

A18. Possible answers:

a. Because the wooden bed (with posts) was moved aside. The metal 'rape-bed' or van seat, was brought in, and Teresa was tied by her wrists to it, and chained by her ankles. The pink fluff was removed from the chain leg-cuffs, purchased by Avery on October 9th. After, Avery wiped the ankle chains clean, and reattached the pink fluff.

b. Most likely – as Brendan said, the yellow nylon rope was tied tight around the round posts, and left no marks. We conducted an experiment using a 'turned wood pot-plant stand' and with yellow nylon rope, we tied a member to it. With vigorous thrashing, no marks were discernable to the naked eye.

Q19. What would be the point of Mr. Avery using *67 to allegedly conceal his identity if his *67 calls are documented in his phone records along with Ms. Halbach's phone number? (STATE1582).

A.19. Several points:

a. Force of habit; however, Teresa was the only person that Avery used *67 when calling the entire day.

b. He didn't know what was, or was not documented in these logs - like any Joe citizen.

c. Maybe Avery simply believed that the star 67 prefix would conceal his contact with Teresa from any scrutiny. Maybe this is why Avery initially told police - who were looking for the missing Teresa - that *she* had not shown up at his place. Shame Bobby Dassey saw her, and her teal RAV4 at Steven Avery's.

This brings us to 'stupid'.

No one but Zellner has accused Avery of being smart, let alone a savant.

Avery has an IQ below 80 - and despite Ms Zellner's hype, Avery will never be smart. But as is noted with criminals with low IQ; they grow survival adaptations and cunning in a criminal kind of way, that, from-time-to-time, makes them appear smart. IQ is also a test of high-school based pattern problems, and is not a good indicator of things like criminal cunning, or practical intelligence. Someone with a high IQ will be good at puzzles, but may be a terrible businessperson.

Q20. Explain how Ms. Halbach, on 10/31, was unwittingly "lured" to the Avery salvage yard, when she was given the "Avery Road" address for the appointment and she had been to Avery Road no fewer than 5 times previously.

A.20. Several points:

a. Firstly, a lure - like a fishing lure - is something that attracts by way of reward. Therefore, there was no 'lure' for Teresa. She was working. She got paid for turning up at unsavory people's homes, and photographing their cars - take the crazy George Zipperer for example.

b. Teresa knew she was going out to Avery Auto. The idea of 'luring' comes more from the deception behind whom Teresa would be meeting for the shoot.

c. Avery made the appointment under 'B Janda' and gave Barb's phone number. Although Barb was at work all day. Avery justified this by saying Barb was the seller. Barb said she didn't even want to sell the van.

d. This made Teresa and Auto Trader (in Stevens 80 IQ mind) think that Teresa would not even see Steven.

e. Steven may have thought that the October 10th, towel incident had put Teresa off. This *is* reasonable.

f. Kratz said lured. Lured, no. Disguised the client, yes.

Q.21. Explain how Ms. Halbach, on 10/31, was unwittingly "lured" to the Avery salvage yard when Ms. Halbach told Dawn Pliska of AutoTrader in a 2:27 p.m. call that she was on her way to the Avery Property.

A.21. As above. Not lured, but deceived. Teresa thought she was meeting a B Janda, and not a man. Teresa even rang Barb's phone and left a message asking for her address. Teresa didn't believe she was meeting the 'towel man'. But we don't think she was scared of Steven either - just weirded out. Just because it's a murder investigation it doesn't mean we can't do real.

Q.22. Explain how Ms. Halbach, on 10/31, was unwittingly "lured" to the Avery salvage yard when there is a large sign that reads "Avery's Auto Salvage" at the entrance to the property on Highway 147. Did Ms. Halbach have her eyes closed as she drove down Avery Road?

A.22. Teresa told Dawn over the phone that she was on her way out to the Averys'. But we think if Teresa were your daughter, and Avery made an appointment under a female name, which he intended to make himself, and then she was raped and murdered, maybe you would feel deceived too. Avery took the afternoon off work at the yard to meet Teresa - and then he told his co-worker that Teresa never turned up.

Of course, the 'luring' is a Kratz-ism. Teresa was not lured - she was working.

Q.23. If Ms. Halbach were afraid of Mr. Avery, why did she allegedly confirm with Dawn Pliska at 2:27 p.m. on 10/31 that she was driving to the Avery salvage yard for her appointment?

A.23. Teresa was working.

a. Teresa had started a photography business. Teresa wanted and needed work, was a committed self-employed photographer, and was hesitant to turn down work.

b. She wasn't afraid, but possibly wary. We don't know what was in Teresa's mind from the information available, so how did Kratz? Kratz' idea is irresponsible speculation that he unnecessarily tried to pass off as fact.

c. The fact Avery displayed himself in his towel on Oct 10, we can safely guess, would have concerned Teresa to some degree. A young woman on a salvage yard, in the middle of nowhere, alone, and a man presents in a towel. This would cause most 25-year-old females some concern. It is a sexual display. He knew what time Teresa was arriving. However, fear cannot be a conclusion drawn from the encounter.

Q.24. Explain why Ms. Halbach's sub-key was not discovered in Mr. Avery's bookcase by Sgt. Colborn on November 5, when he searched the bookcase for 1.5 hours.

A.24. He hadn't put it there yet.

  a. Sgt. Colborn planted Teresa's sub-key after finding it on the Avery property. He did this to bolster the case against Steven, because it would be harder to convict an exonerated man who had served 18 years of wrongful imprisonment, than any other killer. This is not intended to justify the dupe and idiot, Colborn.

  b. Or, he is an idiot, and just bumbled it the first 6 times.

Q.25. Provide any re-enactment videos or photographs, conducted with a similar bookcase, which demonstrate that Ms. Halbach's sub-key could have been dislodged by the "none too gentle" twisting and turning of the bookcase, fallen through the gap between the back panel and the frame of the bookcase, and landed by Mr. Avery's slippers located on the northwest side of the bookcase. (Trial Exhibit 210)

A25. No re-enactment can be done, because the sub-key - complete with it's lanyard - (making it the key that Teresa and the killer used) - was planted by Colborn. This is why Colborn was shitting his pants in court, and why he suddenly got the squeaky voice of a pre-pubescent boy when Buting trapped him on the stand.

Q26. Explain why, if Sgt. Colborn twisted and turned the bookcase, all of the loose change and other items on top of the bookcase remained in place and did not fall to the floor. (Trial Exhibit 208, 209).

A26. Because Colborn is lying about how the key appeared. He planted it, but did it so badly that his actions alone will free Avery the killer from his life sentence.

Q27. Explain why Ms. Halbach was using a sub-key (RAV-4 Manual) and not the master key which she is holding in a photograph of her with the RAV- 4. (Trial Exhibit 5).

A27. The points:

a. The image showing Teresa holding the master key is inconclusive. The key in her hand is not necessarily the master key in this photo. There are two other keys on the ring that could have been taken off later.

b. The image is quite old, as the rear guard of the RAV4 is covered in rub marks, which were later touched up, and;

c. Teresa may have lost the Toyota's main-key just before her sister bought her the lanyard, which was/is attached to the sub-key. The sub-key was Teresa's main-key at that point. The lanyard proves it. At no point after receiving the lanyard, did Teresa stop using it. How could the lanyard be attached to the main-key in this older photo, and then attached to the sub-key found in Avery's trailer?

The only way is if Teresa's sister gave Teresa the lanyard after the main-key was lost, and replaced by the sub.

This is the image that apparently shows Teresa was using the main key. All we can decipher are two extra keys hanging below her right hand. The lanyard is there.

Q28. Explain why Ms. Halbach's DNA was not on her sub-key, which prosecutors claim she used every day, but Mr. Avery's DNA was on the sub-key.

A28. Because either:

a. Avery wiped the key clean. Avery's DNA was re-applied by police.

b. Police wiped the key clean. Avery's DNA was applied by toothbrush.

c. Ed Edwards wiped the key clean, broke into Avery's trailer, planted the Zander Rd note, and used Avery's toothbrush to apply Avery's DNA.

d. If not (*a*), what of the lucid Dassey confession? How did Dassey know that branches and a hood had been put on Teresa's RAV4, if the killer had not told him, or he had never seen it?

Q29. Describe and identify any experiments that you have conducted with a similar sub-key in which you have been able to remove the primary 5 owner's DNA and substitute another individual's full DNA profile by simply having that individual hold the key in their hand.

A29. It cannot happen. We asked this question of a crime-lab specialist.

Q30. Or, in the alternative, describe any experiments with an exemplar sub-key and blood in which the blood of one individual concealed the DNA of another individual on the exemplar sub-key.

A30. It cannot happen. We asked this question of a crime-lab specialist.

Q31. If you successfully perform this experiment, explain why the blood that was used to conceal the other individual's DNA would not be detectable, as none of Mr. Avery's blood was detected on the sub-key by the Wisconsin State Crime Lab.

A31. Avery did not bleed on the key.

   a. He wore a Band-aid, and (in all probability) gloves.

   b. Police planted Avery's DNA on the sub-key via a groin swab, buccal swab, or Avery's toothbrush. The police planters most likely cleaned the key first - but we cannot know everything that happens. Avery could have also cleaned the key. But the key point is already made.

Q32. Provide an explanation of how Mr. Avery was able to leave his full DNA profile on the key from his skin cells only and to mask any DNA of Ms. Halbach left on her sub-key.

A32. As above. Key was cleaned; Avery's DNA applied.
This alone proves that Colborn planted the key in Avery's
trailer. Police needed something of Teresa's inside Avery's
trailer, other than the book.

Q33. Provide an explanation of why a microscopic
examination of Ms. Halbach's sub-key revealed an
abundance of debris, which ruled out that the sub-key had
been used frequently.

**A33. Debris is held in microscopic grooves. Cleaning
would remove any surface material, and some sub-
surface material. To know if DNA existed within the
microscopic groves, the groves would have to be
harvested specifically. We understand that, in this case,
that was not done; only exterior swabbing was carried
out. The sub-key appeared freshly cut, but how long does
it take for a key to become as worn as Ms Zellner
requires it to be? It depends when Teresa lost the main-
key.**

Q34. Why would Mr. Avery leave his full DNA profile on
Ms. Halbach's sub-key, when he had allegedly successfully
removed all forensic traces of Ms. Halbach from his
bedroom?

A34. Points:

a. Key was planted, and the planter's DNA needed to be
removed, for safety. Brendan does state that Steven had the
key in his trailer, but Steven owned 6 vehicles and had many
keys. If Colborn did 'find' the key and stupidly picked it up
and put his own DNA on it, he has just destroyed the one
piece of evidence that puts Teresa inside Avery's trailer – so
does he clean off his DNA and put Avery's on? Or does the

crime-lab test it and find Colborn's DNA? This is less likely, as technicians would know how dodgy this would look.

b. We have covered the bedroom. Avery's room was rearranged. A rape-bed was possibly brought in. The bedding was burned. Nothing else remained.

c. Remember, Avery likely struck Teresa in the head, knocking her senseless at the rear of her jeep. This is how he got her inside without a fight, and restrained her to the bed. As for blood; there could have been blood matting in her hair, but not dripping to the carpet. This thicker, congealing head blood would have adhered to bedding - which was later burned. The later 'garage blood' came from stabbing and shooting her abdomen on the garage floor. The blood on the carpet in the rear of the RAV4 was from the bullet wounds.

Q.35. Why would Mr. Avery keep Ms. Halbach's sub-key when he could move Ms. Halbach's vehicle to the crusher by using a frontloader, making it unnecessary to start the vehicle's engine with a key?
A.35.

a. It is unnecessary to keep the key.

b. Avery locked the RAV4 to keep family out; he put the key in his pocket out of habit. He inadvertently brought the key home.

c. Avery locked the RAV4 to keep family out; he put the key in his pocket out of habit. When he removed the license plates and threw them into the Mercury Wagon, he tossed the key in also. This key was found by Law Enforcement and was then planted in Avery's trailer.

d. When Hillegas took Fassbender into Teresa's home, he found Teresa's sub key; however we rule this out due to the lanyard. If that lanyard was on the sub-key, then it was the key that Teresa was using.

Q.36. Explain why Mr. Avery would not have crushed Ms. Halbach in her vehicle rather than burning her body in an open fire pit 30 yards from his trailer at 7:30-11:00 p.m. when family members were coming and going and approaching the fire.

A.36. Crushing the body into the RAV4:

a. When the body started to decompose, the smell would have attracted attention on the yard.

b. The car-bodies are removed by a contractor for further recycling; they would notice the smell, or see the body. Crushing a car does not flatten it totally.

Q.37. Why doesn't any Avery family member describe the distinct smell of a burning body on October 31?

A.37.

a. The smoke is not drifting over the Dassey home.

b. It would smell like roasting meat until it burned off, but the tire's high-potency smell covers the smell.

c. The 5pm visitors at Avery's only go to the front of the trailer, not to the fire-pit. They report smelling burning plastic from the drum, because that was located right there, on the driveway where they stopped.

d. Aside from Brendan, the only other members who saw the fire, viewed it from a distance or from inside.

e. Brendan initially said that he did not smell anything in the fire; however, Brendan later told Fassbender that the bonfire 'smelled real bad'.

Q.38. Why do Mr. Avery and Brendan Dassey allegedly leave Ms. Halbach's body burning in the burn pit, in plain sight, while they drive Ms. Halbach's vehicle to the southeast corner of the Avery salvage yard?

A.38. It was night-time, and:

a. They cover the body with the tires, seat, cabinet, and brush. Brendan says the body was under the tires. One would have to be right beside the fire to see anything in the bottom.

b. If they burned the body at 5:30pm, and stashed the RAV4 at 9:30pm, then the body had been burning for 4 hours. With 200 - 400kw from each tire alone, the fire would have reached 1400°F and the body would have been mostly destroyed. Steven had apparently broken the body up with his shovel, and mixed it around - before Brendan had gone home at 10pm.

c. The fire was *behind* Steven's garage. The fire-pit could be seen from the Dassey property from certain points because there were no fences, but the fir-pit was obscured from the driveway. Scott, Barb, and Bobby all entered their house from the drive.

Q.39. Why would Mr. Avery so thoroughly clean up every speck of forensic evidence in his trailer and the garage, but leave 6 easily-detectable blood spots of his in the RAV-4?

A.39. Avery's 6 blood daubs in the RAV4 were planted.

Q.40. Explain why the prosecution claims that, after Mr. Avery shot Ms. Halbach on his garage floor, he put her body into, and then removed it from, the RAV-4.

A.40. As said by Brendan, Steven's first disposal plan was to take Teresa's body to the small pond where the

**RAV4 was found; the RAV4's rear seats were folded
down, a liner inserted, and her body was then put into
the rear cargo area and driven to the pond. Avery then
decided that the pond was too shallow, and that burning
was the better option. They drove back, Teresa was
removed from the RAV4, and carried to the fire.
Brendan said Steven had the top, and he had the feet.**

Q.41. Why did the prosecution have 2 inconsistent theories
in the Avery and Dassey trials about the cause of death?
(Avery = gunshot to the head; Dassey = stabbing and throat
cut).

A.41. Premature Conclusions, but:

a. Two small caliber entry defects holding trace led, were
found in the skull bone fragments removed Avery's fire-
pit. Tissue from the shinbone removed from the same fire-
pit revealed that 7 of the 16 loci matched Teresa's DNA
profile. The bones in Avery's fire-pit were Teresa
Halbach's. Teresa had therefore been shot twice in the
skull.

b. Brendan said Avery shot Teresa between 5 and 10
times; but when he forced himself to think about it,
Brendan recounted 5 shots. Brendan said – before the
over-eager investigators let it slip – that Steven shot her
twice in the head. Brendan claims he didn't see the
shooting, as he didn't 'like that stuff', and was looking
away or had his eyes closed.

c. Brendan recanted the throat cutting, and the hair cutting
on May 13th. There was no throat cutting. Never
happened. But the prosecution had already built their case
against Dassey on this false premise.

d. The prosecution used some of Dassey's incorrect confession in his trial. Why? You'd have to ask them; they had *all* the information to work out what had actually happened. But after Mr. Kratz' emotive pre-trial press conference, preceding Avery's trial, how could the same prosecution team change what they had *prematurely* claimed had happened to Teresa? They were forced into using false parts of Dassey's 'distancing' confessions. The result: Avery shot Teresa in the garage - and Dassey cut Teresa's throat in the trailer.

e. Why the prosecution believed Teresa's throat could have been cut in the trailer with no corroborating evidence is lazy and irresponsible. The only thing we can think of is: the prosecution may have thought Teresa was dead before Brendan cut her throat. If so, the blood would have pooled in Teresa's legs and abdomen, and that was why no blood flowed from her neck, soaking through into the mattress. However, Brendan does confirm that Teresa was alive in the garage, negating this possibility as fact.

Q.42. Explain how the prosecution acted in good faith when it changed its theory of the murder by moving all of the events of the crime to the garage, after the Wisconsin Crime Lab could not detect any forensic evidence in the trailer. (Dassey v. Dittmann, 860 F.3d 933 (7th Cir. 2016), footnote 13).

A.42. The prosecution did not act in good faith.

a. Because of Ken Kratz' pre-trial press conference outlining the throat cutting, we think it forced them to maintain this premise even though they knew it to be false.

b. Dassey confirmed on May 13, 2006, that Teresa was stabbed and shot in Avery's garage – and never the trailer.

Q.43. Explain why Brendan's confession is so similar to the fictional story in James Patterson's book/movie "Kiss the Girls," which Brendan admitted to reading and/or watching. *Is this just an amazing coincidence?*

A.43. Subjective, but worth investigation:

a. Firstly, if Brendan can read the novel, *Kiss the Girls*, understand its plot and theme, and then use this to distance himself from a murder investigation - then he is pulling the wool over your eyes.

b. The novel and the movie have different 'scenes' and endings. So which is it?

c. The novel has a scene where a girl is tied to a bed and raped. In the *movie version* only, a woman has her hair cut. Whilst trying to think of a way to avoid the question, "what happened to her head?" Brendan said, "that he (Steven) punched her." and then, "That I cut-off her hair." He may or may not have gotten this idea from watching the *movie version*, but if so, he was using it as a tool to avoid answering truthfully. This idea that Brendan based his *entire* confession on the novel reeks of clever defense tactics.

In the novel a girl is tied to a bed and raped, but she did not have her throat cut, and was not taken to a garage and shot twice in the head, and was not put in the back of her car, and was not dumped in a pond, and was not burned in a fire - yet all of these things that did not happen in the novel are corroborated on the Avery property by evidence; specifically, the garage clean-up, the rifle wipe-down, the fire, the bones enmeshed in the tire belts, the knowledge that Steven put a hood against the RAV4, the cadaver-dog indications on November 5th along the same track that Brendan said he and Steven drove Teresa's RAV4.

d. If Brendan is to ever get out of prison, Brendan's lawyers must've told him to recant any admission of guilt, and to come up with a plausible reason as to why he confessed in so much detail. Was the 'kiss the Girls' defense Brendan's idea, or his lawyers'?

e. The idea that Brendan was pressured into a false confession is plausible, because this happens regularly. However, almost all false confessions result from plea bargaining. An innocent person will confess to murder if the weight of evidence against them suggests that they will likely be convicted, and the plea bargain offers them a safer option, or the only option for survival. Did this happen to Brendan? No. Brendan suggested and gave details of Steven's involvement in Teresa's disappearance *before* investigators employed underhanded coaching tactics.

f. **Is this just an amazing coincidence?**

It is far less of a co-incidence than series of co-incidences that had to have occurred if Avery is innocent; such as:

The girl that Steven makes an appointment with disappears the same day. Her cell phone stops communicating with the cell tower 5 minutes after arriving at his home; (arrives 2:36pm, last cell phone ping at 2:41pm.) Co-incidentally, on the same night she disappears, the person Steven was with says that Steven shot this girl in the garage, twice in the head. Co-incidentally, she was shot twice in the head. Co-incidentally, this is the same garage that Brendan and

Steven clean with bleach on the same night she vanishes. Teresa's skull has two .22cal sized bullet holes in it that did not exit the head. Despite having 2 .22 rim-fire rifles in his trailer, Co-incidentally, only one has just been wiped clean. Co-incidentally, the rifle that has been wiped clean of all fingerprints is the exact rifle that Steven's accomplice says was used to shoot Teresa. Co-incidentally, her car and bones are found on the property. Co-incidentally, they had been burning tires and a van seat. Co-incidentally her cremains are enmeshed in the van seat and steel-belts in Avery's fire-pit. Co-incidentally, the accomplice gives details of hiding her RAV4, that only the hider could know - its location, and that a car-hood and branches were put against it. And, Co-incidentally, according to a defense attorney, this story apparently matches a bits of a James Patterson novel.

Q.44. Explain how Mr. Kratz recently denied that the two bullets found on the garage floor went through Ms. Halbach's head when he told the jury that Ms. Halbach was killed on the garage floor when she was shot twice in the head. Note: Kratz' proof that Ms. Halbach was shot twice in the head, according to him at Mr. Avery's trial, was that "two bullets were found," referring to the bullet fragments found on Mr. Avery's garage floor.

A.44. Mathematics:

a. Brendan's final estimate of how many times Teresa was shot is 5 times.

b. The .22 long-rifle round only carries enough velocity, weight, momentum, and therefore penetration power to enter a skull. The two projectiles stayed inside Teresa's head. No exit holes were found in any other parts of the skull.

c. At least three more shots were fired into Teresa's body; Dassey does not know where in Teresa's body, because he was looking away or had his eyes closed. He knew Teresa was shot in the head, because later, when lifting her body in and out of the car, he saw her head.

d. Two of these body-shots were found and recovered by investigators.

e. This leaves at least 1 more projectile inside Avery's garage, as the rim-fire rifle round is not like a high-powered or centre-fire round that could exit the building. The .22 rim-fire projectile would not carry the velocity or power to enter a body, hit hard material, ricochet, and exit the timber structure and cladding. No bullet hole was found in the window or doors. **Or;**

f. The bullets were doctored by police from the test fired projectile recovered for tool-mark analysis; but:

Q.45. Explain why the bullet fragment (Item FL) has **wood**, but no bone, embedded in it if it entered and exited Ms. Halbach's **skull** and landed on the garage floor.

A.45. Facts:

a. The shots to Teresa's head remained inside her brain cavity; these projectiles melt around 1200°F or 600°C, so they would have melted in the fire-pit. Automotive tires have a very high ignition temperature of 800°F. Avery's fire burned the 6 tires to their metal belts; so Avery's fire got above 800°F. A comprehensive study of automotive tire burning characteristics was carried out by, Fire Technology, *(50, 379–391, 2014_ 2012 Springer Science+Business Media, LLC (Outside the USA). Manufactured in The United States DOI: 10.1007/s10694-012-0274-)*

Individual tires were found to give a peak heat release of 450kw, and burn from 16-47minutes. Avery burned Teresa *under* 6 tires, and used gasoline to intensify the burning. The fire was already burning well before Avery put Teresa and the tires on the fire. The lead projectiles in Teresa's brain would not have survived the intensity of this blaze.

b. The bullet fragments recovered, (if un-doctored), were not the headshots, but were body-shots. There were a minimum of three body shots. Only 2 were recovered.

c. Avery shoots the .22 caliber bullet into Teresa's abdomen. The bullet does not strike bone. The bullet exits Teresa, hits something wood, collects the profiles, and lands on the concrete floor.

d. If the projectile fragment carries wood embedded in its micro grooves, this may prove that it was not doctored or doped. The crime-lab test facility fires the bullets into a ballistics gel, and then recovers them; they do not strike wood during forensic tool-mark testing.

e. Sherry Culhane applied Teresa's DNA to the 'real' recovered body-shot projectile, which held wood, but no bone.

Q.46. Explain why the bullet fragment (Item FL), which Mr. Kratz claimed had Ms. Halbach's DNA on it, did not have detectable **blood** on it if it entered and exited Ms. Halbach's skull.

A.46. The recovered bullet *did not enter* Teresa's skull; it was a body shot.

a. Not all bullets fired into and through a body will carry biological trace material. When they do carry biological material, it is in very small amounts.

Q.47. Identify in the trial transcripts where Mr. Kratz tells the Avery jury that the bullet fragment Item FL, which had Ms. Halbach's DNA on it, entered any part of her body other than her skull.

A.47. Mr. Kratz failed to do the math.

Q.48. Explain how the bullet fragment (Item FL) got red paint on it by being shot through Ms. Halbach's skull and landing on the garage floor without any evidence of having ricocheted off any items that were painted red.

A.48. Facts:

a. The recovered bullet did not enter Teresa's skull; it was a body shot.

b. It is difficult to track a ricocheting bullet's exact flight path with the information available. What evidence is available that suggests that the bullet did not hit something painted red?

c. If the bullet fragment had red paint on it, it hit something painted red.

Q.49. Identify any evidence that would establish that the bullet fragment (Item FL) exited the skull of Ms. Halbach (in light of Mr. Kratz's recent statements that it is very unlikely that a .22 would have sufficient power to exit the skull).

A.49. The bullets that entered Teresa's skull did not exit.

a. Both defect holes were examined microscopically and found to be traveling forward, into the skull. Therefore (Item FL) went through Teresa's body.

b. We can't explain why Mr. Kratz failed to recognize basics.

Q.50. Explain how the bullet fragment, if it did not enter and exit the skull, entered and exited a vital organ of the body but left no evidence of organ cells on the bullet fragment.

A.50. Likely conclusions:

a. Item M05-2467#FL did not enter a vital organ.

b. Although bullets recovered from shootings can carry tiny amounts of biological trace, not all do. Just because a bullet went through a person, does not mean that it *must* hold biological material. The bullet fragment in question was highly damaged, probably due to ricochet. The projectile is made of led. Lead is soft. Areas on the lead will have scraped and chipped off during ricochet. Or;

c. Item FL did carry a tiny amount of biological material, but the crime-lab technician screwed up the testing. Projectiles only carry a tiny amount of biological evidence; usually only enough for *one* test.

Q.51. Explain how the bullet fragment (Item FL) has wood embedded in it if there were no bullet holes in the garage **wall** in the area where it was found.

A.51. Possible conclusions:

a. The bullet ricocheted off wood, or glanced wood, and did not leave a hole per se`.

b. Any impact marking was simply not found.

c. Wood, wood chips, or sawdust was present on the floor; and as the projectile impacted – going from a pointy shape, and collapsing into its mushroom shape, collected a timber profile.

d. The bullet did not collect its wood from the wall. Perhaps rafters, wall-framing, tools, other items.

e. The bullet struck a knot in a wall-framing stud, collected the wood profile, and left the hard knot visibly undamaged; the list goes on.

Q.52. Explain the trajectory of the bullet that resulted in wood and paint being embedded in fragment FL but not bone.

A.52. We can only say here, that the bullet could have been genuine evidence that passed through Teresa's body; or it was doctored.

a. If doctored: How did the projectile acquire wood and paint?

b. If genuine: If bone was not embedded in the bullet, it is likely that it did not hit bone as it passed through Teresa's body; but it also could have glanced bone, but not collected the bone's profile. We maintain that the 2 skull bullets went into the fire inside Teresa's head.

c. M05-2467#FL's trajectory took it through Teresa's abdomen; the bullet struck wood, and then struck something painted red. This suggests that Item FL is a genuine piece of evidence; if so, what a shame investigators screwed up by planting other evidence. This will cost the State tens of millions of dollars.

d. We asked: why was the paint on the bullet never compared to painted items in the garage, like the red metal tool chest, or the red paint spots on the walls. If forensic testing was thorough, we would know where the paint came from, and have a better idea of the bullet's trajectory.

e. If a bullet had no DNA on it, it cannot be said that the bullet actually went through Teresa. With the amount of .22 rabbit, gopher, and target shooting going on the property, the bullet may have been historical. However, only 2 projectiles were recovered from Avery's garage. The murder victim was shot with .22 rim-fire (provable). Avery had a .22 rim-fire rifle that was wiped clean, and Brendan tells police that Steven shot Teresa with this exact .22 rifle in Steven's garage - a garage that Brendan and Steven partially cleaned with bleach on the night that Teresa went missing, at the location that Teresa was last seen. *"Some of it."*

Q.53. Explain why Mr. Kratz never told the jury about the bullet trajectory that accounted for the wood and paint on Item FL.

A.53. Speculations:

a. Kratz and the crime scene investigators could not work out FL's path of travel, or;

b. They never tried to discover accurate trajectory; we don't know.

c. They did not do a paint comparison analysis with other red painted items in the garage, or;

d. They did do a paint comparison but did not find a match.

e. It was the prosecution's prerogative.

Q.54. Explain how the size of the entrance skull defect is consistent with a .22 caliber bullet and not any other caliber bullet.

A.54. Can't, but significantly:

a. The entry defect diameters are consistent with calibers ranging from .22 rim-fire, up to 5.56mm center-fire (.223cal). Pistol ammunition is larger in diameter, 7mm – 9mm, or larger.

b. The two bullet holes in Teresa's skull do not prove that she was shot with Steven's .22 rifle, however, centre-fire ammunition at close range, would have exited the skull producing two *exit* defects.

c. Avery had a Marlin-Glenfield .22 rim-fire above his bed – that had been wiped clean of all DNA and fingerprints.

d. Brendan Dassey said Steven shot Teresa 5 times with this exact .22 rifle.

e. Blood was cleaned up with bleach from the place Teresa was said to have been shot. This is corroboration. The partial bleach clean-up happened on the same night Teresa disappeared - or was last see, or heard from. A lot of co-incidences are needed to align here for Avery to be innocent.

Q.55. Explain how Steven and Brendan removed **all t**races of **forensic** evidence from the **garage**. Describe the cleaning solutions and chemicals used to accomplish this feat.

A.55.

a. The prosecution presented the case that not all forensic evidence was removed from the garage: they presented the bullet fragment holding Teresa's DNA.

b. Steven and Brendan used household bleach, paint thinners, and gasoline on the floor to clean up Teresa's blood, leaving behind a detectable 3ft by 3ft bleach smear.

c. Bleach is a chemical known to break down blood, and DNA's structure.

d. Forensic evidence was found inside Teresa's RAV4. Brendan specifically said the RAV4 was *backed* into Steven's garage. *"Some of it".*

Q.56. Explain why the bullet fragments were not discovered in the earlier searches of the garage.

A.56. Possibilities:

a. Poor crime-scene investigation and management.

b. Investigators believed that Steven and Brendan had stabbed Teresa, and that Brendan had cut Teresa's throat, causing her death by homicidal violence. They believed this nonsensical story until March 1st, 2006 – 4 months after Teresa's murder. The crime-lab had found the two bullet *entry* holes in Teresa's skull. Coached by investigators Wiegert and Fassbender, Brendan says that Teresa was shot 10 times; however, Brendan was not coached to say: twice in the head. It may have been a good guess, but it was what happened. First Brendan says Teresa's shooting happened outside; then after what appears to be coaching, in Steven's garage. Investigators gain a search warrant and re-enter the garage.

c. Either investigators find the two .22 projectiles, one holding Teresa's DNA, or;

d. The projectiles were never there, and investigators used two test-fire projectiles and apply Teresa's DNA to one - along with wood and red paint. We have shown that officers the world over are not above evidence tampering, fabrication, and planting – but we don't believe this level of corruption extends into the crime-lab.

e. The wood and paint on one projectile suggests *(c)* is true.

f. The high-level of mushrooming and damage to one of the projectiles suggests that it was not recovered from the crime-lab's ballistic gel. This projectile fragment has hit something much harder than gel.

Q. 57. Why, if Mr. Avery removed the forensic evidence of Ms. Halbach from his garage, did he leave his own DNA in the garage?

A.57. Facts:

a. Steven and Brendan only wiped up the blood. They do not clean the entire garage. They only clean a small part of the garage floor leaving the remainder of the floor filthy.

b. Why make the effort on Halloween to only clean part of a floor with 3 types of chemical? Was it co-incidence that these two were cleaning the small section of garage floor on the same night Teresa disappears? And is it co-incidence that one of them confesses (albeit over a very long time whilst distancing himself from the crime using lies) to Steven killing her in that garage? That is a lot of co-incidence to get one's self past to conclude that Dassey's confession was invalid. *"Some of it".*

Q.58. If Mr. Avery removed the forensic evidence of Ms. Halbach from his garage, how did he distinguish between his DNA and Ms. Halbach's DNA?

A.58. Teresa's DNA was only found on the .22 projectile.

Q.59. Explain why the creeper, which the State claimed Mr. Avery used to transport Ms. Halbach's bloody body, had no forensic evidence of Ms. Halbach on it.

A.59.

a. **The creeper was not used** to transport Teresa to the fire. Early in Brendan Dassey's 'confession' interviews, Brendan was trying to distance himself physically from the murder. By saying Steven dragged Teresa on the creeper (and also sled) Brendan was creating the narrative by which Steven was able to get Teresa to the fire alone. Brendan maintained that Steven had *told* him about this. When Brendan did admit his direct physical involvement, he said that both he and Steven had carried Teresa to the fire. Brendan had the feet, and Steven had the shoulders.

Q.60. Why would Steven and Brendan carry Ms. Halbach's body from the trailer to the garage, but then decide to place her on the creeper to roll her to the burn pit 15 yards away?

A.60. As above for A.59. We believe that both Brendan and Steven carried Teresa from the trailer to the garage – this specific point was not raised when Brendan quit 'distancing' and finally admitted his physical involvement. They did not place Teresa on the creeper, or the sled, they both carried her, as Brendan said on May 13th. Some believe that everything Brendan said to investigators was coached or fed to him - but this is simply ignorance. (I know no one *likes* to be called ignorant) They have not read the transcripts thoroughly. Investigators led Brendan to some conclusions; like seeing body parts in the fire; and that Steven shot her in the head; this makes these statements involuntary and unreliable, but not necessarily untruthful. The May 13th confession – 2 months after Brendan's evidential confessions

- is the only confession that we believe is reliable, voluntary, accurate, and admissible.

Q.61. Why wouldn't Mr. Avery dispose of Ms. Halbach's body somewhere other than his burn pit which was 30 yards from his back door between 7:30 and 11:00 p.m.?

A.61.

a. This is why Avery's initial plan was to drop Teresa's body in the pond, next to where the RAV4 was found. But the pond was too shallow. We believe that Teresa's body was put into the rear cargo space on a liner, and driven by Avery to the pond. When he tested the pond's depth, he then drove Teresa's body back to his garage, or fire-pit.

b. Avery already had the Halloween bonfire going. He thought that the fire would consume all of Teresa's body. A much better solution to having a body lying in the pond. Avery did not realize, that much of the bone would survive the fire. The bone and small sample of tissue may not have survived the heat if the body had been put on top of the tires, instead of underneath.

c. Psychopaths often, (if not always), think they can't be, or won't be caught. They think they're smarter than everyone else; and they think they can talk their way out of anything. Steven Avery's list of other acts, his family history, and Brendan's confessions suggest that Avery was indeed a psychopath. Brendan never wavered on the fact that Steven had threatened him with stabbing and burning, *the same as what Teresa got*, if he ever talked. The only inconsistencies in Brendan's confessions were about what Brendan had physically done in the crime, and the covering up of the crime.

Q.62. If Mr. Avery cleaned his garage so thoroughly, why did he leave the bullet fragments on the floor?

A. 62. Speculations:

a. He looked but couldn't find them, or;

b. He looked and found the one unaccounted for projectile, or;

c. He assumed that they were still in her body.

d. He didn't think to look.

e. After Law Enforcement had searched his garage and found nothing, Avery though it unnecessary to continue looking or worry about the garage.

Q.63. Explain how the prosecution's blood spatter expert was **correct** in describing the blood on the **inside rear cargo door** was **impact** blood rather than cast-off blood.

A.63. One expert says one thing, and another expert says another. How much faith can be put in experts that are being paid? What will the next expert say?

However, we agree that with a second look, and a second opinion, it is likely that Kratz' blood expert was wrong. We think that the blood on the RAV4's rear cargo door is cast-off blood pattern from a heavy blow to the head by a blunt object. Steven could have hit Teresa with a blunt object whilst she was accessing the rear of her vehicle. This explains how the cast-off blood got on the inside of the door; and how Steven got Teresa inside his trailer, and tied her up without her fighting.

Bear-in-mind that the inside of the cargo door could have both impact blood from the loading and unloading of her body after her murder, *and* cast-off blood patterns from the bludgeoning before she was taken into Steven's trailer. Just an observation.

Q.64. Explain why there is not more of Ms. Halbach's blood on the carpet of the RAV-4 cargo area when the prosecution never claimed that Ms. Halbach was placed on a tarp.

A. 64. It has always appeared to us that:

a. There should have been much more blood in the rear of the RAV4.

b. This could only have been controlled and avoided by the laying down of a liner, like a tarpaulin, plastic sheet, or blankets. This should've been asked of Brendan.

c. However, when one examines the small blood stain of Teresa's against the wheel arch carpet in the rear cargo area, it seems that part of her body went over the edge of the liner, and blood from this body part (probably hair or head) contacted the carpet.

Q.65. Explain why the prosecution failed to tell the jury that Ms. Halbach's bloodstain pattern in the rear cargo area demonstrated that the RAV-4 was moving while Ms. Halbach's body was in the rear cargo compartment.

A.65.

a. It did not fit with their narrative.

b. It has been our theory that this could have happened:

When we view the Cadaver-dog tracks, we see two routes that both lead to the pond where the RAV4 was found – why would this be?

The reason surmised is this: Teresa's body is loaded into the rear of the RAV4 and **driven** by way of the berm beside Steven's house, to the pond. Steven accesses the pond but its dark. He decides that it's too shallow and some other means of disposal is needed. Did Steven think 'fire' or something else? The cadaver track goes back around the quarry, and to the Kuss road cul-de-sac, and back up to Steven's. This initially gave weight to the third-party bones planting, but did Steven take the body in the RAV4 to or from the quarry this way?

The point is, the RAV was taken to the pond twice. One with Teresa in the back.

Cadaver-dog tracks corroborate this idea.

Q.66. Explain why the bullet fragment (Item FL) had no garage dust on it even though the concrete in the garage was jack hammered and all other items in the garage were covered in dust as the crime scene photographs illustrate.

A.66. Speculation:

a. Item FL was collected first. The finding of the bullet prompted further, more aggressive searching, like jack-hammering.

b. It was planted. But considering the other details and evidence we don't favor this idea.

c. It was somehow shielded from the dust.

Q.67. Explain why the prosecution contended that the RAV-4 could not have been driven onto the Avery property from the Radandt pit despite at least 4 entry points from the Radandt pit onto the Avery Salvage Yard.

A.67. Mind-boggling isn't it.

a. They believed Brendan's initial story that Steven took the RAV4 past Chuckie's house. I.e. through the main entrance to the salvage business. However, to conclude this they;

b. Ignored the evidence of the cadaver-dog tracks that indicated from the RAV4, through the quarry to Kuss rd, and back to Steven's, and then back down the berm that runs from Stevens' to the yard.

c. Brendan Dassey said, in his reliable and voluntary interview on May 13th, that He and Steven took the RAV4 that particular way.

Q.68. Explain why a civilian, Ryan Hillegas, was allowed to lead the search party on November 5, 2005?

A.68. We think the 'civilian search party' was organized by Law Enforcement as a way around not having a search warrant or probable cause.

a. Hillegas was tapped for this task by Law Enforcement; the 21 phone calls he received the night before compliment this notion.

b. Because Law Enforcement had already located Teresa's RAV4 on Avery land, they focused in on Steven; as Steven had made an appointment with Teresa that day.

c. This meant that Hillegas was not even suspected. Because Hillegas was temporarily living with Teresa, he became proactive and involved with the police efforts.

d. Although some criminals inject themselves into investigations, this does not prove Ryan was the killer. The weight of evidence falls on Avery.

Q.69. Explain why only Pamela Sturm was given a camera and allowed onto the Avery salvage yard on November 5 when the other searchers were sent to other locations not on the Avery property.

A.69. Facts:

a. The police knew where Teresa's' RAV4 was. Strum was briefed on the location, and the need for secrecy. If Law Enforcement were found to influence the search, it would become inadmissible (but maybe not in Wisconsin ☺). For safety, best to limit the illegal scheme to two *civilian* people: Hillegas and Sturm. (Sturm's daughter need not have known.) We think Teresa's RAV4 was initially picked up during an aerial over-flight by light plane. Brendan said: when the plane flew over, Steven thought they (LE) might be onto him.

b. She was given a camera to photograph the RAV4, because they knew where it was.

c. Sturm was allowed on to the Avery property, because she approached Earl Avery at the salvage yard office and asked permission to look around the yard. Earl's permission was granted. The other Avery family members were off site.

Q.70. Provide an explanation (other than by divine intervention) of how Ms. Sturm and her daughter could have located Ms. Halbach's vehicle within 20 minutes among the 4,000 vehicles on 26.9 acres of the Avery salvage yard if they had not been told where the car was located prior to their search.

A.70. Sturm had clearly been briefed as to the RAV4's location.

a. Unless 'He' loves watching torture-rape, murder, and mutilation by fire, why would God allow Teresa's rape and murder without intervening, yet take the time to lead Pam Sturm to the raped and murdered girl's car?

Q.71. Explain why Pamela Sturm was the only searcher provided with a camera by Mr. Hillegas.

A.71. Law Enforcement knew Sturm would 'find' the car.

Q.72. Explain why Ryan Hillegas was never questioned about the 21 unknown phone calls he received on November 4 between 3:45 p.m. and 7:25 p.m.

A.72

a. Avery was Law Enforcement's pure focus; they were considering no other suspects.

b. They knew who had called Ryan on the 4th.

c. Avery's defense council failed to investigate Ryan Hillegas fully and present him as their third-party suspect.

Q.73. Explain how Steven and Brendan could be the killers when unidentified blood deposits on the rear cargo door excluded both of them.

A.73. Unidentified blood means we don't know whose blood it is either, but:

a. Unidentified blood does not exclude Steven; it only suggests someone else could have bleed in the car, then, or at any other time. We do however realize the significance of unidentified blood, and what it could mean.

b. Because the elimination process was not extended wide enough, this process will have to recommence.

c. Elimination exemplars for blood were isolated to those on the Avery property at the time. Exemplars should have included: Scott Bloedorn, Ryan Hillegas, George Zipperer, Andres Martinez, All Avery and Dassey males, All Halbach males, and all males in conflict of interest with the accused. New elimination testing should include all of these, and Edward Wayne Edwards.

d. Steven and Brendan can still be the killers because the weight of the total evidence (excluding planted blood and key) crushes any other theory.

e. Is the unidentified blood Charles Avery's? Did Chuck assist Steven and Brendan? A cadaver-dog indicated in Chuck's bedroom, giving a 90% chance that human cadaver sent was brought in there. Steven called Chuck at 5:57pm on Halloween. When investigators asked Brendan if Chuck 'saw anything', Brendan answered, 'probably'. Chuck needs to be eliminated from the unidentified bloodstain. This casts doubt over the validity of Chuck Avery's statement, that at around 8:00pm on November 4th, Chuck saw headlights down in the area where the RAV4 would be found the next morning. Brendan Dassey said that he and Steven hid Teresa's RAV4 by the pond on Halloween night, and walked home along the berm track, arriving back by 10pm.

Q.74. Explain why Ryan Hillegas accessed Teresa Halbach's Cingular account at 5:48 p.m., before the investigators arrived at Ms. Halbach's residence.

A.74. Speculations:

a. Hillegas was concerned, and genuinely trying to find Teresa. Ryan also called Brad Czech, whom Teresa had recently broken off an affair with, presumably looking for Teresa.

b. Ryan Hillegas had possibly left offensive messages on Teresa's phone. Thinking Teresa had left home because of this, Ryan wanted to delete them before police heard them; or realizing that Teresa would be reported missing, police would listen to these messages. Messages were deleted before Mike Halbach later listened to, and deleted around 10 messages on November 3rd.

c. Hillegas was certainly up to something - but deleting a dead person's voice messages, a killer does not make. Why? On Nov 2nd, he knew she had not come home, and wanted to find her. If he deleted messages on the night of Oct 31st, or on Nov 1st, then one could say Teresa had not been away long enough, and this person may know more than they are letting on.

Q.75. Why was the Cingular account accessed a second time at 7:18 p.m. when Mr. Hillegas was not present?

A.75. Mike Halbach; Mike went through Teresa's messages attempting to find anything to indicate where she might be; he deleted at least 10 messages. He said he knew her password from helping her set up a website.

Q.76. Why didn't the investigators investigate that Ms. Halbach had appointments in Sheboygan on the morning of 10/31?

A.76. They already had Avery for the murder.

a. Teresa arrived at Avery's.

b. Teresa's cell phone pinged a distant tower 5 minutes after her confirmed arrival at Avery's. Steven said she left at 2:50pm, 9 minutes after the ping (CFM).

c. Avery lied to Earl, Chuck, and police, saying Teresa never arrived.

d. On Nov 5th, Brendan lies to police, saying Teresa never arrived.

e. Blaine lies about the fire.

f. Why all the lies?

g. Police think why worry about Sheboygan?

Q.77. Why did Ryan Hillegas and Scott Bloedorn tell the investigators that Mr. Bloedorn did not have a romantic relationship with Ms. Halbach?

A.77. Teresa had sex with Bloedorn twice, and then broke it off. Possibilities:

a. Hillegas was envious, or resentful as he still held feelings for Teresa. He could not bring himself to admit the sexual exchange.

b. They/ or Bloedorn, did not want to admit this connection to Teresa and come under police suspicion - who would in Wisconsin?

c. In Wisconsin, if Law Enforcement decides it's you - you will likely go down for it.

Q.78. Why did Ryan Hillegas claim that Scott Bloedorn called him about Ms. Halbach being missing when the phone records show that Mr. Hillegas called Scott Bloedorn first at 2:19 p.m.?

A.78. Possible reasons:

a. He was mistaken.

b. He lied.

Q.79. Why did Ryan Hillegas claim to be with Kelly Pitzen at Ms. Halbach's house on November 3 all afternoon until midnight or 1 a.m. when Pitzen called him at 5:16 p.m. and Ryan called Pitzen at 7:18 p.m.?

A.79. Possible reasons:

a. He was mistaken.

b. He lied.

Q.80. Why did Ryan Hillegas testify inconsistently that he went to Ms. Halbach's house once a week and that he went to Ms. Halbach's house three nights in a row?

A.80. Dates:

   a. It depends on the dates in question; specifics required.

   b. Ryan had recently moved in to Teresa's house, in a temporary capacity.

Q.81. If the original burn site for Ms. Halbach's body was the Avery burn pit, why are 60% of the bones and all of the teeth but one missing? Why are bone fragments found in the grass several feet from the burn pit? Why is the suspected human pelvic bone from the Radandt pit never microscopically examined? Why are the bones not melded into the wire in the burn pit? Why is the skeleton not in the normal anatomical position described at other open pit cremations?

A.81. There are several questions here:

Q81.1. If the original burn site for Ms. Halbach's body was the Avery burn pit, why are 60% of the bones and all but one tooth missing?

A.81.1:

   a. Teresa's bones were enmeshed and inter-twined in some of the steel belting, and the van seat. This suggests that she was burned *with* those tires and that van seat. It more specifically suggests that Teresa was burned under these items. The rims and some of the steel-belting was dragged out of that fire-pit (from the fire Avery denied having) and stacked for Brendan to remove, says Chuck Avery. Brendan said that he collected the tires and the van seat before and after burning. Those tires and that van seat were burned in that pit, so we concluded that if Teresa was burned with those items, then she was burned in that same pit.

b. Human bone will burn to ash at 1400°F. Avery's fire reaches temperatures between 800° and 2500 degrees Fahrenheit. Below 800°F the tires won't burn; Above 2500°F the steel would have started melting, but did not. However, the bone would not melt or soften, until it reached 3038°F. Bone has a much higher melting point than pure calcium. This makes bone very hard to melt; the fire must be at a temperature of 3038°F before the bone is put in, or it will combust and not melt.

c. The fire will be at different temperatures at different parts of the fire pit. Temperature distribution is not even, and in-fact can fluctuate by several hundred degrees. Roughly, 60% of Teresa's bones reach 1400°F and burn to ash, but some areas do not reach the required 1400°F; meaning 40% of her bones survive intact. The steel rims would act as shielding to certain bones.

d. Brendan said (un-coached) that Teresa was **underneath** the tires. Heat rises. Therefore, the full heat of the tires does not reach Teresa; enough heat is produced to cremate 60% of her body, but leaves 40% of her bones intact. If she was put on top of the tires, a higher degree of burning would have occurred, and less bone would have remained.

e. It appears possible that the 3 potential pelvis bone fragments found elsewhere could be Teresa's.

f. Brendan said Steven wanted to get rid of the pelvis bone and took it out there to the gravel pit. There is also a 'suspect' area of digging at Kuss rd, where cadaver-dogs indicated strongly. Did Steven attempt to bury it, but decide to put it down in the quarry instead?

g. The teeth and the jaw bones reach temperatures in excess of 1800°F, and burn. One tooth survives because it does not reach this temperature. The surviving tooth may have been knocked loose during Avery's mixing and banging with the shovel. Kayla, Blaine, and Brendan all confirm Steven was using a shovel in the fire. The shovel was found partially burned.

Q81.2. Why are bone fragments found in the grass several feet from the burn pit?

A81.2:

a. Avery's dog dragged them out.

b. The bone fragments came out when Steven dragged out the burned steel tire belts and the 6 steel rims. Remember Chuck Avery said that the day after the bonfire, Steven had the 6 rims, and some of the steel belting stacked up ready for Brendan to take down to the yard. Brendan had been called and asked to remove it to the steel collection pile.

c. The bone fragments came out when Steven transferred some of the larger bones to the burn barrel. He would do this to hide un-burned bone from view; or to continue burning after the big fire was no longer burning.

Q81.3 Why is the suspected human pelvic bone from the Radandt pit never microscopically examined?

A: Odd. Very odd. Probably because they could not get a DNA profile from it; but it should have been *typed*. Human remains should not just be laying around the countryside. Do they not care if it's animal or human?

Q81.4 Why are the bones **not melded** into the wire in the burn pit?

A: Human bone melts at 3038°F, but burns to ash above 1400°F. Bone in a cremation oven, at 1800°F, does not melt or soften, it burns to dust, ash, and smaller bone fragments.

a. Melded means melting; Bone melts at 3038°F. However, bone will burn at 1400°F to ash, and ash-like fragments. The answer is of course, Avery's fire reaches temperatures between 800° and 2500° Fahrenheit.

Why 800°F? The tires won't burn below this temperature.

Why 2500°F? If the fire exceeded 2500° then the steel rims would have started melting.

b. **No** bone melts. Zero. This is because the fire would be unlikely to exceed 2000°F, and clearly did not reach 2500°F, as evidenced by the steel rims not melting. Theoretically, if some of the steel belting did reach 2500° and started to melt, the bone in the belting still needs another 538° of heat to reach the required 3038°F, the melting point of human bone. Brendan said (un-coached) that Teresa was ***underneath*** the tires. Heat rises. Therefore, the full heat of the tires does not reach Teresa; enough heat is produced to cremate 60% of her body, but leaves 40% of her bones intact. If she was put on top of the tires, a higher degree of burning would have occurred, and less bone would have remained.

Q81.5. Why is the skeleton not in the normal anatomical position described at other open pit cremations?

A: Movement:

a. As reported by Brendan, Steven "*banged on the bones with the shovel*", and, "*mixed it around*", presumably to keep the parts burning hot.

b. Un-burned Bones were taken out and put in the barrel, presumably to hide them from view.

c. Steven pulled out the 6 steel rims, and some of the steel belting for Brendan to take away. This would disturb the skeletal alignment.

Q.82. Why did the missing person poster describing Ms. Halbach's vehicle not describe the front-end damage to the parking light if the damage existed prior to her disappearance?

A.82. The broken parking light was not broken prior to her disappearance.

Q.83. Explain why Scott Bloedorn, who claimed Ms. Halbach was never gone overnight, never reported her missing?

A.83. Possibilities:

a. Ms. Zellner means that Teresa never stayed away overnight without saying so. As to why Scott Bloedorn, Teresa's roommate and two-time fling, failed to report her missing is strange. But we have an idea. Hillegas and Bloedorn were friends, so:

a. If Hillegas *had* sent Teresa a nasty phone message (for whatever reason) then maybe Ryan and/ or Scott thought Teresa was angry or scared and had taken off for a couple of nights. This would not be something they would want to admit; or:

b. Bloedorn felt rejected by Teresa and perhaps said something nasty to her; again, perhaps they thought

Teresa was angry or scared and had taken off for a few nights. This would not be something they would want to admit.

c. Whether they murdered her together or separately, they would not have wanted to report her missing until they had framed Avery; but with the staggering weight of evidence against Avery becoming more coherent, do you really think anyone else killed her?

Q.84. Why do the investigators not discover who had possession of Ms. Halbach day planner?

A.84. We understood that Teresa's day planner was at her home when Fassbender was let in by Hillegas. Investigators clearly don't think it relevant at the time. By this time as well, investigators were well into their set-up of Avery.

Q.85. Why does Mr. Kratz tell the jury that the RAV-4 is not visible on the flyover video on November 4 because it is covered in branches when the edited flyover video given to the defense does not show the area where the RAV-4 was located?

A.85. Several points:

a. We believe a fly-over was conducted on November 3rd.

b. Considering that Teresa's RAV4 was the only car on the yard concealed by branches, it would have stood out.

c. Was such a fly-over illegal? Perhaps Kratz did not want to admit finding the RAV4. Perhaps this is why Kratz edited the RAV4 out of the video.

d. Is the insinuation here, that the RAV4 was not yet planted? If so it does not fit with Colborn finding the RAV4 on the 3rd, unless:

e. On Nov3rd the RAV4 is sitting in the quarry, with it's plates still attached. Colborn finds the RAV4 in the quarry. This is possible but raises points that both suggest a third-party, and Mr. Avery alike. However, by the 4th, the RAV4 must be by the pond.

Q.86. Why does the microscopic examination of the hood latch swab fail to reveal any evidence that the swab ever touched a hood latch?

A.86. These observations come from Ms. Zellner's latest forensic testing. If Ms. Zellner says that the swab labeled 'hood latch swab', was swapped for one of the swabs taken from Steven Avery, then we believe her; period. Answer: The prosecution's hood latch swab never touched the hood latch.

Q.87. Explain the exact evidence that excluded Ryan Hillegas as a potential suspect.

A.87. None.

a. By planting Mr. Avery's blood in the RAV4, police had excluded Hillegas.

b. Ryan had no alibi.

c. Ryan was not properly excluded.

d. Once Avery's blood match was made to the blood in the RAV4, the crime-lab protocol is to cease elimination exemplars. But this doesn't explain the 'unidentified blood' found in the RAV4. Blood elimination exemplars should have continued. Investigators did not case a wide enough net.

Q.88. Explain the exact evidence that excluded Scott Bloedorn as a potential suspect.

A.88. Scott Bloedorn was not properly excluded as a
potential suspect.

Q.89. Explain the exact evidence that excluded Bobby
Dassey as a potential suspect.

A.89.

> *a.* Bobby was alone, but alibied by Scott Tadych at
> 3:10pm. Nothing alibis Bobby from the crime between
> 2:36pm and 3:06pm. But if Bobby was involved in a
> crime at this time, it was on the Avery property. Steven
> Avery maintained Teresa left the property in her RAV4 at
> 2:50pm, after Bobby. Bobby returned home around
> 5:30pm; Barb was home and Steven had just returned
> from the Two River gas station. Tadych arrived 2 minutes
> after Bobby, saw Steven, Brendan, and Barb standing
> outside talking. Tadych remained in his car, Barb got in,
> and they drove away.
>
> *b.* An elimination blood sample was taken from Bobby to
> specifically eliminate him from the male blood found in
> the RAV4. Crime-lab protocol has them stopping
> elimination exemplars as soon as a match is made, but as
> Bobby was on the property, Kratz wanted him compared.

Q.90. Explain the exact evidence that excluded Scott Tadych
as a potential suspect.

A.90. Bobby alibied Tadych at 3:10pm.

> *a.* Tadych arrives at Barb's at 2:46pm. He leaves at
> 3:00pm, and sees Bobby on H-147 near Mishicot at
> 3:10pm. However Brendan sees Teresa and her RAV4 at
> 3:40pm near Steven's trailer. According to Brendan,
> Teresa is alive when Tadych is off the property. Lisa

Buchner also said she saw Teresa alive or her RAV4, or both, at 3:40pm.

The problem here is that Ms. Zellner wants forensic evidence to corroborate every question, but this is rarely possible in all circumstances. The case against Avery, and Dassey, is built more on a totality of facts: timeline, phone records, and the witness statements: the May 13th Dassey confession to investigators, and Dassey's admission to his Mom on the recorded prison phone carry huge weight to those prepared to study them. By the nature of the confessions to Law Enforcement, it should be easy to have the confessions ruled as involuntary and unreliable - but this does not mean that Dassey's May 13th confessions are untruthful. Not every case can lean on forensic evidence; but it was *forensic evidence*, which the State planted, believing it would seal the deal, and put Avery back in prison. A fair point here is that the elimination exemplars should not have been stopped, and a wider exclusion net cast.

Q.91. Explain the relevance of the 'other acts' evidence repeatedly mentioned by Mr. Kratz in post-conviction interviews, since the evidence was excluded from the trial by Judge Willis as having zero probative value.

A.91. Other-acts:

a. 1982, Avery soaks a cat in accelerant and throws the animal into a bonfire. We declare this an act of cruelty, which Avery has downplayed as a joke. Burning animals alive is psychopathic behavior, which shows Steven's lack of remorse. Relevance to Teresa is clear. It was 1982, but psychopathic traits do not go away over time. Time is not a factor in remorseless killing; yet it is only the period of time between this incident and Teresa's burning that Judge Willis raises against this 'other-act'.

b. Threatening with a firearm. Relevance; Teresa was shot twice in the head. Once again, it was 1985. This firearm incident was bad enough for Avery to receive a 6 year sentence - this clearly carries probative value.

c. Relevance is subjective.

d. The probative value of Avery's other-acts evidence is sufficiently helpful in establishing his character; but in Avery's case it is also strong enough to prejudice jurors against him. So rather than having Zero probative value, Avery's other-acts have high prejudicial value; and Avery had already been prejudiced enough by Kratz' pre-trial press conference that ran a false narrative of throat cutting.

Q.92. Explain why 60% of Ms. Halbach's remains were missing from the burn pit including all but one of her teeth, if the pit was the primary burn site.

A.92. This is the same as Q.81.1.: 60% of Teresa's bones were missing, because 60% of them reached 1400°F or higher, and burned to ash; at higher temperatures above 1800°F, the any bone-fragments would burn to ash dust. The remaining 40% did not reach 1400°F and remained intact.

    a. Teresa's bones were enmeshed and inter-twined in some of the steel belting, and the van seat. This suggests that she was burned *with* those tires and that van seat. It more specifically suggests that Teresa was under these items. The rims and some of the belting was dragged out of that fire-pit (from the fire Avery denied having) and stacked for Brendan to remove, says Chuck Avery. Brendan said that he collected the tires and the van seat before and after burning. Those tires and that van seat were burned in that pit, so we concluded that if Teresa was burned with those items, then she was burned in that same pit.

b. Human bone will burn to ash at 1400°F. Avery's fire reaches temperatures between 800° and 2500 degrees Fahrenheit. Below 800°F the tires won't burn; Above 2500°F the steel would have started melting.

c. The fire will be at different temperatures at different parts of the fire pit. Temperature distribution is not even, and in-fact can fluctuate by several hundred degrees. Roughly, 60% of Teresa's bones reach 1400°F and burn to ash, but some areas do not reach the required 1400°F; meaning 40% of her bones survive intact.

d. Brendan said (un-coached) that Teresa was **underneath** the tires. Heat rises. Therefore, the full heat of the tires does not reach Teresa; enough heat is produced to cremate 60% of her body, but leaves 40% of her bones intact. If she was put on top of the tires, a higher degree of burning would have occurred, and less bone would have remained.

e. It appears possible that the potential pelvis bone found elsewhere could be Teresa's.

f. Brendan said Steven wanted to get rid of the pelvis bone and took it out there. There is also a 'suspect' area of digging at Kuss rd, where cadaver-dogs indicated strongly. Did Steven try to bury it, and then think 'too hard' I'll put it down in the quarry?

g. The skull clearly was in an area approaching 1400°F, but some skull surviving proves that part of this area of the fire-pit did not reach 1400°F.

h. The jaw and teeth reach temperatures exceeding 1800°F. The surviving tooth did not. Temperature distribution varies greatly in this type of open fire where accelerants and tires are burned.

Q.93. Explain why the CD recording of Ms. Halbach's call to the Zipperers' answering machine at 2:13 p.m. was never turned over to the defense and is now missing from the prosecution's case file.

A.93. The prosecution are old dogs, but:

a. The recording should have been given to the defense in discovery materials, as Jerry asked specifically for *all* recorded messages relevant to the trial.

b. Maybe the prosecution though it was inconsequential.

c. Maybe the prosecution did not want the defense to know what message Teresa had left on the Zipperers' voicemail. Maybe they thought it would give the defense options, or allow a third-party to be presented.

d. We surmise that the voice message left by Teresa at 2:12pm on October 31st on the Zipperers' phone likely made it look like Teresa had not arrived, or no longer intended to go there, as she did not want to be late for B Janda. This message could have created jury doubt; but if we look at the timeline, we believe Teresa found the Zipperers' soon after leaving this message:

2:12pm *exactly* — Teresa calls George Zipperer's home landline, looking for directions. The call is not answered and Teresa leaves a voice message. Joellen Zipperer (George Zipperer's wife) testified in court that Teresa arrived soon after this call, some time between 2pm and 2:30pm on October 31st *(from Witness Statement Exhibit 28)*. Just like

Avery said, Joellen said Teresa left an invoice and a copy of
Auto Trader.

2:13pm *exactly* — Teresa calls her voice mail, and checks
messages. We can now say that if Teresa arrived at the
Zipperers' it was between 2:14 and 2:20pm. A phone
conversation at 2:27pm exactly, confirms Teresa had left the
Zipperers'. Joellen also said that Teresa had spoken to
George, and had permission to take pictures of their son
Jason's, Firebird.

    Why then, when police later came to George
Zipperer's home investigating Teresa's disappearance, did he
rant at police, demanding Teresa be 'prosecuted for
trespassing' on his property?

    This could have been a ploy by Zipperer to suggest
he believed Teresa was still alive and could still be
prosecuted.

    Joellen's testimony is critical, as it suggests Teresa
had completed her gig there, and would not go back after
Avery's. Some suggest that Teresa couldn't find Zipperer's
and proceeded to Avery's. However, Teresa never called the
Zipperers' phone again, as she was accustom to do when
running late or re-scheduling. Joellen could have been under
pressure from her husband to lie; but if this were true, Teresa
would have disappeared at 2:28pm, and should not have
been seen later at both 2:35; and possibly again at 3:30pm at
Avery Salvage.

    If Teresa went back to the Zipperers' after Avery's,
she would have phoned them, but did not.

2:24pm *exactly* — Avery calls Teresa's cell phone. He
blocks his phone number by using the *67 feature. The call
is recorded by Teresa's phone company, Cingular Wireless,
as lasting 8sec, but it was not answered. We asked: is Avery

really trying to conceal his ID? Because if Teresa answers, she will know it's Steven anyway.

2:27pm *exactly* — Auto Trader Magazine operator, Dawn Pliska, calls Teresa. Teresa answers and the call lasts 4min 45sec. Teresa tells Dawn that she is heading out to Avery Salvage. Teresa has just left the Zipperers' area. It is a 10 minute drive from Zipperer's to Avery's. This would mean that Teresa left Zipperer's at 2:25pm. It usually took Teresa 10 minutes at each vehicle shoot, so we could say Teresa arrived at Zipperer's at 2:14pm, and left at 2:24pm. 3 minutes later she received a call that lasted 5 minutes - and 3 minutes after that she arrives at Avery's. 11 minutes from Zipperer's to Avery's.

2:35pm *exactly* — Avery calls Teresa's cell phone again, and again blocks his caller ID with the *67 feature. Teresa does not answer, probably because she is arriving at Avery rd.

2:36pm *approx* — Avery states to police (during a later interrogation after initially denying her arrival), that Teresa arrives at his trailer soon after this unanswered call. We showed this is likely true. However, in initial police inquiries, whilst police were looking for Teresa as a missing person and trying to piece together her movements, Steven Avery said Teresa never showed up.

Later Avery said that she did show up, but he never spoke to her.

Steven Avery's statements about Teresa's arrival changed 3 times. First he said Teresa never arrived; then he said that she did arrive, but he never talked to her; and then he stated that she did arrive, and that he talked to her and paid her $40 and received a magazine. Steven also told his brothers that he never saw Teresa that day, and that she never arrived on the afternoon he took off salvage work to meet her. However, Steven eventually changed his story to the version that is most accepted as accurate, and that of his affidavit.

> [M]r. Avery recalls that when he looked out of his trailer window, he saw Ms. Halbach snap one photograph of the Janda van. Mr. Avery put on his shoes and went outside. Ms. Halbach began walking towards Mr. Avery's trailer, but when she saw Mr. Avery, she waved and turned around to go to her car to get his magazine. When Mr. Avery approached the car, Ms. Halbach was in the driver's seat with the door open and the engine running. Mr. Avery approached the driver's door, which Ms. Halbach left open, and handed Ms. Halbach cash totaling $40.00. Ms. Halbach handed an AutoTrader magazine to Mr. Avery. Mr. Avery remembers there was no mud splattered on Ms. Halbach's car, or visible damage to the driver's side bumper or parking light of her vehicle, and the back seats were in the upright position. Ms. Halbach turned left on Highway 147 after leaving the Avery property. (Affidavit of Steven Avery, P-C Exhibit 4).

2:35pm *approx* — Bobby Dassey, Brendan's older brother has been sleeping after a night-shift at Fisher Hamilton in Two Rivers. Bobby wakes, gets out of bed, looks out of his window, and sees Teresa. She takes two photos of Barb's van, and then walks toward Steven's trailer. Bobby doesn't stare at Teresa for ten minutes, as some suggest, he showers for 5-10 minutes before work. Bobby stated in a police interview that he got out of bed between 2pm and 2:30pm. It seems that Bobby didn't take note of accurate times on October 31st, which is clearly common, who does? Police ask witnesses to guess or offer times, but these can be inaccurate. We assume that for Bobby to see Teresa walking toward Steven's trailer the time must have been 2:36pm, as this is when Steven said she arrived, soon after not answering his call at 2:35pm exactly. Teresa didn't go to Janda's, because she did not have the address for the *B Janda* customer. Teresa may have approached Avery's familiar trailer to confirm the missing details.

Two people, Bobby and Steven put Teresa at Steven's door at 2:36pm; as do our calculations based on phone records, and the 10 minute drive time from Zipperer's to Avery's.

e. **If Teresa had abandoned the Zipperer job, she would have arrived at Avery's at around 2:25pm; so when Dawn Pliska called, Teresa would have been at Avery's, not 10 minutes drive away.**

Q.94. Explain why Mr. Hillegas was not asked by the investigators to provide an alibi.

Q.94. Explain why Mr. Hillegas was not asked by the investigators to provide an alibi.

A.94.

a. Poor police work.

b. The RAV4 on Avery land, and Avery's initial lying about Teresa not arriving, forced police down an all too common tunnel; they lost sight of any other possible suspects, and.

c. Ryan made himself available to lead the illegal land search, and help frame Avery.

A.95. As above, but:

a. The crime-lab apparently has a protocol that ceases elimination exemplars after a positive match is made; in this case Avery. However, there are unidentified fingerprints and unidentified blood in, and on, Teresa's RAV4, so elimination samples should have been taken for every person that knew

Teresa, especially ex-boyfriends, sexual partners, roommates, and family. Law Enforcement showed their pedigree by focusing only on Avery. But nonetheless, they got it right.

Q.96. Explain why Scott Tadych was not asked to provide his DNA or fingerprints to the police.

A. 96. As above, but:

a. They reduced the elimination sample net to people only on the Avery property at the time; for us this would include Tadych. But Tadych had a (weak) alibi, and his timeline and movements eliminated him from the Avery timeline.

b. It appears elimination was only being used, at this point, to eliminate or connect Avery's accomplice(s).

Q.97. Explain why Mr. Hillegas was not asked by the investigators to provide his DNA.

A.97. Shockingly bad police work!

Q.98. Explain why Mr. Hillegas was not asked by the investigators to provide his fingerprints.

A.98. Shockingly bad police work, and:

a. Because Hillegas was rooming at Teresa's home, and could have had contact with her vehicle, and any of her other property, Hillegas should have given elimination samples. It is simply not good enough, lazy, and tunnel vision.

Q.99. Explain why Mr. Hillegas told the investigators a false story that the Halbach family told Mr. Hillegas that Ms. Halbach had damaged the driver's side parking light of her vehicle, made an insurance claim, received compensation, but had not used the proceeds to repair the parking light.

A.99. The reasons are limited:

a. Ryan is the killer.

b. Ryan was mistaken.

c. Teresa had later repaired the light herself. Possibly, Teresa does not see the value in putting in a claim and paying excess on a $40 light, and gets it fixed at an auto wrecker.

d. Teresa had recently hit something and broken the light. She *would* pick up the broken parts and put them inside her car.

Q.100. Explain why the following statements by Mr. Kratz **are true**, in light of the **evidence** refuting these statements:

A.100. Ken Kratz has written a book titled, *Avery.*

Note that Ms. Zellner uses speech marks to denote Kratz' quotes, however these are written quotes from Kratz' book, *Avery.*

100.1

Kratz: "Beginning six years after the trial, in January 2013, Steven Avery and I exchanged a series of letters. He knew that I was no longer a DA and no longer represented the state, and **he invited me** to visit him at the prison in Boscobel, Wisconsin." Avery at 164-165.

Zellner: Although Mr. Kratz does not specify who initiated their correspondence, the record is clear that Mr. Kratz wrote to Mr. Avery first with a letter dated January 14, 2013. In this letter, Mr. Kratz asked Steven to meet with him "for [Mr. Kratz's] own personal use." In fact, Mr. Kratz has not produced any correspondence from Steven Avery wherein Steven invited Mr. Kratz to visit him. Rather, Mr. Kratz invited himself with the intention, later revealed in his letter dated September 6, 2015, of writing a book about Steven.

Our Explanation: Who are we to believe, Kratz or Steven? No evidence is provided to say true or false; but Kratz is used to twisting words to suit his agendas.

100.2

Kratz: "Steven [Avery] calls to tell Auto Trader employees that Teresa never showed up on October 31st, but that she called to tell him she couldn't make it. He asked that they reschedule the appointment." Avery at 163.

Zellner: Investigators concluded that Steven Avery did not call AutoTrader between 4:30 and 5:00 p.m. on November 3. (STATE5509-5514).

Our Explanation: We could not verify Kratz' claim. *False.* However, Avery told his brothers that Teresa never showed up. Avery and Brendan both told police on November 5th, that Teresa had never showed up.

100.3

Kratz: "Steven [Avery] tells Scott Bloedorn, Teresa's roommate, that Teresa 'never showed up' for her appointment on October 31st, and is upset that he was even contacted in connection with the disappearance." Avery at 163.

Zellner: Scott Bloedorn called Steven Speckman, not Steven Avery, on 11/3 at 4:10 p.m. (STATE5509-5514).

Our Explanation: The refutation does not match Kratz statement. We watched a non-police video interview with Avery where he says that he is upset that he was even contacted in connection with the disappearance. *Both True.*

100.4

Kratz: "Without Brendan's statement as to where the murder occurred, the investigators would never have gotten a search warrant and found that bullet." Avery at 108.

Zellner: The magic bullets were magically found during a search on March 1, 2006, after Brendan's confession. However, law enforcement had previously searched the garage 5 times between November 5 and 12, 2005. Mr. Kratz is correct in saying that law enforcement would not have found the damaged bullet if not for the March 1, 2006 coerced statements of Mr. Dassey. Most importantly, Brendan's statements about where the murder occurred are entirely inconsistent. Brendan first described shooting Ms. Halbach outside the garage, then inside the vehicle in the garage, and, finally, on the garage floor (only after being told about the shell casings in the garage). The Seventh Circuit Opinion stated that there were clear efforts by the interrogators "to have Dassey move all of the events to the garage, as no forensic evidence was found in Avery's trailer." (Dassey v. Dittmann at 68).

Our Explanation:

a. Brendan lied in his interviews prior to May 13, 2006, attempting to distance himself from the crime.

b. He said Teresa was stabbed in the car, not shot in the car.

c. If the 'magic bullets' were doctored, why did FL carry wood and red paint?

d. We only put weight behind Brendan's May 13th confession to Investigators; and the May 13th confession to his Mom.

e. Mr. Kratz statement is true. Ms. Zellner confirms this by writing: *Mr. Kratz is correct in saying that law enforcement would not have found the damaged bullet if not for the March 1, 2006 coerced statements of Mr. Dassey.*

f. The Dassey statement leading police back to Avery's garage was coached. But whether the bullets were doctored evidence is less clear, and probably impossible to prove.

100.5

Kratz: "[Brendan] describes the horrible smell of a burning body — a smell that those unfortunate enough to experience can tell you they will never forget." Avery at 106.

Zellner: In his May 13, 2006, interrogation, Brendan said only that the fire smelled "real bad." Before, when asked if he could smell burning body parts, Brendan told Fassbender and Wiegert that he could not. Brendan does not describe "the horrible smell of a burning body."

Our Explanation: Good point; Brendan spoke of his own free will on May 13th.

a. The burning tires would have 'smelled real bad' too. So why did Brendan *initially* say that the fire did not smell at all - when he was in his distancing phase? Why did he not say the tires smelled bad? Was it because it was the cooking meat that he could smell?

b. If it was only the tires, why distance yourself from that, when you have already said that you collected said tires and set them by the fire?

100.6

Kratz: "The rape was initially reported to authorities by the girl's mother; the girl herself only agreed to cooperate with prosecutors after Avery was safely locked up for the Halbach murder the following fall." Avery at 35.

Zellner: These allegations were investigated by the Calumet County Sheriff's Department in 2004 after they were reported by the girl's mother. The complaint was unfounded because the alleged victim denied any sexual contact with Steven. The only credible investigation declared that these allegations were unfounded. According to Mr. Kratz, the alleged victim agreed to cooperate with prosecutors after Mr. Avery's detention. This is a misstatement. The alleged victim did cooperate, i.e., agree to be interviewed, with investigators when the allegations were investigated in 2004. While cooperating with the investigation at that time, the alleged victim denied any sexual contact with Mr. Avery and the investigators concluded that the allegations were unfounded.

Our Explanation: On point of law, one must agree with Ms. Zellner. This 'incident' was not allowed in to trial as part of Avery's 'other acts' motion, and was sealed by judge Willis to prevent jury prejudice. Nevertheless, people in Avery's family were scared to stand up to Steven. It is surmised that Avery's niece, in 2004, thought it better to withdraw her charge, rather than risk retribution. Avery had threatened to burn her house down and hurt her parents if she talked. This fact was sealed by Judge Willis.

a. Kayla Avery pulled out of her testimony in the Dassey trial claiming she had lied. Why then, was she shaking and terrified when she took Brendan's story to her school counselors? A school counselor testified in Dassey's trial as to Kayla's demeanor, and Kayla appeared to back out because of fear.

b. Brendan said Steven suggested that he would stab and burn anyone who talked. i.e. get the same as Teresa.

c. Could the rape victim have been scared of retribution?

d. The Defense Bar is ruthless when they victim shame a victim of rape. Many rapes go unreported because of intimidation tactics.

100.7

Kratz: ". . . officers jack-hammered chunks of concrete out of [Steven Avery's garage] floor, looking for blood that might have soaked through the cracks . . . . Analysts did follow-up tests to more precisely identify the substance as human blood, but in this case those tests came back inconclusive. No expert would be willing to testify that blood was present in Avery's garage in great quantities." Avery at 88.

Zellner: Here, Kratz conflates three sets of evidence collected from Steven Avery's garage:

1. Ten swabs from stains on the garage floor, taken on November 6, 2005.

2. Sixteen chunks of concrete cut from the garage floor on March 1, 2006

3. And numerous swabs from the concrete floor of the garage collected on October 4, 2006.

There is no evidence that suggests, as does Mr. Kratz, that swabs from the jack-hammered chunks were analyzed for the presence of blood. Mr. Avery's DNA was identified on

one of those swabs and Ms. Halbach's DNA was not
identified on any of the swabs. The ten swabs taken on
November 6 were sent to the crime lab, where nine of them
tested positive for the presence of blood. Further, six of
those swabs yielded Steven Avery's DNA profile. Mr.
Kratz's assertion that the stains on the garage floor tested
inconclusive for the presence of blood is false. Mr. Avery's
blood was present in the garage in sufficient quantity to
yield his DNA profile. None of Ms. Halbach's blood was
detected in the garage. If Ms. Halbach was shot in the head
in the garage, her blood would be detectable in the garage. If
Mr. Avery had sufficiently cleaned the garage so as to
destroy every trace of Ms. Halbach's DNA, he would have
cleaned up his own blood. STATE 5244-46; 5648. In fact,
the State's DNA analyst, Sherry Culhane, testified
consistently with this analysis. TT:2/26:112-115.

Our Explanation: Both statements are true, however:

a. Kratz writes, *No expert would be willing to testify that
blood was present in Avery's garage in **great quantities***. It's
a play on words, but his point is related to the 3ft by 3ft
bleach smear. Bleach can destroy blood's structure. Blood
was possibly what had been cleaned with the bleach, causing
the 3ft by 3ft bleach smear, but was sufficiently broken
down, rendering tests inconclusive. There is also deer blood
in this area.

b. The jack-hammered areas: sections of concrete were lifted
around the smear. In relation to the garage floor area, the
bleach clean-up was a small area, 3ft by 3ft. It was thought
that blood could have seeped down into the concrete, and
was missed by the bleach - but bleach is more viscous than
blood. The bleach would penetrate the concrete further than

blood could. Nothing could be found in or under the 3ft by 3ft bleach smear.

c. Brendan says Steven reopens his cut and puts a Band-aid on his finger at this point. Although we think Avery's blood in the RAV4 is planted, we think the small amount of Avery's blood in Avery's garage was from Avery's cut finger, before he put on the plaster.

d. A dead persons does not move around the garage. A dead person stays where they are. Avery did move around the garage, and dripped a tiny amount of blood outside of the area that he and Brendan bleached.

e. It is plausible that Teresa's blood on the floor was bleached into inconclusiveness; while Avery bleeds outside of the clean up. The idea that Avery's blood was inside the bleach smear is not correct.

100.8

Kratz: "In fact, Avery not only doesn't mention the fire, he denies even having a 'burn pit,' and then eventually allows that he has one, but that nothing had been burned in it for two weeks." Avery at 38.

Zellner: Steven Avery, when asked if any of the garbage in the salvage yard pit was burned "in burn barrels or open pits," replied: "Not in the pit, no." Steven Avery readily admitted that there were burning barrels in the residential areas on the Avery property and that the last time he used his burning barrel was about two weeks earlier when he burned regular garbage. Clearly, Mr. Kratz is mischaracterizing Mr. Avery's statement. The Averys did not burn garbage in the business or salvage yard areas of the property; they did, however, burn garbage near their homes. Marinette County Interview 11/6/05.

Our Explanation: The pit and the barrels were for burning garbage.

a. Blaine Dassey said there was never a fire in the pit or the barrel on Halloween, when others (in-fact everyone) said there was a fire in Avery's pit: Kayla, Bobby, Tadych, Chuck, Earl, Robert, Candy, Brendan - everyone but Blaine. However, Blaine later recants, and says that yes, there was a bonfire behind Steven's garage; and yes there was a fire going in the burn barrel, and that *Flame and smoke were coming from the barrel.* Blaine then says he saw Steven put a plastic bag into the burning barrel on Halloween. Robert and Earl then report that this barrel was alight around 5pm, when they called on Steven; they could smell burning plastic. Ms. Zellner states: *Avery readily admitted that there were burning barrels in the residential areas on the Avery property and that the last time he used his burning barrel was about **two weeks earlier** when he burned regular garbage.*

But this is shown to be another lie; why so many lies?

b. Brendan Dassey said they collected tires and a van seat from the yard to burn in the pit behind Avery's garage. So that time, yard junk was burned in the garbage only pit.

c. In Kratz' defense, Avery *did* deny having a fire on Halloween. Avery said he had not burned garbage for 2 weeks. However:

Nine people saw Avery's bonfire. (Josh Radandt excluded, who saw the burn barrel fire.)

Avery was seen filling a gas-can at 5:15pm on Halloween.

Brendan says Steven put gas on the tires to get them going.

Did Blaine deny the fire because Steven told him too?

100.9

Kratz: "When [Scott] Bloedorn called Steven Avery on Thursday, November 3rd to ask about his appointment with Teresa, Avery said she's never shown up." Avery at pg10.

Zellner: Steven Avery never spoke with Teresa's roommate, Scott Bloedorn on November 3, 2005, or any other day. Law enforcement investigated these allegations and determined they were false.

Our Explanation: As Scott refuses to talk to police, we only have phone records to go on. Mr. Kratz will have to stump up some evidence to validate his claim; or remove it from his book.

100.10

Kratz: "[On October 31st], Avery took steps to conceal himself. Unwilling to give his name or phone number to Auto Trader when booking the shoot, he provided "B. Janda" as a contact name and a telephone number belonging to his sister, Barb Janda." Avery at 22.

Zellner: Dawn Pliska, the AutoTrader employee who took Steven Avery's call on October 31, 2005, informed law enforcement that she guessed at the contact name for the appointment when she typed "B. Janda" because the caller was difficult to understand, not that he told her the appointment was for "B. Janda." There is no evidence that Steven Avery told Pliska that the contact name for the appointment was "B. Janda." TT:2/13:60-63.

Our Explanation: Dawn changed her story a couple times. She said Teresa had called her at 2:27pm on Halloween; but in fact, she had called Teresa. Dawn said she didn't know if it was a woman making the appointment or not. If Dawn now says she *guessed* B Janda, why did Avery's defense claim that Steven had made the appointment under the name B Janda because the van was Barb's? If dawn now says she guessed the name, then we see no reason to doubt her; but we do see how others could.

100.11

Kratz: ". . . after phoning Teresa directly, to set up the appointment on a forty-six degree October 10th, Steven Avery answered his door clad in only a small white towel. Creepy, thought Teresa. She told friends and coworkers she didn't want to return." Avery at 23.

Zellner: Mr. Kratz's assertions are false. There is no evidence that 1) this incident occurred on October 10, 2005; 2) Ms. Halbach thought it was "creepy"; and 3) she told coworkers that she did not want to return. No one reported that Ms. Halbach did not want to go back to the Avery property. TT:2/13/60-63. Another AutoTrader employee, Rachel Higgs, told investigators that Ms. Halbach was not uncomfortable going to the Avery property to take photos and that Mr. Avery was harmless.

Our Explanation: Ms. Zellner is correct. Kratz is guessing or making this story up.

100.12

Kratz: "Steven doused the cat in gas and oil before the stricken animal was thrown onto the fire. It jumped off and ran around the yard, still ablaze, until Avery caught the cat, applied additional fuel, and threw it back on." Avery at 29.

Zellner: Kratz's assertion that Steven Avery threw the cat into the fire is false. In fact, there is only evidence that someone else threw the cat into the fire. Further, the trial judge ruled this evidence inadmissible because it has "zero probative value." Motion to Allow the Introduction of Other Acts Evidence pg. 3-4.

Our Explanation: Hang-on. Avery actually says he was playing with the cat and it accidentally went in the fire.

Let's look at the 1982 judgment.

Avery **pleads guilty** to animal cruelty and is sentenced to 9 months in prison to be served concurrently with breech of probation. We want the evidence that suggests *someone else threw the cat into the fire.*

The following two images are Avery's judgment of conviction for burning his cat.

CSCF-371

| STATE OF WISCONSIN | CIRCUIT COURT | MANITOWOC COUNTY |

STATE OF WISCONSIN,   PLAINTIFF   CASE FILE NO. 82 MD 371

-vs-
                                                    JUDGMENT OF CONVICTION
STEVEN A. AVERY   ,   DEFENDANT   SENTENCE TO COUNTY JAIL
Route 1
Maribel, Wisconsin

UPON ALL THE FILES, RECORDS AND PROCEEDINGS,

IT IS ADJUDGED that the defendant has been convicted upon his plea of

        (x) Guilty

        ( )   Not guilty and a verdict of guilty

        ( )   Not guilty and a finding of guilty

        ( )   No contest

on the __23rd__ day of __November, 1982__, of the crime(s) of
party to the crime of cruelty to animal, committed on or about September 2, 1982,
at the Town of Gibson, Manitowoc County, Wisconsin, contrary to Section 948.02
and 939.05 of the Wisconsin Statutes.

MANITOWOC COUNTY
STATE OF WISCONSIN
FILED
DEC 6 2005
CLERK OF CIRCUIT COURT

On __November 23, 1982__ the Court inquired of the defendant whether he
has anything to state why sentence should not be pronounced and no sufficient grounds
to the contrary being shown or appearing to the Court,

IT IS ADJUDGED that the defendant is guilty as convicted.

IT IS ADJUDGED that the defendant is hereby committed to the county jail of Manitowoc
for a term of __nine (9) months__, to be served concurrently with the sentence defendant
will be serving as a result of revocation of probation on Case File No. 80 CR 773.

Defendant to report to the county jail at 9:00 A.M., on November 29, 1982.

IT IS ORDERED that the clerk deliver a duplicate original of this judgment to the
sheriff who shall forthwith execute the same.

Dated __November 23, 1982__.

                                BY THE COURT,

                                Joan A. Hoffman
                                Clerk of Court

                                By: *Shirley Tilleson*
                                    Deputy Clerk

Judge   Leon H. Jones
s't.District Attorney Elmo E. Anderson
Defense Attorney   Michael J. Bally

MANITOWOC COUNTY
STATE OF WISCONSIN
FILED
NOV 23 1982
CLERK OF CIRCUIT COURT

PLAINTIFF'S EXHIBIT NO. 9

This document is a full certified copy of the
original on file in the Office of the Clerk of
Circuit Court, Manitowoc County, State of
Wisconsin

Date: _____ _____
                Deputy Clerk of Circuit Court

11/18/2005 13:26   9206832733   CLERK OF COURT   PAGE 05

STATE OF WISCONSIN

CIRCUIT COURT
MANITOWOC COUNTY
STATE OF WISCONSIN

MANITOWOC COUNTY

FILED

SEP 2 1982   CASE FILE NO. 82 MD 371 J

STATE OF WISCONSIN,

CLERK OF CIRCUIT COURT

PLAINTIFF

CRIMINAL COMPLAINT

vs.

JERRY L. YANDA, D.O.B. 01/02/64
1034 - 23rd St.   and   STEVEN A. AVERY, D.O.B. 07/09/62
Two Rivers, Wis.   DEFENDANT   Route #1
                                    Maribel, Wis.

JAMES J. MEIDL, Lt., Mrwc. Co. Sheriff's Dept........ being duly sworn on oath says (on information

and belief) that on the 2nd .... day of .... September ...... 19 82 .... at the

.... Town .... of .... Gibson .... in said County

and State, JERRY L. YANDA and STEVEN A. AVERY .... did
as parties to the crime, intentionally mistreat an animal, to-wit: Poured gas and oil
on a cat and started it on fire, contrary to Section 948.02 and 939.05 of the Wis. Stats.
This offense is punishable upon conviction by a fine not to exceed $10,000 or by
imprisonment of not more than nine months, or both. (Class A Misdemeanor)

The complainant further alleges that he is informed by the reports of Kenneth J. Petersen,
known to the complainant to be an officer with the Manitowoc County Sheriff's Dept.,
that on September 2, 1982 he reported to the Two Rivers Police Dept. where he was inform
by Sgt. Wilda that Jerry Yanda had reported to the department and informed Sgt. Wilda
that he along with Steven A. Avery had started a cat on fire and burned it to death.
That Officer Petersen after advising Jerry L. Yanda of his Miranda Rights, received a
written statement from Jerry L. Yanda wherein he admitted that he along with Steven A.
Avery, took a cat which belonged to Steven A. Avery and poured gas and oil on it and
threw it in a bonfire and then watched it burn until it died. That Officer Petersen
was further informed by Peter A. Dassey, that he was present at the Steven A. Avery
residence when Steven A. Avery suggested burning a cat. That Peter A. Dassey informed
Officer Petersen that Jerry L. Yanda and Steven A. Avery started a fire and then got
the cat and poured gas and oil on it and threw the cat in the fire.

The information provided by Kenneth J. Petersen is believed because he has provided true
and accurate information in the past as a police officer. The information provided by
Peter A. Dassey is believed because he is providing information as a citizen informant
with no ulterior motive. The information provided by Jerry L. Yanda is believed because
he is providing information against his own self interest.

James J. Meidl
Complainant

Subscribed and sworn to before me this .... 2nd .... day of .... September .... 1982 ....

District Attorney

Approved for filing ....
District Attorney

Page, 2 states:

Jerry L. Yanda, and Steven A. Avery, as parties to the crime, Intentionally mistreat an animal, to-wit: poured gas and oil on a cat and started it on fire.

That officer Petersen, after advising Jerry L. Yanda of his Miranda rights, received a written statement from Jerry L. Yanda, wherein he admitted that along with Steven A. Avery, took a cat which belonged to Steven A. Avery and poured gas and oil on it, and threw it in a bonfire, and then watched it burn until it died.

That officer Petersen was further informed by Peter A. Dassey, that he was present at the Steven A. Avery residence when Steven A. Avery suggested burning a cat.

That Peter A. Dassey informed officer Petersen that Jerry L. Yanda and Steven A. Avery started a fire and then got the cat and poured gas and oil on it and threw it in the fire.

~

Points:

a. The cat burning was premeditated; Avery had talked about burning the cat with Jerry, and inadvertently, Peter had overheard him.

b. How does a gasoline soaked cat 'accidentally' go in a fire? Someone does not put gasoline on an animal and take it near a fire, if they don't intend burning the animal.

c. The only reason someone would need to further soak the cat in oil, is to provide fuel for prolonged burning.

d. The event was not a joke. It was the planned, cruel and remorseless burning of an innocent animal for entertainment.

e. Avery was jailed for 9 months.

f. Probative value is always subjective; and such an incident will not always be accepted into other acts.

g. We believe this incident has clear probative value; but that is only our opinion. We also believe that any felony conviction, leading to a prison sentence, should be entered into other acts; once again, our opinion.

h. Avery actually appeals to us to feel sorry for him for the cat burning. I was young; I accidentally talked about burning the cat: I accidentally soaked him in Gasoline; I accidentally poured oil on him; I accidentally took him near a bonfire; I accidentally threw him in; I accidentally did nothing to help him; I accidentally got caught.

This people, is a pity play: If you feel sorry for 'Avery the cat burner', then he has played you. Non-delusional, or high-functioning psychopaths *always* use pity plays to excuse their actions or to get 'back on side'.

"I'm sorry I beat your face in, Darling, It was because of x,y,z. It'll never happen again."

Sympathy ploys are a hallmark of non-delusional psychopathy.

XI

HISTORY NEVER REPEATS

Ms. Zellner will free Avery.

The evidence tampering by police will elicit a mistrial, and Avery will walk.

But what kind of man is Zellner releasing on the woman of Wisconsin?

From 1985 through 1988 - from behind prison walls, for the rape he did not commit, Avery sent his wife Lori menacing letters. Avery also sent threats to kill Lori, through their children.

The letters included:

I hate mom - she will pay.

I will kill you. I will get you when I'm out.

Daddy will git Mom when daddy gets out. [sic]

Fuck you Lori, you are going to die. Yes you are.

The divorce file states: [Mr. Avery is impulsive, had threatened to kill and mutilate his wife, and refused to participate in programming.]

Prior to 1985, Lori states Avery beat and choked her. Threatened to kill, and threatened to mutilate her. Once Avery tracked her to a domestic abuse shelter and tried to drag her out; Avery had to be forcefully removed from the facility. Lori believes, if Avery did not go to jail in 1985, that he would have killed her.

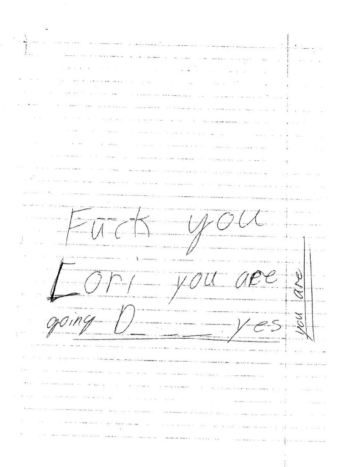

I will get you when I'm out ded you

On trial for murder, this history was put before Judge Willis as Other Acts Motion 1.

Avery's Other Acts Motion was 14 pages long, and these are only the serious offenses, that the defense thought were relevant to rape, murder, and mutilation.

Ms. Zellner rests easy in the fact that - in her opinion - Judge Willis thought all of this raping and violence *towards women* was lacking in probative value, despite having been kept away from Wisconsin's women for 18 years of his life.

Rape is rape.

Violence against women is violence against women.

Escalation leads to murder.

This is the true nature of this level of violent crime against women.

Why did Judge Willis hide from Avery's horrific past - and why is Kathleen Zellner down-playing the horror?

ORIGINAL

STATE OF WISCONSIN	CIRCUIT COURT	MANITOWOC COUNTY
	BRANCH I	

STATE OF WISCONSIN		STATE OF WISCONSIN'S
	Plaintiff,	2nd SUPPLEMENTARY
vs.		MEMORANDUM IN SUPPORT
		OF OTHER ACTS EVIDENCE FILED
STEVEN A. AVERY,		**[Submitted Under Seal]** AUG 1 4 2006
	Defendant,	
		Case No. 05-CF-381 CLERK OF CIRCUIT COURT

PURPOSE

After the State submitted it's nine separate motions to allow the introduction of other acts evidence, a memorandum of law in support of it's motion, and a supplementary memorandum, the Court requested additional specificity from the State, in correspondence dated August 1, 2006. Specifically, the Court requires the State submit, as to each proposed other act: (1) the charge for which the evidence is offered; (2) how the evidence relates to an element of the charge; and (3) what witnesses will testify, and what they will say.

The State here attempts to more clearly explain it's theory of admissibility, and comply with the Court's request for additional specificity as to the nine other acts offered, although incorporating by reference the detailed information previously provided to the court.

ELEMENTS OF OFFENSES

Although the Court may already be aware of the charges the defendant faces, and the elements which must be proved by the State for each charge, the list below may be of assistance. It must be noted that Count 1 (First Degree Intentional Homicide), Count 2 (Mutilating a Corpse), and Count 4 (First Degree Sexual Assault) are charged as a "party to the crime" and can be proved whether the defendant committed each of the elements individually, or aided and abetted another in the commission of those elements. The State also paraphrases the elements to be proved, for simplicity of analysis.

114
(1)

Jodi Stachowski was Avery's girlfriend throughout the Halbach Murder trial. During the *Making a Murderer* docuseries, Jodi supported Avery - or appeared to.

But once Avery was convicted, and Jodi felt protected from his vengeance, Jodi changed her story too.

Jodi said Steven had repeatedly punched, choked, and raped her.

She had also said Avery had threatened to burn down her parents house, with them inside it.

Where have we heard that before?

It's no wonder Jodi turned to alcohol.

From prison, Avery intimidated and threatened Jodi in the same way he had menaced Lori 17 years earlier.

Letters threatening to kill.

Demands for money to be given to his mother, Delores.

More threats.

Of all the 14 pages of Avery's 2005 'Other Acts' Motion, not one incident involves a male; all Avery's violence is against women.

We asked: how does a sequential and consistent history of violence against women not qualify as relevant?

Violence against women is violence against women.

Judge Willis suppressed and sealed the 'other acts' that Avery had committed because if he didn't, Avery's jury would've been prejudiced. Willis has the idea that each trial be judged on its own merits.

History shows, however, the best indicator of future behavior, is past behavior.

A jury that does not see Avery's violent history will think: did this guy just get up one morning and think, *I'll murder an innocent woman today?*

Avery's history gives context to an escalating continuum.

But then comes the oscillation to pity-plays.

The psychopath does not feel emotion like 'normal' humans. He does not care if people pity him - he simply uses it as a tool.

The psychopath's brain, for whatever reason - genetic, developmental, childhood abuse - does not have the neural network to process emotion.

"Poor people loose. Poor people loose all the time." Is a pity-play.

I've raped, I've beaten, I've choked, I've intimidated, I've tortured, I've killed - but I was poor, and now I'm in prison - please feel sorry for me - I'm a nice guy, really.

Martha Stout, PhD, says:

"After listening for twenty-five years to the stories my patients tell me about sociopaths who have invaded and injured their lives - when I'm asked, "How can I tell whom not to trust?" the answer I give usually surprises people. The natural expectation is that I will describe some sinister detail of behavior or snippet of body language or threatening use of language that is a subtle give-away.

Instead, I take people aback by assuring them that the tip-off is none of these things, for none of these things is reliably present. Rather, the best clue is, of all things, the pity play.

The most reliable sign, the most universal behavior of unscrupulous people is not directed, as one might imagine, at our fearfulness. It is perversely an appeal to our sympathy."

[There] is an excellent reason for the sociopathic fondness of pity. As obvious as the nose on one's face, and just as difficult to see without a mirror, the explanation is that good people will let pathetic individuals away with murder, as therefore, any sociopath wishing to continue his game, should repeatedly play for pity.

When deciding whom to trust, bear in mind that a combination of consistently bad or egregiously inadequate behavior with frequent plays for your pity is as close to a warning mark on a conscienceless person's forehead as you will ever be given. (*The Sociopath Next door, Martha Stout, PhD.*)

Zellner will free Avery.

Law Enforcement made a colossal mistake in setting him up.

When Avery walks -

Who Will Be His Next Victim?

XII

TYING UP LOOSE ENDS

The Zander note is one such loose end. Who wrote it? If not Avery, how did it get into Steven's shelf? 3302 Zander Rd leads to a creepy, abandoned cottage, near a site Ed Edwards was said to have committed murder.

But that is all we have.

An assessment leads us to believe that Steven Avery towed a vehicle from outside 3302 Zander Rd; and that he wrote Teresa's cell number on the card separately.

If the Zander Road note was from Edwards, something more occult or obvious would have accompanied it at the crime scene.

The swab of unidentified blood taken from Teresa's RAV4 is a loose end, but not one that we have the power to rectify. People do cut fingers and do leave tiny amounts of blood in all sorts of places. It is most likely that this blood is someone who had a lot to do with Teresa; a family member or roomate. It is possible, even likely, that the blood could belong to Scott Bloedorn or Ryan Hillegas - as they would have had recent contact with Teresa's car. Blood *seems* suspicious, but is not always. It was said that Ryan had scratches on his hands; and it was assumed from that that he had killed Teresa. Does a scratched hand prove murder? People scratch their hands all the time - I have a scratched hand from gardening as I write this. Even if the scratch from Ryan's hand left blood on Teresa's car, this does not prove murder. It proves he knew Teresa and had a scratched hand.

Why Ryan Hillegas told the court that Teresa had damaged the front light of her RAV4 and claimed insurance without repairing it, is a question that we cannot answer, except for pure assumption.

We see the bullet (FL) as genuine, un-doctored evidence. The bullet means Teresa was shot in Steven Avery's garage.

The Dassey confessions, when assessed by a psychologist, suggest that he lied to distance himself from the crime; that he told him Mom the truth during his multiple confessions on the phone; and that his May 13 confession was truthful.

Dassey's post conviction defense counsel has run the pity-play.

By making Brendan appear pathetic, the defense is trying to elicit sympathy from the general public. The general public is rarely exposed to the cunning deceptions employed by top-end lawyers. They made us think that because Dassey was led and coached on several questions during his interrogations, that *all* of his answers were coached. Even that Brendan was mentally tortured.

Brendan was coached on seeing toes, and that Teresa was shot in head, and that the shooting happened in the garage. Most answers Brendan gave initially involved him putting obstacles between himself and the investigators. But in his May Day interview, Brendan speaks un-coached, and spills the beans about the planning of Teresa's kidnapping.

Brendan's defense counsel wants you to feel sorry for, him, because if you do, you will think that this poor pathetic kid could not be a rapist.

That you will think that this poor pathetic kid could not put a woman's body into a fire and then go home to bed.

Brendan said that raped Teresa, and helped burn her.

He did not feel sorry the next day.

He did not feel sorry the day after that - he felt 'something' after two weeks, probably because by then the investigation was breathing down their necks, and he was scared of going to jail.

Brendan is no innocent kid; if you sum the facts, he is a rapist and a monster - and people feel sorry for him.

If you have an unexplained loose-end involving either Steven Avery, Brendan Dassey, or related evidence, please email us; no attachments - put all detail in the email's body; and send to:

dionysusthinktank@gmail.com

Printed in Great Britain
by Amazon